Turks, Moors, and Englishmen in the Age of Discovery

Turks, Moors, and Englishmen in the Age of Discovery

✳

Nabil Matar

COLUMBIA UNIVERSITY PRESS

New York

Columbia University Press

Publishers Since 1893

New York   Chichester, West Sussex

Copyright © 1999 by Columbia University Press

Library of Congress Cataloging-in-Publication Data

Matar, N. I. (Nabil I.)

Turks, Moors ,and Englishmen in the age of discovery / Nabil I. Matar

p.   cm.

Includes bibliographical references (p.   ) and index..

ISBN 0–231–11014–6 (cloth : alk. paper).

1. Middle East—Relations—Great Britain.
2. Great Britain—Relations—Middle East.   3. Africa, North—Relations—Great
Britain.   4. Great Britain—Relations—Africa, North.   5. Middle East—
History—1517-1882.   6. Africa, North—History—1517–1882.   7. Great Britain—
History—Elizabeth, 1558–1603.   8. Great Britain—History—Stuarts, 1603–1714.
9. Indians—First contact with Europeans.   I. Title.

DS63.2.G7M38   1999

303.48'256041—dc21   98–44812

CIP

∞

Casebound editions of Columbia University Press books are printed on permanent and durable acid-free paper.

Printed in the United States of America

10 9 8 7 6 5 4 3 2 1

For Ibrahim and Hady

CONTENTS

Preface　　*ix*

Introduction　　3

1. Turks and Moors in England　　19

2. Soldiers, Pirates, Traders, and Captives: Britons Among the Muslims　　43

3. The Renaissance Triangle: Britons, Muslims, and American Indians　　83

4. Sodomy and Conquest　　109

5. Holy Land, Holy War　　129

Conclusion: Britons, Muslims, and the Shadow of the American Indians　　169

Appendix A: English Captivity Accounts, 1577–1704　　181

Appendix B: The Journey of the first Levantine to America　　185

Appendix C: Ahmad bin Qasim on Sodomy　　193

Notes　　195

Bibliography　　231

Index (Prepared by Marilyn Goravitch)　　257

PREFACE

From the Elizabethan period and throughout the seventeenth century, Britons from England and Wales, and to a lesser extent, Scotland and Ireland, were exposed to the civilization of Islam. This civilization was experienced by means of its literature, culture, and languages, chiefly Arabic and Turkish. It was also experienced as a theology that English and Scottish clerics confronted—either in polemical texts or in disputations. Such an Islam could be written about, debated, denounced, admired, and scrutinized without bringing the Briton into contact with a single Muslim man or woman. It could be praised for its sufi models, attacked for its "Mahometan berry" (coffee), threatened by eschatological destruction, or denounced for its "renegades"—all from the safety of Britain's insular borders. It is a testimony to the vast impact of Islam on Renaissance England and the British Isles that despite the limitations of this exposure, the Arab-Islamic legacy permeated English discourse and thought. In *Islam in Britain, 1558-1685,* I attempted to examine that legacy and showed that although a centripetal relation governed Islam and Britain, by the end of the seventeenth century, that relation had become centrifugal and oppositional.

In this book, I shall show how that change was effected by focusing on the Age of Discovery, the period that corresponds in England to the time between the Elizabethan period and the beginning of the Great Migration in the Caroline period. Specifically, I shall examine this interaction in the light of England's concurrent encounter with another non-Christian people—the American Indians. Students of the English Renaissance have ignored the importance of the fact that Britons encountered Muslims at the same time they encountered American Indians. Only three years after the Turkey

Company had been established in 1581, Sir Walter Raleigh's first project for settlement in Roanoke, Virginia, was launched (1584), and in 1585, two years before the second Roanoke project was undertaken, the Barbary Company was formed to strengthen England's trade with Morocco, which had existed since the 1550s. The ventures to North America and to North Africa and the Levant occurred so close together in time that, throughout the period under study, the English were in a triangular geographical relationship. They lived and traded among the Turks and Moors while simultaneously or subsequently trading with the American Indians and living in their lands.

The encounters with the Muslims and the American Indians took place at different political, colonial, and military levels. But within the Elizabethan and Stuart discourse of Otherness and empire, the two encounters were superimposed on each other so that the sexual and military constructions of the Indians were applied to the Muslims. These constructions might well have remained a symptom of cultural stereotyping and ignorant representation had they not made possible the ideological discourse that accompanied the conquest of Islam in the eighteenth and nineteenth centuries. In the Renaissance conquest of America lay the groundwork for colonialism and orientalism.

I wish to thank many colleagues and friends who have read all or parts of this book, and who have been of great help to me. First and foremost is Dr. Jane Patrick, former Humanities Department head at Florida Tech, who always organized my schedule in a way that allowed me to travel to libraries and conferences. She also read, patiently and willingly, every typescript I gave her. For the past twelve years her advice, prudence, and encouragement have been invaluable to me. Now enjoying retirement with her family, she will always be remembered as a dear friend.

I also wish to thank Alex Baramki for patiently reading the galleys; Dina for helping me with translations; Daniel Vitkus of Florida Tech for his numerous insights; Mordechai Feingold of Virginia Tech for his encouraging reading; Raymond-Jean Frontain of the University of Central Arkansas for commenting on chapter 4; Salim Kemal of Dundee University for his perceptive emails; Mohammad Shaheen of Jordan University for many discussions at Oxford; and the tourist guide, John (he never bothered to tell me his surname), a Native American who walked me through the Chaco Canyon in 1995 and told me the "other" history of America.

I am grateful to Chris Larson of UCLA for inviting me to participate in the "Seminar on Toleration" in 1997, which taught me a lot. I am also grateful to the editors of *Journal of Islamic Studies, Explorations in Renaissance Culture,* and *Literature Interpretation Theory* for permission to use some of the material I had published in their journals: "Muslims in Seventeenth-Century England," *Journal of Islamic Studies,* 8 (1997): 63–82, copyright Oxford University Press; "English Renaissance Soldiers in the Armies of Islam," *Explorations in Renaissance Culture,* 21 (1995): 81–95, copyright South Central Renaissance Conference; and "The Traveller as Captive: Renaissance England and the Allure of Islam," *Literature Interpretation Theory,* 7 (1996): 187–196, copyright Gordon and Breach Publishers. Many thanks are also due respondents at the following conferences: "The Image of the Other," at The American University in Cairo, 1996; the "South Central Renaissance Conference," in Austin, Texas, 1997; and the "Seventh International Conference," in Durham, England, 1997. I am particularly grateful to Donald Dickson of Texas A & M University for allowing me to test my thesis as a presentation before the "Interdisciplinary Colloquium."

Any shortcomings that remain in this book are my own.

I wish to thank the staff and librarians at Houghton Library, Harvard University; the University Library, Cambridge University; the British Library, London; Durham University Library, Durham; the Public Record Office, London; the University of Florida Library; and the Baylor University Library. In particular, I wish to thank Ms. Victoria Smith at the Inter-Library Loan desk at Evans Library, Florida Tech, and Ms. Linda Khan at the microfilm center, for their continued assistance and kindness. Both always went out of their way to help.

Finally, I wish to thank Marilyn Goravitch, whose computer wizardry, intelligence, and sincere cooperation made this and other projects possible. I also want to thank Sue Downing and Peggy Machado for their moral support and help; my mother in the solitariness of her octogenarianism; and my children, Ibrahim and Hady, to whom this book is dedicated, with apologies that, while writing this book, I could not compete with Richie's dad, who built a car all by himself.

Turks, Moors, and Englishmen in the Age of Discovery

INTRODUCTION

The English Renaissance was the Age of Discovery and exploration, of the westward venture to America and beyond, that dramatically changed English and world history. But from the Elizabethan to the early Caroline periods, Britons undertook another venture as they entered into an extensive commercial, diplomatic, and social engagement with the Turks and Moors of the Muslim empires. No other non-Christian people interacted more widely with Britons than the Muslims of the Ottoman Empire, the Eastern Mediterranean, and the North African regencies of Tunisia, Algeria, and Libya, along with Morocco (which was not under Ottoman domination). These Muslims were real in a physical and linguistic sense, and represented the most widely visible non-Christian people on English soil in this period—more so than the Jews and the American Indians, the chief Others in British Renaissance history.[1]

The numerical evidence about the concurrent interaction with Jews and American Indians shows that Renaissance Britons were far more likely to meet or to have met a Muslim than a Jew or an Indian. In the case of Jews, Britons would have known them as Marranos: in the Elizabethan period, between eighty and one hundred New Christians/Marranos were known to be living in London. These outward Christians, all of whom were Portuguese, had felt settled enough to buy houses and congregate in London, in the north and west of Tower, chiefly in Crutched Friars (the Anes Family), in Aldgate (the Alvarez family), in Tower Ward (the Nunez family), in Hart Street (the Pinto family), and in Holborn, the residence of the queen's physician, Dr. Roderigo Lopez, who often entertained foreign coreligionists there. Under James I the numbers dramatically declined and Jews/Marranos nearly disappeared from London until the Interregnum when Oliver Cromwell permitted them to resettle in England.[2]

In the case of American Indians, only a few came (or were brought) to England. Not only were they fewer than the Jews in number, but they were sometimes encountered not as Indians assured of their identity and history, but as de-Indianized Christians who were learning to become "English" men and women, to dress in English clothes, and to speak the English language. The portraits of the Anglicized and deracialized "Mme. Penobscot," who was abducted along with a few other Indians from Maine in 1605 by George Weymouth,[3] and of Pocahontas, show how such Indians were perceived: they were not being recognized for their Indianness, but for the success of the colonists in changing them into "civilized" human beings. The words under Pocahontas's portrait specifically describe her as having been "converted and baptized in the Christian faith." As far as English society was concerned, there was nothing inherently important or distinctive about the Indians: they were worthy of attention only because they could be transformed. While Londoners, as Shakespeare wrote in *The Tempest*, might "lay out ten to see a dead Indian" (2.2.34), the visit of Mrs. Rebecca Rolfe with her retinue generated limited imaginative and literary excitement.[4] There is not a single play about her or the American Indians in the whole golden age of English drama.

Meanwhile, from the 1580s until the 1630s, there were dozens of plays about Turks and Moors. Not only were these Muslims more familiar on stage and in London than Jews and American Indians, they were much more familiar to Britons than the Muslims of Central Asia (Iran), the subcontinent (India), and the Indian archipelago. Although under Elizabeth and James commercial and diplomatic relations were developed with the Muslims of Savafi Persia and Mughal India,[5] those relations remained much more politically and financially limited than relations with the Levant and Mediterranean Muslims. Actually, it was the Levant interaction that served as the artery through which "Englishmen ultimately went to the East Indies."[6] Before a study of the impact of Persian and Mughal Muslims on Renaissance England is conducted—a project that has yet to be undertaken—

an investigation of the impact of the Turks and Moors of the Ottoman Empire and North Africa must be completed.

* * *

During the period under study, thousands of Turks and Moors visited and traded in English and Welsh ports; hundreds were captured on the high seas and brought to stand trial in English courts; scores of ambassadors and emissaries dazzled the London populace with their charm, cuisine and "Araby"

1. "Pocahontas." Courtesy of the Virginia Historical Society, the Center for Virginia History.

horses. In these venues real meetings took place between Muslims and Britons: the latter ate at the same tables with visiting "Turks" in London, encountered Barbary pirates in the jails of the southwestern sea towns or coastal villages of Ireland and the Channel Isles, and admired Ottoman *chiauses* in their processions to the Banqueting Hall. Britons transported Muslims to the Hajj in Mecca so the pilgrims could escape the depredations of the Maltese pirates,[7] and traded with them in Mediterranean harbors; they fought in Muslim armies, joined the Barbary Corsairs in piracy and pillaging, and entered as slaves into the intimacy of Muslim life, religion, and language. To numerous Britons, the Turks and Moors were men and women they had known, not in fantasy and fiction, but with whom they had worked and lived, sometimes hating them yet sometimes accepting or admiring them. On a few occasions the two had become intimate through sexual and marital relationships. Although it is impossible to attach an exact number to the Britons who had dealings with Muslims, it is not unlikely that in the Elizabethan, Jacobean, and Caroline periods, that number was not less than that of the Britons who saw Moorish Othellos and Turkish Bajazeths on the popular London stage or in the makeshift shows of the wandering theater groups.

The representation of these Muslims in English Renaissance writings has been widely examined in recent scholarship, but it has been nearly always limited—first, by the kinds of sources critics have used; second, by the imprecision with which North African Muslims and sub-Saharan Africans have been conflated and identified; and third, by the method critics have adopted.

In regard to the source material, critics and historians who have examined Renaissance "Islam" have relied predominantly on works by playwrights such as Peele, Kyd, Marlowe, Shakespeare, Greville, Mason, Daborne, Heywood and Goffe, and by travelers such as Morrison, Sanderson, Sandys, Biddulph, Coryat, Blount, Lithgow, and others. Although the writings of these men exhibit the genius of British Renaissance imagination, they have constituted the critics' only source for the study of Renaissance Islam and Muslims. But, from Kyd to Mason and Goffe, Muslims were portrayed on stage without any uniquely differentiating features; they exhibited the moral, or more fre-

quently the immoral, character of Shakespeare's "superstitious Moor" and
Goffe's "raging Turke," but there was no allusion in either the characteriza-
tion or the dialogue in drama to specific aspects of Muslims that could be
traced to actual meetings with them. Although much can be learned from
these and other literary sources about the English representation of Islam
and Muslims, these sources should be supplemented by and contextualized
within the evidence that has survived about the *actual* interaction between
Britons and Muslims. This evidence appeared in contemporary prison depositions, captives' memoirs, Privy Council documents, and other materials
that were produced by Britons who had lived among the Muslims and mastered their language(s), or had spent weeks or months negotiating with them
in London or trading with them in Algiers.

It is therefore surprising that some critics have gone as far as claiming that
Englishmen knew Muslims only as literary representations and imaginary
constructs. G. K. Hunter, for instance, stated that in the Elizabethan imagination, there "seem, in fact, to be Moors everywhere, but only everywhere
in that outer circuit of non-Christian lands." Kim F. Hall agreed that "English
traders went to the markets of Guinea and Barbary, but African traders rarely
went to England."[8] Only Bernard Harris, Eldred Jones, and Jack D'Amico
have alluded to Muslim ambassadors and "blackmoors" in England—but they
failed to distinguish between North Africans and sub-Saharans.[9] As will be
shown in the pages that follow, there was an extensive interaction among
Turks, Moors, and Englishmen on English soil in the period under study.

Second, numerous historians have examined the representation of black
Africans (to whom I shall refer as sub-Saharan) on the same pages where they
have dealt with North African Muslims, the "Moors." No distinction was
established between the two geographical, and more importantly, political,
referents. In her *Things of Darkness,* Kim F. Hall addressed in detail the English
encounter with Africans but, like other critics before her, did not distinguish
between England's dealings with North Africa and with sub-Saharan
Africa.[10] Although it is always difficult to identify exactly the signification of
ethnic and national terms in Renaissance English writings, the conflation of
North Africans with sub-Saharans is misleading because England's relations
with sub-Saharan Africans were relations of power, domination, and slavery,

while relations with the Muslims of North Africa and the Levant were of anxious equality and grudging emulation. When Purchas sought a model of the enterprising trader to inspire his readers, he turned to the "Mahometan, that in places furthest distant, this their Religion hath beene preached, which they trade together with their Marchandize, euen from the Atlantike Ocean vnto the Philippines." Much as Purchas was hostile to the "superstitious" Muslims, he still recognized their ability to combine religious conversion and trade—exactly what he, along with others, wanted his compatriots to do.[11] As Purchas made this statement about the Muslims he was well aware that his English and European coreligionists were already trading in sub-Saharan slaves: while one group served as a model, the other served as a commodity. That is why it is important to distinguish between the English perceptions of "Moors," "Blackamoors," "Negroes" and others[12]—not only to clarify English differentiations of color and religion, but to identify the relations of power and colonization.

Third and finally, the method critics have nearly always employed in the analysis of literary sources has depended on postcolonial discourse. This appeal to postcolonialism is understandable given the fact that the twentieth-century Muslim world has only recently liberated itself from its colonial (but not neocolonial) history. But by adopting the postcolonial template, critics such as Jonathan Haynes, Jack D'Amico, Emily C. Bartels, Jean Howard, Virginia Mason Vaughan, and many others have projected the military and industrial decline of Muslim countries in the modern period on English drama and travelogue[13]—at a time, when, the attitude of a Renaissance Briton to the Turks was not unlike that of "a Chinaman towards Europeans between the fall of Pekin and the victories of Japan"—an attitude of fear, anxiety, and awe.[14]

If one searches for nonliterary evidence of an English "colonial discourse" about Islam and the Muslims, one would come up with very little. In *Utopia*, Thomas More applied the colonial discourse to the Indians of America and argued for subduing, converting, and dispossessing them; two decades later, while awaiting execution, his chief anxiety in regard to international affairs was the formidable success of the Turks in conquering Christian lands in Central Europe and, still more menacing, their success in converting the populations to Islam.[15] Although More was not worried that the Turks would attack England, he was deeply concerned about Muslim imperialism and the islamicization of Europe: as the conquest of the Americas was enlarging Christendom in the West, the thrust of the Ottomans was diminishing it in the East. More than half a century later the situation had become worse. The English lawyer R. Carr lamented in 1600 "how it comes to passe, that so many of our men should continually reuolt, and abiuring all Christian rites, becomes affectors of that impious Mahumetane sect, whilst on the other part we finde none or very few of those repayring vnto vs."[16] As I have already shown in *Islam in Britain*, Christians, seeking to improve their fortunes or end their enslavement, converted to Islam and joined Muslim society and enterprise; no parallel conversion to Christianity took place among Muslims (chapters 1 and 4).

Notwithstanding the dangerous allure of Islam,[17] Queen Elizabeth cooperated commercially and diplomatically with both the Turks of the Ottoman Empire and the Moors of the Kingdom of Morocco, and never entertained or articulated—and nor did her subjects—projects for colonizing them. On the contrary, and instead of exhibiting her superiority to the Moroccan ruler, Ahmad al-Mansur (reg. 1578–1603), Queen Elizabeth repeatedly sought military and diplomatic help from him.[18] In 1603, the last year of his life as well as hers, al-Mansur proposed to the queen that Moroccan and English troops, using English ships, should together attack the Spanish colonies in the West Indies, expel the Spaniards, and then "possesse" the land and keep it "under our dominion for ever, and—by the help of God—to joyne it to our estate and yours." The Muslim ruler then continued:

> **And therefore it shall be needfull for us to treat of the peopling thereof, whether it be your pleasure it shall be inhabited by our armie or yours, or whether we shall take it on our chardg to inhabite it with our armie without yours, in respect of the great heat of the clymat, where those of your countrie doe not fynde themselfes fitt to endure the extremitie of heat there and of the cold of your partes, where our men endure it very well by reason that the heat hurtes them not.[19]**

In al-Mansur's plan, England was to help the Moors colonize America. Obviously, neither did al-Mansur fear English colonization nor was Elizabeth planning to colonize North Africa.

In the Jacobean period the only call for the colonization of Muslim territory came in a discrete missive addressed to King James I by Henry Roberts. [20] Roberts' missive was a true "colonial" discourse because it presented Morocco in exactly the same manner as America was presented: as America was described in promotional literature in terms of its natural wealth and beauty to encourage Britons to emigrate, so did Roberts describe the natural wealth of Morocco, the flora and fauna on which Britons could feast, and the Muslim population which, in his view, was eagerly awaiting conversion to Christianity—exactly as the American Indians were believed to be eagerly awaiting Christianization. But Roberts' colonial call was a private call and was never translated into royal policy; at no point did King James respond to such a colonial discourse in regard to Muslim territory.

Another call was made to King Charles I by his agent in Morocco, John Harrison. In October 1630, Harrison urged the king "to setle a Christian plantation in that part of the world, to Gods great glorie and Your Majesties everlasting honour."[21] A year later, however, Harrison had forgotten about the prospect as he became deeply concerned about the growth of Muslim naval power. The Turks and Moors, he wrote in October 1631, "in short tyme will be maisters of the seas, yea, they are so in these parts already [Salee], and next summer threaten the Channell even our English Channell."[22] Rather than England building a "plantation" in the land of the Moors, it was the Moors who were threatening to land in England.

Historians and critics who have inaccurately applied a postcolonial theory to a precolonial period in British history forget that in the Elizabethan and early Stuart periods, England was not a colonial power—not in the imperial sense that followed in the eighteenth century. Although England had colonized Wales and Scotland and was waging a colonial war in Ireland, at the time Queen Elizabeth died, England did not yet possess a single colonial inch in the Americas. In 1607 England established its first colony in Virginia, but over the next half a century it still had not succeeded further than the small colonies of Massachusetts (1629), Maryland (1632), Rhode Island (1635), and Connecticut (1636)—all in all, far less territory than Spain or France possessed in the New World. [23] Meanwhile, Britons had been facing setbacks elsewhere in the world. In 1558 England lost its last French outpost at Calais (in 1624 Richard Eburne was still lamenting the loss of "Normandy and Aquitaine"),[24] and in 1578, its pro-Portuguese mercenaries were defeated in Morocco. From 1594 until 1603 England encountered an ongoing rebellion against its colonization of Ireland, and in the 1620s its traders were driven out of the Spice Islands by the Dutch and out of Japan by the sho-guns. Although there was a momentum for colonization, inspired by the writings of Raleigh, Hakluyt, Purchas, and others, Elizabethan and early Stuart Britons were not yet capable of fulfilling the imperial enterprise; when the attacks of the Algerian pirates on English and Scottish ships became devastating in 1617, and Lord Bacon met with merchants and sea captains to consider the options for fighting the pirates, it was unanimously agreed that England could not confront Algiers on its own, and that unless it joined forces with Holland, France, and Spain, there could be no hope of success.[25] Even proud and enterprising Britons knew that England did not possess imperial might.

Half a century later the situation changed as England thrust itself through its Cromwellian control of the seas onto the imperial stage. At the end of 1655 Cromwell issued his *Proclamation Giving Encouragement to such as shall transplant themselves to Jamaica*. Cromwell assured the potential colonizers that there would be an army and a fleet there to protect them, and that they could build themselves "castles" on their property.[26] In the "West Indies," the English possessors could be "kings" and build castles (as later Robinson Crusoe called his island abode); for them, as for other Europeans, castles were the most powerful proof of their success in appropriating and coloniz-ing the new world.[27] Such castles were never built by Britons on Muslim soil. As a result, Britons never used the term *colonization* to describe their relations with the Muslims. In the Americas, Ireland, and elsewhere in the western hemisphere, words such as *colony*, *plantation*, and *settlement* were used to define the status of Britons there, especially after they defeated the natives and imposed their military superiority.[28] Such words do not appear in the English discourse about the Muslim Empire. While Englishmen went as "colonists" to America, they went as "factors" to Islam. As Richard Beacon was well aware in 1594, it was the Turks, and not the English, who were establishing colonies in which they reduced Christians to servitude.[29]

* * *

In the interactions between Britons and Muslims there was no colonial discourse, practice, or goal. Muslims were seen to be different and strange, infidels and "barbarians," admirable or fearsome, but they did not constitute colonial targets. There were no equivalents to Plymouth or Jamestown in North Africa—not even to unsuccessful Roanoke. Neither was there a painting of an Englishman gazing at a feminine, possessable, naked Islam, as in Jan van der Straet's depiction of Amerigo Vespucci gazing at "America"; rather the first painting ever made in England of a Muslim, which was coincidentally made in 1600, about the same year as van der Straet's, showed the Moroccan ambassador with a fierce and intimidating look. The ambassador was posing in London, thereby asserting his power in the metropolis of the English, unlike Vespucci who was asserting himself (with his cross) in the land of the naked and languid Americans.

Precisely because the Muslims were beyond colonial reach, Britons began to demonize, polarize, and alterize them. In a frenzy of racism and bigotry that dominated the late Elizabethan, Jacobean, and Caroline periods, dramatists and travelers, theologians, and polemicists created the representations

2. "America." Courtesy of the Smithsonian Institute

that would define early modern Britain's image of the Muslims. They established in their popular and widely read works the stereotype of the Muslim[30]—a stereotype that was presented and re-presented in numerous plays and pageants, and that gained wider appeal and permanence than the stereotype of the Jew or the American Indian. The "Turk" was cruel and tyrannical, deviant, and deceiving; the "Moor" was sexually overdriven and emotionally uncontrollable, vengeful, and religiously superstitious. The Muslim was all that an Englishman and a Christian was not: he was the Other with whom there could only be holy war.

It is important to note here that the creation of this alterity was chiefly undertaken within literary and theological contexts. Government documents, prisoners' depositions, and commercial exchanges show little racial, sexual, or moral stereotyping of the Muslims in the manner of Peele's *The Battle of Alcazar*, Dekker's *Lust's Dominion*, Shakespeare's *Othello*, Beaumont and Fletcher's *The Knight of Malta* or Rowley's *All's Lost by Lust*.[31] It was plays, masques, pageants, and other similar sources that developed in British culture the discourse about Muslim Otherness. Indeed, as in the case of Spain, Portugal, France, and Italy, it was the stereotype developed in literature that played the greatest role in shaping the anti-Muslim national consciousness. Just as *El Cid* and *Don Quixote* defined the genius of Spanish imagination, and *The Lusiads,* the *Song of Roland*, *Orlando Furioso*, *Jerusalem Delivered* shaped Portuguese, French, and Italian imagination respectively, so did Eleazer and Othello become the defining literary representation of the "Moor,"[32] and Bajazeth, Ithamore, and Amureth of the "Turk." The great national literature of Europe sustained the idea of the Otherness of Muslims from the Renaissance into the early modern age: as long as Tasso, Camoes, Ariosto, Cervantes, Marlowe, and Shakespeare, along with *El Cid* and *Roland,* were viewed, rightly, as the supreme icons of European imagination, the polarization with Islam and Muslims could only continue. While the national consciousness of many European countries was being forged in the late medieval and Renaissance periods, the foremost enemy was identified as the Muslim, and the foremost hero was the "ancestral" fighter against the "infidels."

In the case of England, the polarization with Islam occurred when the great heroes of Elizabeth—Drake, Raleigh, and others—were fighting not the Muslims (with whom they often cooperated), but the Spaniards and the "Salvages" of the New World. Unlike, therefore, Spain, France, Portugal, and Italy, England did not produce an anti-Muslim national epic; Spenser's and Milton's epics make only few allusions to "Turks" or "Mahometans." In England the theater took up the cudgel against the Muslims and appealed to a populace that felt threatened by, and confused at, the appearance of the Muslim Other in their metropolis, in their harbors, and across their Mediterranean and Atlantic trading routes. Very few "men of creative imagination," to use the phrase Elliot H. Tokson employed to describe English playwrights who wrote about the "Black Man" between 1550 and 1688,[33] depicted the Muslim accurately or sympathetically. Rather, they developed a polarization that informed the literary and cultural imagination of early modern England. Actually, Tokson continued, and "indicative of a broad racism," these writers "widened the distance" between the European and the African,[34] both North African and sub-Saharan, and transformed contact into conflict, engagement into stereotyping. Not surprisingly, as Tokson and Anthony Barthelemy have shown, not a single play about the Muslim Levant and North Africa that appeared in the Elizabethan, Jacobean, or Caroline periods showed the Muslim in a morally heroic and favorable light; not a single reference in eschatological exegesis spared the "Mahumetans" from destruction either by war or conversion.[35] Although in the actual meeting with Muslims on British, North African, and Levantine soil there was interaction and familiarity along with communication and cohabitation, in literature and theology, and thus in the emergent ideology of early modern Britain, the Muslim was depicted as occupying a place beneath the civilized European/Christian.

This construction of an image that was independent of and contrary to empirical evidence confirms what Margaret Hodgen has shown in her study of sixteenth-and seventeenth-century anthropology—that the representation of the non-European non-Christian in the Renaissance was not so much dependent on facts and experience as on cultural molds and imaginary portraits.[36] That is why, for the first time, Muslims of the Ottoman Empire and North Africa began to be categorized as "Barbarians" by English (and other European) writers.[37] The use of the term at this stage in the history of

Christian-Muslim interaction is striking because in the medieval period, the term had not been used; now, writers began using the term—paradoxically when they had access to extensive and reliable information about the advanced, not "barbaric," military and historical civilization of the Muslim Empire. This use of "barbaric" is not, however, difficult to explain: just as the association with barbarity denigrated the American Indians in the discourse of the New World, it was now brought into use to denigrate the Ottomans and the inhabitants of the 'Barbary' states. And as the alleged barbarity of the Indians justified for the Europeans the domination of the natives, so too did the barbarity of the Muslims legitimate the hope of dominating them.[38] Britons categorized the Muslims as barbaric even though they, the Britons, had not dominated them, perhaps even because of it: the Muslims were doomed to alterity whether they were conquered (as the American Indians had been) or not.

In their discourse about Muslims, Britons produced a representation that did not belong to the actual encounter with the Muslims. Rather, it was a representation of a representation: in order to represent the Muslim as Other, Britons borrowed constructions of alterity and demonization from their encounter with the American Indians. Unable to defeat the Muslims, as they had the American Indians, and unable to situate them in a world view convenient to their colonial and millennial goals, as they had done with the Americans, writers and illustrators applied constructions of differentiation from the American Indians to the Muslims. This process of superimposition was conscious and deliberate. In America, Englishmen and other Britons had encountered a culture to which they could feel superior and could defeat with what Thomas Harriot described in his *A briefe and ture report* (1590) as the "invisible bullets"; in America, they had exchanged their trifles for land and colonies, and had demonstrated to the "Salvages" their technological and national prowess.[39] In the Muslim world, Englishmen posessed no invisible bullets because the Muslims were religiously and militarily powerful, were widely influencing English culture, and were dictating their own terms of commercial and industrial exchange. (The English had to learn to produce what the Turks would buy.) Triumphant in America, the English found themselves humbled in North Africa and the Levant; conquerors in Virginia, they were slaves in Algiers.

As a result, and in order to maintain their sense of national superiority and confirm the image of Englishmen as God's own, they imposed the moral constructions they had devised to legitimate the colonization and (after 1622) the destruction of the Indians on the Muslims: as the American Indians were "sodomites" and therefore were deserving of divine punishment, so too would the Muslims be deserving of the same English/Christian-wielded punishment for their "sodomy." Just as the war against the Indians was a "holy" and "just" war that legitimated the usurpation of their land, so would the war against the Muslims be a "Holy War." But precisely because the Muslims of the Mediterranean basin were powerful and undominated, English writers turned to superimposition as an act of psychological compensation and vicarious assurance. Superimposition provided them with a strategy to confront the non-Christian Other, and helped them redress their colonial and cultural inadequacies before other European countries such as Spain and France. It also assured them of an epistemological control over the Muslims—over those whom they had failed to dominate.

Paradoxically, this superimposition of Indian on Muslim appeared in the society that produced philosophical empiricism and was on the verge of the scientific revolution. While Baconian science was developing the new tools for examining reality based on experience and "particulars," the representation of the Muslims depended not as much on firsthand experience as on constructions produced out of anxiety. Such anxiety coincided with the cultural and intellectual dislocation produced by the encounter with the racial and religious Other. For the English adventurer and trader, the world outside his island presented him with peoples who were different from him, and in the case of Muslims, autonomous of him. In the Mediterranean domains of Islam, the Briton could not have helped realizing that he was in a thoroughly islamocentric environment. In order to come to terms with this threatening new world, English writers entered into a triangular exchange and an interborrowing of discourses: they constructed the sexual and military identity of the non-Christian/Indian Other, and through this construction they initiated a discourse of separation from, and alterity with, the Muslims. Only through such a triangle could they maintain their sense of national superiority over the undefeated Moors and Turks—only through such a triangle could they sustain the eurocentric version of themselves they had developed during their conquest of the Indians.

In America, discourse went hand in hand with colonization. As Hakluyt's "prose epic" was published, republished, and expanded, the groundwork for the ideology of colonization was being laid—a groundwork that by the 1630s became a fully developed enterprise of occupation, destruction, and replacement. In North Africa and the Levant, however, the discourse remained a discourse: English writers dramatized and described a holy war against the Muslims as their compatriots waged war against the Indians, but the anti-Muslim holy war remained a pageant or "paper war." Unlike the Spaniards and the Portuguese who had seized (and in the case of the former retained) territories in Muslim North Africa, Britons did not seize a single inch of Muslim land throughout the Age of Discovery. Even in the second half of the seventeenth century, when the colonies in North America were aggressively being expanded, England not only failed to expand in the Mediterranean but actually had to give up its only outpost on Muslim land—Tangier. In 1683 and 1684, the colony of over a thousand soldiers (and their families) deserted Tangier (after destroying the fort) and embarked for home, leaving no trace behind them—not even of the English gardens they had tended, which, as Patricia Seed has argued, distinctly marked the English "ceremony of possession" in America.[40] They left Tangier not in dignity but, in the words of the Muslim historian al-Wufrani, in shameful flight.[41] The more English writers recognized that their discourse of domination and power was not translating into actual possession of Muslim land, the more they turned to superimposing Indians on Muslims, so much so that the terms "Indian" and "Moore" became, for some writers, interchangeable.

If the orientalism of the late eighteenth century, as Edward Said defines it, is colonialism as a form of discourse, then what the Renaissance English writers produced was merely a discourse—without colonialism—that was generated by superimposing the discourse about the conquest of America on Islam. The Renaissance witnessed the birth of a British/European discourse of conquest that preceded the development of the other constituents of conquest, namely technological superiority and capitalism. Once the Ottoman and the North African Muslim dominions began their military and commercial decline in the eighteenth century, British and other European writers turned to their discourse about America and the Indians during the Age of Discovery and imposed it on Islam, thereby producing the discourse of orientalism and the concurrent enterprise of empire.

Turks and Moors in England

Throughout the Elizabethan and Stuart periods Britons had extensive inter-action with Turks and Moors. It is significant that such interaction took place at all, since neither of the two peoples were permanent residents of England, nor were they subjects of the Crown. The Muslims were totally outside the parameter of English authority because they belonged, and were seen to belong, to an empire of military might and commercial potential. They were not homeless refugees from the continent who, like the Jews, sought new domiciles and work opportunities in England, nor were they defeated and dispersed people like the American Indians. The Muslims had a clear geo-graphical locus and did not as readily seek to emigrate to England as other peoples: while large numbers of Dutch and other Protestant immigrants set-tled in London in the second half of the sixteenth century, along with a small number of Portuguese and Spanish Marranos, only a few Muslim converts to Anglican Christianity (along with possibly some artisans) were known to have settled in the city. The Muslims had a distinct political, geographical, and religious identity that both protected and separated them from the Christian Other.

Despite this strong sense of separation between Christians and Muslims, Queen Elizabeth became the first English monarch to cooperate openly with the Muslims, and to allow her subjects to trade and interact with them with-out being liable to prosecution for dealing with "infidels."[1] Eager to find new markets for her merchants and secure military support against Spain throughout the 1580s and 1590s, the queen offered the Turkish and the Moroccan rulers mutually beneficial and practical agreements. In her correspondence with Sultan Murad (reg. 1574–1595), both agreed to admit English and Turkish traders into each others' kingdoms: the sultan assured her in a letter of 1579 that the English "may lawfully come to our imperiall Dominions, and freely returne home."[2] In turn, Elizabeth assured him: "we will graunt as equall and as free a libertie to the subjects of your highnesse with us for the use of traffique, when they wil, and as often as they wil, to come, and go and from us and our kingdomes."[3] England was now open to "Turks." So extensive was the commercial and diplomatic coordination between the queen and the sultan that Europeans suspected her of planning to offer him "safe port in England, by means of which to set his foot also into the Western Empire."[4] In 1590 King James VI of Scotland was "perswaided that no Christian Prince [except Queen Elizabeth] ever had in the Turk suche great estimation"; and by the end of the century, the Pope viewed Elizabeth as "a confederate with the Turk."[5]

In order to maintain her amicable relations with both the Turks and the Moors, the queen made sure that English sea captains released Muslim slaves from captured Spanish galleys. After the English fleet attacked Cadiz in 1596, thirty-eight "poore wretched Turks" who had been "gally-slaves" swam over to the English side. It pleased the fleet commanders, as it was reported in Hakluyt, "to apparel them, and to furnish them with money, and all other necessaries, and to bestow on them a barke, and a Pilot, to see them freely and safely conveied into Barbary."[6] Like England, France too released Muslim slaves.[7] While some freed slaves returned to their countries, others sought help. In 1591, one "Hamet, a distressed Turk" petitioned Queen Elizabeth to permit him to fight with her forces against the Spaniards.[8] How Hamed came upon this proposal is unclear, but it would not have been unprecedented in England for an alien to assist in military action.[9] From 1575 to 1588, immigrants were repeatedly made to join in national defense, and in 1596, it was reported by the Fugger spy that the English fleet that attacked Cadiz had been accompanied by "five galleys from Barbary" and that the English took with them to Barbary some of the ships they captured there.[10] Evidently the military cooperation between Britons and Moors covered both land and sea operations and was based on what seemed to be (although it was never formalized) a strategic alliance between London and Marrakesh.

Other "Turks" chose to remain in England by converting to Anglicanism—as "Chinano a Turke" did in 1586 and "John Baptista, of Tripoli" in 1605—a man who was later described by Robert Burton as "a Mauritanian priest."[11] Such a choice, however, was made only by a handful of Muslims since Queen Elizabeth was always eager to return Muslim captives in order to maintain her friendship with both the Ottoman Sultan and the Moroccan ruler. What may be truly indicative of the deep rapprochement between England and Morocco is the possibility that money collected at the Spital sermons in London, which were intended for ransoming Britons from "the Turkes or other hethens," may have been used to repatriate Moors who had been enslaved by Spaniards and released in England. Such Christian charity to the "infidels" is striking and shows how much the queen valued cooperation with Morocco: one of her last letters to Mulay Ahmad in Morocco (March 1603) concerned her freeing of "Moros y a Turcos" who had sought refuge in England.[12]

There is no information about how refugee Muslims lived or about how they supported and conducted themselves among the English, who were accustomed to images of the bloody and cruel "Mahometan" on the stage. Still, Muslims continually appear in English documents, either as having been freed by British sailors or having come to England on trading missions. Unfortunately, and because of the brevity of allusions to them, it is not always possible to distinguish between the freed slave and the merchant. In December 1602, for instance, a man, wrote John Manningham in his Middle Temple diary, "attired in habit of a Turke desyrous to see hir Majestie, but as a straunger without hope of such grace, in regard of the retired manner of hir Lord, complained; answere made, howe gracious hir Majestie in admitting to presence, and howe able to discourse in anie language; which the Turke admired, and admitted, presents hir with a riche mantle, & c."[13]

Who this Turk was is not clear, although the fact that he had wealth enough to offer a "mantle" to the queen and was multi-lingual suggests that he was a well-traveled merchant. In October 1617, "Turkish piratts," as

George Lord Carew reported to Sir Thomas Roe, approached the Scilly coast and met with some fishermen "loaden with fishe, of whom they bought commodities, payinge for them more then the wares was worthe." As a result, Carew was suspicious that these Turks were not really traders but actually pirates who were trying to "discover and view the coaste."[14] In October 1622, two "Turkes" were given passes by the Privy Council to "returne into their countrie" and in April of the following year, a pass for "ten Turkes to returne into their country" was given.[15] In March 1631, a pass was issued for "Barke Baha, a Marchant of Santa Crux in Barbary, to retourne thither with his wife and twoe maide servants."[16] In 1654, there was an "Albion Blackamore lately come to Town that is . . . well skill'd in Dancing on the Ropes."[17] This "Blackamore," who might well have been a freed Muslim slave, became quite popular: in September 1657, John Evelyn went to London where he saw "a famous Rope-daunser call'd the Turk."[18]

In the mid-1650s, a Turk by the name of Rigep Dandulo visited England and was entertained by the son of "the Lady Lawrence of Chelsey." As he walked around in "Turkish Habit" he became the center of the community's interest and was later, under the supervision of a number of leading Anglican clerics, converted to Christianity and settled in England.[19] In February 1657, the Levant Company interceded with Oliver Cromwell on behalf of "two Turks, Halil and Hamett," probably merchant delegates who sought "passage hence to their own country."[20] Two weeks after Cromwell's death, on 16 September 1658, "The humble Petition of Mahamet: Mustaoth: Hamat and Abdulah: all of them Turke native borne" was presented to Richard Cromwell: "That they were taken prisoners by the Spanyard and there hath byne detayned slaues for the figure of 22 yeares And it happened that hauing tyme made their escape and gayned into ffrance And by license were granted liberty for to come into this Nation of Englaind for their conduct and passing home into their owne country by some of yor highnes shipping."[21] That same month another petition was presented to Cromwell on behalf of "Abducadir, Achmet Sillau, and Hamet, of Sally."[22] A decade later, in January 1669, a pass was given for " — Hemmet, — Abdra, and — Hammond, Moors, natives of Barbary, to go into their own country."[23] From Elizabeth to Richard Cromwell and then Charles II, and whenever there was war with

Spain or France, England served as a corridor between the Catholic continent and the territory of Islam.

This English accommodation of Muslims was invariably conducted with
an eye to trade. As England expanded its commercial activity into the
Muslim dominions, it not only helped prisoners of war but also welcomed
Muslim seamen into its coastal towns. Treaties signed between Charles I and
the Commonwealth administration on the one hand and the North African
regencies on the other widened commercial links and, as with the
Elizabethan treaties, allowed Turkish and Moorish seamen to use English and
Welsh harbors. In October 1628, King Charles received Mohammed
Calvecho and Ibrahim Mocadem who were sent as commissioners from the
port of Salee in Morocco. Calvecho had arrived in England in June but
waited until his companion arrived in October before they presented their
letters to the king. The purpose of the visit was both military and commercial: the ambassadors sought arms from England in return for trading concessions to the Barbary Company and assistance in England's Mediterranean
confrontation with France and Spain.[24] The visit was successful since a few
years later, the Privy Council ordered the "Barbary merchants to trade only
to the ports in Barbary named in the articles offered to the King of
Morocco."[25] By the same token, "Turkish" seamen used English harbors.
Between November 1631 and February 1632 a treaty was signed between
Mulay al-Walid and Charles I in which "Moores" were to buy and sell goods
in England.[26] In September 1637, another treaty was signed between Mulay
Mohammad Esheikh and King Charles in which the subjects of the Moroccan
king were allowed to "exercise theire religion . . . in the Kingdome of the
King of great Britaine."[27] Less than twenty years later, in October 1655,
Muslim seamen docked in "Falmouth for provisions" much to the anxiety of
the Dutch and the "Zealenders," who feared that if the Turks continued to
find welcome in England they would "destroy" their (Dutch) trade.[28] Three
years later a treaty was signed with the bey of Tunis that allowed ships from
both England and Tunis to use each others' harbors "for washing, cleaning,
and repairing . . . and to buy and ship off any sort of victuals, alive or dead,
or any other necessaries."[29]

England also supported Muslim merchants with stipends and co-opted men of leverage so they could influence the decision making process in favor of British interests. As early as 1584, William Harborne told John Tipton, who had been appointed consul in the regencies, to contact "our Chaus Mahomet, with whom in all things you are to conferre of matters expedient, for the honor of her majesties country, & the commoditie, and libertie of poore captives."[30] Such employment of Muslim middlemen continued throughout the next century. In January 1697, passes were issued for "Cawra Mustapha, a native of Tunis in Barbary, to go to Turkey or Barbary." Further, "an allowance for his subsistence" was earmarked "as a matter which will be of great benefit to his Majesty's subjects living under that government."[31] In March, passes for "Mustapha and Mahomet, Algerians" were given; in April, a passage "for five poor Algerine seamen" was given because such cooperation would "be acceptable to the government of Algiers, and consequently of great use to his Majesty's subjects there."[32] By the beginning of the modern period England was offering financial assistance and bribes to effect the economic and commercial penetration of North Africa and the Levant.

Simultaneous, however, with this commercial and political *convivencia* was an ongoing piracy committed both by Britons and Muslims against each other. Not unlike the Christian-Muslim frontiers in Andalusia in the fifteenth century or in Central Europe in the sixteenth century, amicability and battle went hand in hand with trading and raiding. And it was during Muslim privateering raids or commercial exchanges that numerous "Turkes and Moores" were captured either on the high seas or near the British coast and brought to stand trial as pirates.

Thus the second category in which Muslims were encountered in England was as prisoners. Particularly after the unsuccessful English attack on Algiers in 1621 and the retaliation of the Barbary Corsairs against English traders and pirates, thousands of Britons were captured and hauled to the slave markets of North Africa. Similarly, Muslims were captured and either put to death or hauled into the jails of England. In 1620 it was reported that English ships had captured a "Turkish pirate ship" after which all 200 Turks on board were executed; in 1622 five "Turks" from Algiers who had been captured in a sea battle with the English ship "Exchange" were brought to Plymouth jail; soon after, nine more Turks were brought to Exeter "either to be arraigned according to the punishment of delinquents in that kind, or disposed of as the King and Council shall think meet."[33] Meanwhile, a number of Turks had been captured and kept prisoners in Cadiz in order to exchange them with English captives in Tetuan.[34] Three years later, in February 1625, Sir John Eliot, vice admiral of Devon, wrote from Exeter to the lord admiral, the duke of Buckingham, about bringing the Turks who had been captured in England to trial. By then their number had swelled to twenty-three "Turkes & Renegadoes" along with an Englishman and a Dutchman.[35] He reported that some of these men had been captured near Plymouth while others had been in jail for seven or eight years. Twenty men were sentenced to death and five were reprieved, including a "boy, young, and not capable of the knowledge or reason of doing good or ill." Importantly, Eliot attached the names of these captives, thereby revealing their geographical origins. There were some from Istanbul: "Abraham de Constantinople," and "Mahomet de Constantinople." Others were from Algiers: "Shaban de Arguir" and "Morat de Arguir." The rest came from around the Mediterranean. In this respect they were truly "Turks and Moors" in the precise sense of those terms. Noticeable among the names are those of "Andrew Jaquis als Mahomet" and "Vincent Hammett"; the combination of Christian and Muslim names indicates that these men were "renegadoes," since Christian converts to Islam always adopted a Muslim name.

By April 1625, it was reported to the Privy Council that there were "3 or 4 Turkes or Moores" in Exeter; thirty in Plymouth, three or four in Bristol and ten in "Baronet Seymor."[36] Apparently, these were not all pirates since the officials in those sea towns did not seem to know what to do with them. Similar confusion appeared in a letter of June 1626 by Francis Bassett, sheriff and vice admiral of Cornwall. Bassett, a man more interested in hawking and cockfighting than in Turks, was eager to rid himself of the prisoners he had in custody and bluntly inquired "How to dispose of these Turkes I haue, I am in a maze."[37] The reason for his confusion was that he was hearing different views. His correspondent Sir Francis Godolphin consulted with the commissioners of the Navy and others who urged him "that by noe meanes," should he "not [sic] put them to death." But others expressed different views. Bassett noted that the prisoners, who were forty in number, were in danger because of their "dyett" and some were so old that they were no longer employable. His chief anxiety, however, was that they might "doe mischeffe, & escape." They had asked to be sent to London, but if he sent them into the country they would, he suspected, "lye so neere the sae, as it may be easie for them to steale a Boate, or take a Barque . . . and so escape." Evidently, like other destitute prisoners in England and the rest of the British Isles, the Muslims were being forgotten in jail. They were in ill health as a result of eating foods—what little they would get—that were very different from what they were used to. But most importantly, they were totally ostracized by the populace; as Bassett noted, he could not find any "man so madd as to meddle with them."

One man, however, who had thought of meddling with Muslim captives was Sir Thomas Roe, the English ambassador in Istanbul, who spent much of his time in the Ottoman capital trying to secure the safety of English traders and seamen and their liberation once they were captured by the corsairs. On 1 February 1625, he wrote to King James requesting that he authorize a trade-off between the English captives in Algiers and the Turkish captives in Ireland. "God," he wrote, "hath prouided, by sending more [Turks] into Ireland, the liberty of whom will release those fewe [Britons] yet kept as hostage."[38] A few months later he reported to the Privy Council that over four hundred English captives had been released, but that the rest of the Britons were still in Algiers awaiting the exchange. Roe urged the Council "to giue like liberty to those Moores lately taken on the coast of Ireland and Plimmouth; who will fully, and with ouerplus, counteruayle and fullfill the couenant made on behalfe of the English; and being returned together with Jafer aga, wilbe a great and efficacious meanes, to strengthen and confirme this beginning."[39]

The king did not comply with Roe's request—actually he appeared to Roe not to be honoring the English part of the agreement with the Algerians that had been reached earlier that year. In June 1626, Bassett wrote to his friend Edward Nicholas complaining about the "dyvers Turkes which were brought in within my viceadmyraltie" and added that their number had increased since the English sailors on a Cornwall ship that had been captured by the Turks later overpowered their captors and brought more Turks as prisoners.[40] Because they had not been brought to trial as Bassett had hoped, the Muslim captives became so desperate that in July of that year they petitioned the Privy Council for assistance: "The humble petition of Jeffera Reys Captayne Joffer Ballu Basha and 36 more Turkes and Moores in a shippe of Argeir mored at Plymouth."[41] In their petition there is some information about their background and condition. They reported that having been "distressed at Sea" and "presuming uppon the late league made by his Ma:ties Ambassador" with Algiers, they "put into" his Majesty's "port of Plymouth." Evidently whenever commercial treaties were signed between England and a North African regency, Muslim sailors assumed that it was safe for them to use British port facilities in the same way that Britons were using their own harbors.

Unfortunately, such assumptions were not always shared by the English, who were not unwilling to exploit men in such desperate conditions. For, continued the petitioners, soon after they had docked, they were captured and treated as pirates of "Salley" although they had not intended "to revenge [harm] any English." Their advocate, who prepared the petition for them, reminded the addressees that by virtue of England's league with Algiers, the prisoners ought to be released and returned to their homes. After examining the petition the Privy Council concurred: in order "to maintayne with those of Argier and Tunnis" the "league and good corespondencie which his Mejesty desires," the Council ordered that "all the said Turkes and Mores should be at libertie to returne back for that countrie, and putt aboard theire owne shippe, and to have restored unto them all such monyes, armes, munition, provisions and furniture whatsoever belonging to them or theyre shippe as were seazed." It was also decided that all expenses incurred in preparing the ship would be met by the "Turkey Companie," which was urged to speed up their departure so that "the Board be noe further troubled therewithall."[42]

The number of Muslim captives in England grew that year: in June of 1626, forty-one "Turks" were captured at sea and brought to St. Ives in Cornwall.[43] Meanwhile, the ruler of Algiers, who was angry at Charles for breaking their agreement to exchange captives, dispatched his ambassador with over one hundred freed English captives to press the case of the Muslim captives in England. But the ambassador was unsuccessful in his mission and, after spending nine months, returned to his country in a rage. Apprehensive of what might ensue, the duke of Buckingham urged that the king send a letter and a "present of a ring from his Royal hand" to Algiers.[44] Nothing, however, was done to placate the Algerians. As a result, their attacks on English ships escalated thereafter. In September 1630, the Moroccan ruler, Sidi Ali bin Mohammad, sent a letter to King Charles in which he demanded that the king release all Muslim captives and send them back to the lands of Islam ("li-bilad al-Islam") regardless of whether or not they were Sidi's subjects. After doing so, Charles could be assured that no captive from the "English tribes" ("qaba'il al-Ingleez") would remain in North Africa.[45] With regard to the Muslim ruler, the English king and his piratical subjects were behaving in a manner comparable to the marauding desert tribes!

The question of what to do with prisoners was problematic to prison wardens, especially when the prisoners were old and incapable of work. There is no evidence that Muslims were sold and bought as slaves in Elizabethan or early Stuart England. But later in the century, as Muslim power declined, references begin to appear to Moorish and Muslim slaves owned by Britons.[46] A certain Hamet Tanjawi, for instance, was captured and enslaved during the Restoration period; he became a servant of the duke of York, from whom he learned a wide variety of naval lore, and later escaped back to Tangier where he put his English warfare training into Muslim use as he led the attack on the English fort in Tangier in 1676.[47] In his account of captivity in Morocco in the 1680s, Thomas Phelps recalled meeting with an "antient Moor, who formerly had been a slave in England and spoke good English, and who was set at liberty by our late Gracious King Charles the 2d."[48] Another captive/slave was the corsair Abdallah bin Aisha, who spent three years in England and was released by King Charles without ransom upon the intercession of James II.[49]

While these are the only allusions to North African Muslim slaves in England, there are numerous indications that Britons hauled Muslim captives to the Barbary Coast and exchanged them for English captives.[50] In 1635 Robert Blake was authorized to take forty-five Moors to Barbary to exchange them for English captives.[51] But he immediately ran into difficulty. There were more English than Moorish captives . So when two poor women pleaded in October 1636 with the Lords of the Privy Council to have their husbands exchanged with the Muslim captives, they were told that the captives had already been exchanged with English captives in Salee—probably men with royal or merchant connections. "Except there be some of the prisoners remaining in co. Dorset, he [Jerome, earl of Portland] knows not how these women should be relieved."[52]

While imprisoned Muslims sometimes petitioned for their freedom, at other times it was Britons who petitioned the Privy Council on their behalf. In September 1626, Charles Barrett complained from Cornwall that he and other inhabitants were being burdened by expenses incurred in "retaining and relieveing manie Turkes brought as prisoners into this kingdome."[53] Just as Francis Bassett had been anxious earlier about the possibility of the Turks' escape, Barrett too was concerned about their intelligence-gathering ability. That is why, he explained to the Council, the prisoners were kept in "inlande townes remote from the sea to prevent their view and survey of the portes, harbors and other landing places." Barrett feared that after returning to their countries, the prisoners would provide information about the English coastline—information that could prove disastrous in the hands of pirates and privateers. So extreme was the anxiety Barrett generated in the Privy Council that he was told to get rid of the prisoners as quickly as possible by exchanging them with English prisoners in Barbary.

A crisis seemed to have developed over these prisoners, for the keeper of the prison in Lanceston, Cornwall, refused to hand over the prisoners in his custody until the expenses he had incurred had been met. A warrant was therefore sent to him on 12 December from the Privy Council ordering him to deliver to Barrett all the prisoners who had been apprehended before 29 September, and to deliver to John Harrison, the king's agent in Barbary, all prisoners apprehended after that date—evidence that the number of Muslim captives in England was growing.[54] Harrison had been given a commission by the king to exchange English captives in Morocco with Muslim captives in England. The king had declared: "And wee doe hereby give and graunt unto the saide John Harrison full power and authoritye to transport and carry with him into the parts of Barbary such and so many Moores as are at this tyme prisoners in this our realme of England, and them there to deliver in exchaunge for the redemption of such of our owne subjects beinge prisoners in any of the places aforesaide."[55] Unfortunately, however, as Harrison reported to Secretary Coke, his ship that "was to have transported Moorish prisoners to Barbary had sprung a leak." He suspected that there was a "design" by Barrett to transport the captives on a ship in Dartmouth to Leghorn and sell them there "for slaves" rather than exchange them with the British captives in Salee and Algiers.[56] But no such design was carried out since, soon after, it was reported that numerous Turks and Moors were "wandering and begging about the City of London."[57]

Indeed, in February 1627, the Council learned that ten or more of the prisoners whom Barrett was supposed to use for redeeming British prisoners had escaped "out of the Westerne parts and doe hearber themselves in the cittie of London."[58] A request was made to the officers of the Lord Mayor of the city of London to search for the Muslims and upon their capture to return them to Barrett. Another report in that same year mentioned forty "Turkes leaving" in England, some of whom (probably those who had been released by Harrison) were employed in the following manner: three as tailors, two as shoemakers, two as menders, two as button makers, and one as solicitor.[59] That Muslims were living and working in London raises the fascinating possibility of a community infrastructure. Was there a prayerhouse or mosque where they assembled? Were they able to sustain their daily prayer ritual, their Friday gathering, and their avoidance of pork and wine (or for the English, ale)? Also intriguing is the reference to a "solicitor" (and, significantly, not a barrister). Was he simply a provider of social advice or had he learned a smattering of English law? Unfortunately, there is no further information about this group of London Muslims, although it is quite possible that the community was still in the city in the early 1640s, when an anonymous writer referred to a sect of "Mahometans . . . here in London."[60] If these or other Muslims had actually settled in London, they would correspond to the artisans, skilled workers, small merchants, and other European immigrants who had settled in England during this period, and who did so for purposes of commercial gain.[61] Many single men crossed from the continent to England for work; Muslims would not have been unlike them. Just as there were English workers among the Muslims, so were there Muslim workers among the English.

In September 1636, two Moors were captured—one "Mahammet aged twentie seven or thereabout" and "Hammet aged fortie foure yeares or there-about"—from Salee. They had been sailing with "foure Moores, eighteen [sailors] of Sallie, five Renegadoes Dutch one English their Pilott."[62] When their ship reached the English coast the renegades turned against the Moors after being called "to stand upp for their liues & liberties" whereupon "they drove the Moores into the hold, hoisted saile, and brought their Barque into the first [English] port."[63] Writing to the Lords of the Admiralty, the earl of Portland included "coppies of the examinations of two of the moores."[64] Mohammad seemed to have done more talking than Hamed, for he informed Portland that he had been in "about twentie seven" voyages "on the coast of Spaine, save one the last yeare on the coast of ffrance, there they tooke thir-tie ffrench & ten packs of cloth." Earlier both men confessed that their ship had been "set out by merchants of Sallee for the taking of Chrystians" and that the "Turk & Renegadoes" wanted to do "them service against the Spaniards." But then they arrived near the coast of England where they "mett two fish-ermen whome they would not have pursued being too neare Land, but the Captain commanding & guiding the helme" made them capture one, after which the English renegade pilot and the captured English made "themselves [masters] of the Turks . . . and brought them in."[65]

Portland assured his addressees that "if they [Moors] shall confesse as much att tryall as they haue," there would be no need for "other euidence against them." Once the Moors admitted to their piracy, Portland hoped for speedy action against them because "they lye heere att a great charge." In that same period, six "Moors or Turks of Sallee" were "distressed" and forced to land on English soil; their ship, as Lord Portsmouth reported, was brought into Hurst Castle.[66] Like earlier seamen they believed that the commercial and military treaties that had been negotiated between the king of Morocco and Charles I allowed them to use English ports for victualing and safety. Much to their horror they found themselves imprisoned and arraigned at Winchester, along with other coreligionists who had been captured on the Isle of Wight. Confused about how to proceed further, Lord Portland wrote to Thomas Wyan asking him to help in the "Tryall of certaine Mores or Turkes" that was set to take place at Winchester. The prisoners had to wait for over a year before being brought to trial, and in October 1637, Sir James Bagg wrote to the Lords of the Admiralty about it. He confirmed that the six "Moores or Turkes of Sallye" had been "inforced to land out of their boate" but the "evidence against them of taking a small boate in Tourbay" led to their conviction as pirates. Bagg added their names: "Ama Dela, Abdala, Hammett, Hammett, Muhammett & Rubely."[67]

Muslim seamen were continually taken prisoners, sometimes rightly as pirates and sometimes wrongly as merchant seamen who were accused of piracy, so they could be sold as slaves or exchanged with British captives in North Africa. Sometimes Muslims were brought in groups; at other times they were alone, as was the case with the "More" whom Robert Swyer kidnapped from Tetuan in Morocco in 1627.[68] In 1637 two Moorish boys were captured and brought to England for the purpose of converting them to Christianity.[69] That same year, Captain William Rainsborough told the vice admiral to allow the Algerian "Alcado" to check for Moors among the renegade prisoners on his ship.[70] More than thirty years later, in March 1669, it was reported that the English ship *Morning Star* had had on it "a Moorish boy" who was subsequently rescued by an Algiers man of war.[71] In 1670 a ship with ten Turks and two renegades was "driven on shoar near the Port of Trally in Ireland," after which the Muslims were captured and made prisoners.[72]

The third and final category of Muslims who came to England was that of ambassadors. Official Muslim delegations began to arrive in England as early as the second half of the sixteenth century. Such visits introduced the London community to the Muslims in a manner different from that of the previously discussed groups. As refugees and prisoners who were ostracized in jail or wandered the London streets, Muslims were unable to project their culture or religion. Ambassadors, however, arrived in pomp and enjoyed the protection of the monarch, and therefore could and did practice their religious observances openly, abide by their dietary rules, and appear in their national dress with its conspicuous turban. Such visitors provided the populace with the only real portrait of how Muslims—wealthy Muslims, that is—lived, worshipped, and conducted themselves. Although they numbered far fewer than refugees and prisoners, it was this elite group that provided Londoners with their most authentic image of Muslims.

The first Muslims to arrive in London as representatives of their monarchs were "two Moores, being noble men, whereof one was of the Kings blood," who were brought by Thomas Wyndham in 1551.[73] In September 1579, a Turkish envoy arrived with a letter to Queen Elizabeth in which the sultan offered "unristricted commerce in his country to Englishmen."[74] This envoy is important because he probably was the first Turkish official to visit Elizabethan England—and to bring with him the first communication from Sultan Murad III to the queen.[75] In 1580 the sultan sent a merchant/envoy by the name of Ahmed to make some purchases in England.[76] Three years later the first Turkish ambassador arrived, bringing presents that represented the wealth and exoticism of the Levant: lions, Turkish scimitars, horses, and unicorn horns.[77] In January 1589 an ambassador from Morocco, Ahmed Belkassem, visited England with the English agent Henry Roberts, and was received by over forty members of the Barbary Company, "well mounted all on horsebacke," and escorted into the city of London by torchlight.[78] In 1595 another ambassador, al-Caid Ahmed ben Adel visited England, accompanied by two other caids and a retinue "of twentye five or thirtye persones." That the visitors were caids is significant: the caids were the leaders of the corsairs who attacked European shipping vessels in the Mediterranean and Atlantic. Was England entering into secret negotiations with the Barbary Corsairs—to the extent of welcoming them openly in the metropolis? According to the Fugger informant, who disliked the English for their piracy and pillaging, the answer was affirmative.[79]

Not much information has survived about those visits of the ambassadors and caids, unlike the visit in 1600 of the Moroccan ambassador, "Hamet Xarife," as he was known in England, or 'Abd al-Wahid bin Mas'ood bin Mohammad 'Annouri, as Mulay Ahmed listed his full name in the letter to Elizabeth on 15 June 1600. This ambassador arrived with two merchants, "Arealhadgel Messy, and Alhadge Hamet Mimon," along with thirteen others—all told, sixteen Muslims.[80] They arrived in August "strangely attired and behauiored" and stayed for six months, lodging in the house of the alderman in the Royal Exchange.[81] During their visit the problem of their "dyet" arose; as Muslims they could only eat *halal* meat, and therefore they slaughtered their meats at home in accordance with Islamic law: "They kild all their owne meate within their house, as sheepe, lambes, poultrie and such like, and they turne their faces eastwrad when they kill any thing," noted one observer.[82] Another problem may have arisen when one of the retinue died; where, as a non-Christian, could he be buried? Meanwhile, they traveled around the city, observing much of English social and commercial custom, attending royal celebrations, and looking at and being looked at by Londoners. They were so ubiquitous that Londoners considered them "rather espials then honorable ambassadors."[83] These swarthy men with their strange clothes and habits alienated the Elizabethan community, especially since it was reported that they refused to offer any alms to the local poor and "used all subtiltie and diligence to know the prises, wayghts, measures, and all kindes of differences of such commodities, as eyther their country sent hither, or England transported thither."[84] That is why, when they were making preparations to leave England, John Chamberlain noted that neither "the marchants nor marriners will . . . carrie them into Turkie, because they thincke yt a matter odious and scandalous to the world to be too frendly or familiar with infidells."[85] Indeed, judging by the surviving portrait of the ambassador, with his stern face and fierce look, the English painter, like the populace, may have found the Moors not just alienating but intimidating too.

Elizabeth was the only monarch to entertain so many Muslim ambassadors. She was so fascinated by things Islamic that she requested from her ambassador in Istanbul some Turkish clothes; like her father, she wanted to dress in the oriental fashion.[86] Elizabeth's successor, James I, received a certain Mustapha in 1607 who, unlike earlier visitors, was willing to "dispense with some of his Turkish fashions, and to accustome himselfe to ours."[87] Still, he paraded in "many changes of garments very rich, and several turbants" and remained in England for a few months.[88] In 1611, "Two Chiaus or Messengers from ye Turke" came to London,[89] and on 3 November 1618, another "Chiaus" had his audience with the king at the Banqueting House which, as Master of Ceremonies John Finet noted, "was purposely hung for him with rich hangings." In an unprecedented gesture in England, the king touched one of the chiaus's retinue, "said to be his Son, for cure of the Kings Evill, useing at it the accustomed Ceremony of Signing the place infected with the crosse, but no prayers before or after." Such an episode is noteworthy for its openness to religious interaction: although the chiaus would not allow the recitation of a Christian prayer over his son, he accepted the signing of the cross.[90] Either the chiaus believed in Christian medicine or his son was so sick that he was willing to try any cure—even if that involved what to a Muslim is the highly objectionable sign of the cross. That James, a monarch who was notoriously hostile to Islam, was willing to apply his royal miracle on a Muslim may have stemmed from his desire to demonstrate not only Christianity's superior medicine to the Muslims, but the international efficacy of his royal touch to his subjects.

Soon after his accession to the throne Charles I received, in April of 1625, an Algerian "chiaous" who brought with him to England a present of Barbary horses, tigers, and lions, and who remained in England for nine months—without, however, making much of an impression on the king, who did not give him the customary present before he departed.[91] When the plague broke out in London a house in Deptford was requested by the London agent in Algiers, Mr. Leat, for the ambassador. But the request was denied and the house was given to one "Mr. Bell [who was] more worthy to be respected and accommodated, being a committeeman, than a stranger, especially he being a Turk."[92] At a time when there were thousands of English and Scottish captives in North Africa, it would have been unlikely for London merchants to assist the representative of the king who was enslaving their compatriots. In June 1627, two ambassadors from Salee arrived in London, Mohammad ben Sa'd and Ahmad ben Hussein, accompanied by Harrison, the English agent there, for Charles to negotiate with them over the possible use of Salee as a base of operations against Spain.[93]

Neither these ambassadors nor Calvecho and Mocadem left their mark on the popular or royal imagination. The Moroccan ambassador of 1637, however, did, and actually stunned London and its court. In October of that year, Alkaid Jaurar bin Abdella came to England on the first visit of a Muslim given detailed coverage in the London press. When the ambassador and his retinue landed at Tower Hill, Finet wrote, over a hundred aldermen and citizens of the city were there to welcome him, dressed in their "scarlet gowns" and "chaynes of gold,"[94] in a spectacle that was "attended by Thousands, and ten Thousands of Spectators."[95] He was then "lighted with 5 or 600 torches to his lodging" in Wood Street near St. Lawrence Jewry—which meant that his procession passed through a good part of East London; later when he went to see the king in Whitehall he crossed the breadth of the metropolis, which was "throng'd and crowded by innumerable multitudes of people of all sorts."[96] Alkaid was seen by thousands of Londoners.

English society saw in this ambassador the full flourish of Islam.[97] He went to his public audience with the king on horseback (and not in a coach), a servant preceding him with his "scymetar" and "Moors in their country habits on horseback" following. He brought with him a present of "four hawks," which the king insisted on having presented to him soon after the ambassador arrived in London and before the official audience, lest they be mistreated by "unskilled keepers." There were also "four horses, two of them with their rich saddles and furnitures on covered with cloths of damask, and other two with their cloaths only, each of them led by a black Moor." When the ambassador came before the king and queen he spoke to them in "Arabick by the interpretation of his Associate"—very likely the first time Charles had ever heard Arabic spoken by a Muslim. Significantly, the ambassador, who was a Portuguese convert to Islam, knew various European languages, which he later used and for which he was admired; but he insisted on Arabic in that first meeting as evidence of political and cultural assertiveness. There was such commotion and "intruding presse" about his visit that soon after his arrival the London populace was able to read about the official welcome for the ambassador in a publication that included a picture of him. Appropriately for a man who had been liked, the frontispiece showed the turbaned face of a benign and sweet man. (He was, after all, a eunuch).[98]

One of the reasons this ambassador made such an unprecedented impact on the English was that he had brought with him from Morocco 366 British captives, 350 having been ransomed by the king himself, and 16 released free of charge by the Moroccan ruler as a sign of good will. No other ambassador had had such an advantage; the Moroccan ambassador in 1600 had brought with him nine Dutch captives, and the 1626 ambassador had brought one hundred Britons.[99] Alkaid enjoyed the advantage of being at the head of a procession that not only paraded his wealth and authority, but also captives who were returning to their families and communities. As Finet reported, the sixteen captives walked behind him as he went to see the king, all having received new clothes at the ambassador's own expense. This procession is particularly significant as it could be viewed not only as a welcome to him, but as a public celebration for the returning captives—a celebration that was very common on the Continent but unprecedented in England. In France, Italy, and Spain, such public celebrations were frequent and served as a means to fuel anti-Muslim sentiment as well as raise funds for redeeming captives, but there is no record of any similar celebration taking place in England before this.

While King Charles wanted to establish peace with Morocco and to reduce piracy, some of his subjects were unwilling to give up their attacks on Muslim shipping.[100] Two years after the arrival of al-Jaurar another emissary was sent to coordinate a treaty with England: Mohammad ben Askar arrived in April 1639 to "demaund justice against" English pirates.[101] Little seemed to have been accomplished by this emissary because his arrival coincided with the king's departure for the north to wage war against the Scots. A year later, in September 1640, a chiaus along with "15 or 16 followers" visited London as a personal messenger from the Ottoman sultan. As in the case of the 1618 chiaus, when this messenger went to the Banqueting House for his audience with the king, the place was "purposely" decorated for him.[102] Finet's emphasis is important because it reveals a sense of rivalry with the Ottoman court: as the sultan in Istanbul exhibited his wealth before foreign ambassadors, so did the English king—especially because the decoration consisted of fine English cloth, one of the primary exports to the Ottoman Empire. The chiaus was accompanied by numerous merchants from the Levant Company, and was again seen by large crowds of Londoners, who by then must have become accustomed to exotic visitors.

The key episode that occurred during his visit was the exchange of foods: Finet sent him some sweetmeat and received in return various dishes of "meat dressed a la Turkeska." Finet was aware of the tension that might ensue were he to send the chiaus some meat dishes: it was known to the chiaus that, either out of malice or ignorance, Christians sometimes presented to him religiously "unclean" meats. Evidently the ambassador was widely accessible to the community, and the community, insular in its Englishness, was not unwilling perhaps to try some pranks on the foreigner—especially a foreigner whose dietary codes clashed with their pork-eating delights. Food played a major part in bringing the Christians and the Muslims together, for, aside from pranks, the English were quite curious about Turkish cuisine. Shortly before the chiaus was to leave for home the Lord Marshall and the Lord Chamberlain asked Finet about Turkish food and secured an invitation from the chiaus to eat supper at his residence. Having paid the expenses themselves they had the chiaus's servants prepare food "a la Turkeska," and then the two lords, along with "other great lords," had a wonderful meal with the messenger that was "so unusuall a mesure and manner." English and Turk sat around the same table, with the highest seat reserved for the chiaus, "observing theyr content of appetite." Turkish cuisine had arrived in England.

No visits of Muslim ambassadors are recorded during the civil wars and early Interregnum, but in May of 1657 an Algerian messenger arrived in London to "confirm," in the words of the Venetian resident, "the good relations and trade between this country [England] and that mart [Algiers]."[103] Three weeks after his arrival a "present of animals" that was to be presented to the Lord Protector was brought over by "another Turk of lower ranks, who is a renegade Greek." In light of the good relations between the two countries the messenger was given, upon his departure a month later, "200 pieces of eight and a bolt of scarlet cloth."[104] It is possible that King Charles II entertained in 1667 an international fraud who may have been a Muslim in Christian disguise,[105] but the most famous and publicized visitor of his reign was the Moroccan ambassador Mohammad bin Hadou, who arrived on 29 December 1681 and departed on 23 July 1682.[106] There were poems written about the occasion, descriptions in private correspondence and diaries, and most importantly, news reports about the ambassador in the *London Gazette*. Bin Hadou was entertained by royalty and seen by commoners; he wandered in the court and the city, and traveled to Oxford and Cambridge. He visited the Royal Society, met some of its members, and examined its research, attended banquets and concerts, and engaged in public activities.

Along with his retinue he was widely observed and scrutinized; it was reported by John Evelyn that he did not drink wine, was courteous to women, was magnificent on horseback in Hyde Park, and was interested in Arabic manuscripts and scientific innovation. For the duration of their stay in England, the ambassador and the Moors became "the fashion of the season" generating so much excitement that Evelyn was embarrassed at the "concourse and tumult" of Londoners as they gathered to see the ambassadorial processions.

Clearly the Moors and Turks were "everywhere,"—not just in the literary imagination of English dramatists and poets, but in the streets, the sea towns, the royal residences, the courts, and the jails of Elizabethan, Jacobean and Caroline England and Wales.

* * *

The meeting with Muslims in the seventeenth century took place within the previously discussed categories of merchants/refugees, pirates, and ambassadors. What is significantly missing is the category of the Muslim traveler who would visit England on his own initiative. While numerous English and Scottish travelers wandered into the Muslim empire and described in detail the custom, history, and religion of Islam, no Muslims seem to have similarly ventured into the British Isles. This is perhaps because there was no holy site to attract Muslims as Christians were attracted to Palestine, and because Muslims may have feared their rulers, who might accuse them, upon their return, of being spies for Christian potentates—as indeed did happen to bin Hadou.

The Muslims who came to England and the British Isles were in the hundreds, and may have reached a few thousand, although during no period were there more than a few score together on British soil. All the meetings with Muslims took place among the inhabitants of the southern parts of England and Wales, extending from the coastal towns to London and some of its surrounding areas—areas in which the majority of immigrants from the continent (the Low Countries and France) settled.[107] Although Turkish and North African naval activity did reach Scotland and Ireland, there are no records of Muslim refugees, merchants, or ambassadors in either of these two areas or in the northeast of England. There are accounts of Muslim pirates attacking (and sometimes being captured) in Ireland, but that does not change the fact that Muslims predominantly appeared in southern England and Wales. Finally, the Muslims who were seen in England were all men. In all the surviving records of captured Moors and Turks , there is not a single reference to a Muslim woman. While numerous British women were captured and sold in North Africa, no Muslim woman seems to have ever set foot on English soil, either as a refugee or a prisoner. There is no indication that any Muslim ambassador included women in his retinue.

In the actual interaction, therefore, between Muslims and Christians in seventeenth-century England, there was no transgressiveness that was seen to be inherent in the Muslim/Moor.[108] There were social engagements marked by ambivalence and reciprocity, attraction and repulsion, but there was no violence. No Muslim ambassador was ever pelted with stones, as was the Spanish ambassador in the Jacobean period. Actually, and in terms of deep personal relations between Muslims and Britons, it is striking that the only marriages that occurred, or were about to occur, in all of English Renaissance history between English women and non-Christian men, took place with Turks and Moors. While there is no reference to an English woman ever marrying or thinking of marrying an unconverted or un-Christianized Jew or American Indian, there are numerous references to English-Muslim marriages and sexual liaisons. Muslims were clearly viewed as a different non-Christian group from the rest—and a group with whom miscegenation was passable if not desirable. In 1614, for instance, negotiations were conducted for the marriage of the sultan of Sumatra and the daughter of an English "gentleman of honorable parentage" because it was felt that such a marriage would be "beneficial to the [East India] Company." Although some London clerics objected to the marriage on the grounds that the husband was a Muslim, the Company marshaled its own theologians to prove "the lawfulness of the enterprise . . . by scripture." The marriage never took place, but it is important that the marriage of a Christian woman to a Muslim man was seen to be theologically (and not just practically) legitimate in some circles.[109]

A little over twenty years later, in 1636, as the number of British captives

rose in Algiers and funds dried up to ransom them, an anonymous sugges-
tion was made to King Charles I that he send English prostitutes to ransom
the captured seamen—six prostitutes for every one seaman.[110] Although
the king did not act upon this advice, the idea that English (and other British)
women would practice the oldest profession with "Turks" suggests an environment that did not view miscegenation as totally objectionable. In his
memoir of captivity in Algiers between 1639 and 1644, T. S. described an
amazing range of sexual affairs he had conducted with Muslim women—
because he was handsome women, both married and widowed, were
attracted to him. [111] One in particular was so courageous in pursuing him
that he finally fell in love with her and offered to marry her if she would be
willing to escape with him back to England. Unfortunately, "She had two
Children, a Boy and a Girl, that kept her in that place otherwise I think I had
then got my Freedom and carried her away." Later she gave birth to "a pretty
little Girl, somewhat whiter than ordinary; the old Fool [her husband]
thought himself to be the Father of it."[112] When other women made themselves available to T. S. he did not decline but told his Turkish master, who
was happy to take his place in bed. Muslim master and Christian slave shared
in the pleasures of illicit sex with Muslim women.

In the second half of the seventeenth century one of the wives of the dey
of Algiers was English, and so too was one of the harem of Mulay Ismail, the
powerful ruler of Morocco. She bore him two sons.[113] In 1682 a Christian
convert to Islam by the name of Hamed Lucas accompanied the Moroccan
ambassador Mohammad bin Hadou to London, and during his stay married
an English servant girl.[114] The episode was recalled by Thomas Rymer a
decade later: "With us [in England] a Moor might marry some little drab, or
Small-coal Wench." Rymer concluded from this match that the English people as a whole were unlike the Venetians in that they did not feel "hatred and
aversion to the Moors," and therefore were willing to marry them.[115]

* * *

Between Britons and Turks and Moors there was engagement and conflict,
piracy and trade, sexual affairs and marriage—a whole scope of relationships
and associations, some conducted within and some outside the law, some

ambiguous and some unprecedented, some clandestine and some public. The shifts in the relations were chiefly governed by the diplomatic climate and were not dissimilar from shifts that occurred between Britons and Christian Europeans: when there was alliance or trade, relations were receptive and cooperative, and when there was rivalry and military confrontation, there was fear and anxiety. But among all the non-Christian peoples who came to England and interacted with Britons, whether in London or overseas, the Muslims entered into the most open and extensive relationships. They most widely permeated English literature, drama especially, in a manner different from any other non-Christian. In numerous plays there are references to Muslim-Christian and Muslim-English marriages—marriages that could not have taken place or even been dramatized between Britons/Christians and unconverted Jews or American Indians.[116]

Although Muslims were different from Britons in religion, culture, language, and sometimes skin color (especially in the case of the Moors), Britons treated them as they did other European aliens and pirates, merchants and ambassadors—what mattered was social and economic rank, profession, diplomatic role, and other marks of status. A Turkish pirate was not treated any worse than a captured Spanish pirate. Actually, he was often treated better; a Moorish ambassador raised as much suspicion and intrigue as other ambassadors. Significantly, there were never any anti-Muslim riots in London in the way that there were anti-alien riots.[117] Muslims never roused English xenophobia perhaps because there were not as many Muslims as there were Dutch or Walloon families, and because no Muslim ruler ever threatened England in the manner of Philip II and his Armada.

The Turks and Moors belonged to the most powerful of all the non-Christian civilizations with which Britons were engaged. They also belonged to the international community of trade, diplomacy, and military rivalry that marked England's foray into the age of Mediterranean and Atlantic discovery. Although from the Elizabethan period on the English were beginning to develop their anglocentric view of the world, they were deeply aware that they had to contend with a powerful and sometimes confrontational and aggressive islamocentrism—from Salee to London, from Tunis to Istanbul, and from Bristol to New England, Turks and Moors reminded them that the world did not revolve around Albion.[118]

2

SOLDIERS, PIRATES, TRADERS, AND CAPTIVES: BRITONS AMONG THE MUSLIMS

At the same time Muslims were going to England, Britons were going to North Africa and the Levant in greater numbers. They went (or were taken) in the thousands, with the highest proportion consisting of captives who were at one time reported to have numbered over five thousand in Algiers alone. [1] Hundreds of other Britons visited the Muslim Mediterranean world on their own initiative and stayed there either to conduct business, to seek employment, to visit for weeks, or to settle for years. The majority of these Britons were men but there were a few women too. But on the whole the British exposure to Muslims was predominantly confined to the male population.

The writings of a few of these Britons—particularly those of William Harborne, Thomas Roe, and Dudley North—are both fascinating and informative about the Renaissance interaction with Muslims. But the careers and writings of soldiers and captives, along with the sundry other "small" Britons who lived and worked among the Muslims, provide a more intimate and careful portrait. These writings reflect the British experience from a position of defensiveness and sometimes subservience. Hired soldiers and seamen, captives and slaves, traders and artisans, did not enjoy the luxury of ambassadors or royal emissaries, who described the "Turks" from a position of distance and diplomatic carefulness. Nor were they like travelers so secure in

their status that they rarely engaged the Muslims (or learned their language).
Rather these were men who lived among the Muslims as servants or mercenaries, as slaves, pirates or merchants, and were always at the mercy and
whim of the Muslim ruler and his subjects. Despite the agenda some of these
men had for constructing a heroic image of themselves, their writings, along
with documents about them, provide a unique perspective on the interaction
between Britons and Muslims on Muslim soil. Not only do they show a variety of personal interactions with Muslims, they also span the main cities of
Islam along with the hinterlands in an area extending from Morocco to Egypt
and from Mocha to Istanbul. Based on firsthand experience, these texts constitute the first authentic English writings about the Muslim world since the
Crusades.

Soldiers

From the reign of Queen Elizabeth until the Caroline period Britons joined
the armies of the Muslim dominions, both in the Levant, in central Asia, and
in North Africa. Some of these Britons were from the nobility but most were
either common soldiers who found reliable pay among the Muslims or seamen and gunners captured by the North Africans and willingly or unwill-
ingly put to military service. The regencies of Algeria, Tunisia, and Tripoli,
along with Morocco and Persia, offered both attractive employment and
honorable service: "Your Wars are manly, stout and honourable," Sir Anthony
Shirley is supposed to have said to the Persian Sophie/Shah in a play published in 1607. "Your Armes have no imployment for a coward."[2] As a result,
Renaissance Britons entered Muslim military service: North Africa, the
Ottoman, and the Persian Empires fulfilled for Britons their military ideals
and financial needs. It is no wonder that throughout his reign King James
repeatedly issued royal proclamations calling on English and Scottish sailors
and soldiers to return from abroad and serve at home. There was too much
allure in the dominions of the Muslims.

   Some of the Britons who went to the Muslim empires in the
Mediterranean and in Central Asia were men who found themselves without
military employment at a time in Renaissance England when there was no

professional army or class of soldiers with a secure pay. (The first professional army only came into being at the beginning of the Civil War.) Denied
the opportunity for work at home, these men left England to pursue their
careers and fortunes among the Muslims. Surprisingly, rather than being cas-
tigated by their countrymen for serving the "infidels," these men were celebrated in biographies and dramas, and were nearly always viewed as great
English heroes. These men served—and many of them died while fighting
for—the Muslims, and judging from the surviving literary and historical
documents, their numbers were in the hundreds. Although they did not leave
writings behind describing their experiences, they made a strong impression
on Elizabethan and Jacobean imagination and culture. In particular they
showed that it was acceptable and rewarding for Britons to live and work
among the Muslims. These writings, with their heroic image of the Britons,
may have served to promote such a career to the reading and theatergoing
public in England.

Two changes occurred in Renaissance England that were instrumental in
driving Britons to join the Muslim military establishment. The first was the
change that occurred during the reign of the last of the Tudor monarchs and
the first of the Stuarts, concerning the military "career." By the second half
of the sixteenth century, English nobles, for whom military service was an
honorable duty to the sovereign, had to contend with the decline of chivalry
in the "organic scheme" of Elizabethan England.[3] "The humanists' political
and educational ideals" that they had cherished were drastically changing in
what was becoming an "increasingly complex, commercial, and degenerate
society."[4] Simultaneously, the common soldiers, who were conscripted
before battles and disbanded afterwards, were viewed as no better than
unwanted vagrants with "no meanes to maintaine them selves but by
stealinge and lewde practize."[5] They were, as Robert Barret wrote in 1598,
"corrupt weeds" and "scumme of their countrie."[6] In Elizabethan England
the self-image of both the common and the noble soldier underwent irre-
versible changes that resulted in the redundancy of thousands of fighting
men and the marginalization of the military values by which they had lived.
Meanwhile, the Ottoman military establishment was widely known for its
discipline and commitment to its soldiers. As the author of *The Traveller's*

Breviat (1601) wrote, the Muslim army was successful because of its "num-bers . . . and organised provisions" [7]—qualities that would have attracted Britons and other unemployed Christians.

Another change that occurred was in war technology. From the middle of the sixteenth century on, English soldiers found that their reliance on archery, battle-ax, pike, and stave was preventing them from competing with their compatriots and continental soldiers who were trained in gunnery. Military manuals showed how many of the English looked down on gunnery as a retreat from the heroic values of medieval Albion; other manuals showed gunnery as innovative and essential. [8] This change particularly affected the common soldiers, since those who could not adapt to the new technology found themselves without employment or income. What exacerbated their situation were the policies James I adopted: Jacobean drama widely reflected the dwindling battlefield opportunities for the common soldier after the king signed peace treaties with Spain and the Netherlands, and after he per-sistently resisted involvement in what was to become the Thirty Years War on the Continent.

As a result of these transformations in the idealism and technology of war, sizable numbers of Elizabethan and Jacobean Britons sought service in for-eign armies—both Christian (Protestant on the Continent) and Muslim (in North Africa). Such service proved so attractive that as early as 1575, Queen Elizabeth had had to intervene in an effort to end it. In November of that year she passed a bill "prohibiting any of Her subjects from engaging in the service in the Low Countries, or of any other foreign prince or state, as mariners or soldiers."[9] But a bill could not always deter a desperate soldier in search of employment and pay. Indeed that same year Ralph Lane asked the queen for letters to commend his service to the kings of Fez and Algiers. [10] Three years later John Wanton went to Morocco and became the first English arms dealer to reside there and openly serve the North African ruler by arranging shipments of military hardware from England. In 1584, Captain Roger Williams wrote to Secretary Walsingham that unless the lat-ter could help him find work he would go to Holland and get a letter from "the Prince of Orange to the Turk" to show that he was a soldier. [11]

The first English soldier/captain to serve the Muslims and win national

acclaim appears in George Peele's *The Battle of Alcazar* (1591), a play about
the death of King Sebastian of Portugal, "Muly Mahamet king of Barbarie,"
and Tom Stukley in 1578.[12] The play commemorates the failure (although a
heroic one) of English policy in North Africa: Queen Elizabeth had supported the Portuguese contender Don Sebastian, who had promised to assist
Ahmad bin Abdallah to regain the Moroccan throne after the latter was
ousted by Abdel Malek in 1572. In return, Ahmad offered Sebastian all of
Morocco as a fief to Portugal. And England, eager to support anti-Spanish
policy, joined in what was widely viewed as an anti-Spanish campaign, especially because Abdel Malek was supported by Philip II, who wanted to
undermine Sebastian's plans. The battle of "Alcazar," or Wadi al-Makhazin, on
4 August 1578, ended with the total defeat of the Portuguese-Moroccan-
English alliance and the death of Sebastian and Ahmad.

Thomas Stukley was the English captain who joined with a few hundred
of his compatriot soldiers in the alliance against Abdel Malek. Although in
the numerous European and Arabic accounts about the famous battle no
mention is made of him, within a decade of his death on the North African
battlefield he had become a model of English military heroism. When
Stukley comes on stage in Peele's play, which in the title page of the 1594 edition emphasizes the role of Stukley ("The Battell of Alcazar, Fovght in
Barbarie betweene Sebastian King of Portugall, and Abdelmelec King of
Morocco. With the Death of Captaine Stukeley"), he is described as fighting
"against the devill for Lord Mahamet" (3.4.964)—the "devill" being the
Spanish-backed Abdel Malek. As he is fighting with Muslims he is serving
England's cause by opposing its supreme enemy, Spain. This portrait of
Stukley among the Moors may well have mirrored any one of the thousands
of English (and British) soldiers who were believed by Catholic intelligence
gatherers to have been committed to Queen Elizabeth's African war against
Spain. In 1577, when Francis Drake arrived in Safi, the Muslim population
thought that his soldiers were "the forerunners of the King of Portugals,"
who were preparing to join in alliance with the king of Morocco.[13] A decade
after the battle of Alcazar it was reported from Brussels that "30,000 Moors"
and "ten to twelve thousand Englishmen" were joining forces against Spain's
Holy League.[14] By the mid-1590s the cooperation between the queen and

the Moroccan ruler was so widely known that the queen was believed to be preparing to assist the "Moors" against Spain, and to "throw her entire force into Mauretania for the benefit of the Kinge of Morocco and Fez."[15] That there were such high numbers of Britons fighting with the Muslims of North Africa is very unlikely—the queen might have been willing to support the principle but not the expense. Nevertheless, the reports reveal how widely it was believed that English soldiers were serving the Muslims.

For Peele, Stukley was the model soldier who never compromised his Englishness, even while serving the "Lord Mahamet." He was a "warlike Englishman," as Celybin described him (4.1.1023), whose "knell" England would "kindely ring" (5.1.1368) at his funeral. The presentation of Stukley as a heroic captain of high ideals did not correspond to his image in the few surviving Elizabethan sources. During his life Stukley had been described by Camden (and quoted by Hakluyt) as "a ruffian, a riotous spend-thrift, and a notable vapourer";[16] more damning was the report that William Cecil received from the Florentine envoy in London denouncing Stukley as "prodigal, false, vile, without faith, conscience or religion."[17] Furthermore, and just before he had gone to North Africa, Stukley had been given by the Pope—the same one who had excommunicated Queen Elizabeth—the title of Marquess of Leinster, and had been directed to launch an invasion of Ireland.[18] Whatever the official view of Stukley was, however, the popular view Peele dramatized presented Stukley as a model English fighter and confirmed through him the chivalric values of Christendom. To Peele's audience Stukley was a great Englishman who had gained honor while serving with Muslims, and who had met his death at the hands of Italian Papists—the most nefarious of enemies.[19] While the "official" view of Stukley was antipathetic, the popular representation was heroic; it was the latter portrait that defined for writers, ballad singers, and theatergoers the model of the English soldier among the Muslims.

A chronicler confirmed that Stukley had boasted before the final battle that "when you come to action, you shall look after me, and shall see manifestly that Englishmen are no cowards."[20] For readers who included numerous common soldiers who were nearly always represented as cowardly and undisciplined in contemporary drama, Stukley's words would be welcome.

So admired was Stukley that another play about him was entered in 1605—
The Famous History of the Life and Death of Captain Thomas Stukeley—although
it may well have been performed as early as the 1590s. This play covered
more events in the life of Stukley than Peele's, but concluded with the war
in North Africa and the hero's death there. Shortly before he was killed,
Stukley showed his generosity of spirit by reconciling himself with his
English friend and rival Vernon, another English soldier who had joined
Sebastian's campaign into Muslim North Africa. Both soldiers died with
pride as their English blood mixed with the blood of a Portuguese and a
Muslim king (ll. 2721–24). [21] The play confirmed to the English audience
that numerous Britons had fought and died in the battle of Alcazar. The
account written by Hohannes Thomas Freigius and reprinted in Hakluyt
explained "that divers other [than Stukley] English gentlemen were in this
battell, whereof the most part were slaine." [22] There was heroism for both
the English common soldier and gentleman in the battlefields of Islam. Later
in the seventeenth century, when Thomas Fuller reflected on Stukley, he
again praised him for having "behaved himself most valiantly." Nearly everything negative about him had been forgotten. [23]

In the first years of the 1600s there was a surge in the number of English
soldiers and gunners who became involved in Morocco's military affairs. The
last years of Mulay al-Mansur's reign witnessed a violent rivalry among the
claimants to the throne, and with al-Mansur's death in 1603 that rivalry
turned into a civil war (accompanied by plague) in which each of the
claimants sought every military assistance possible. In 1603 it was reported
that Mulay Sidan (Zaidan), one of Mulay al-Mansur's children, "unprovided
of skilfull Gunners for his Ordnances . . . procured from Salie out of certaine
English men of warre, who at that instant were there, two English Gunners,
to whom he committed the charge of his Artillerie." [24] Evidently the English
were not unwilling to sell their services to the Moors, who, in turn, did not
have any qualms (or choice) about having Christians take over the artillery.
Later, Zaidan increased the number of the English gunners, and when he
fought with another of the contenders, Mulay Abdallah, he lost "betwixt thir-
tie and fortie," who were captured by the latter claimant; other Englishmen
fled with the defeated army but were spared by the victor. [25] In 1607 it was

reported that Zaidan refused to release the English (and Dutch) captives in Morocco because they were "cannoniers" on whose military expertise he had grown to depend. [26]

A more detailed account of those English soldiers in the service of Zaidan appeared in R. C.'s *A True Historicall discourse of Muley Hamets rising to the three Kingdomes of Moruecos, Fes and Sus* (1609), which described the actions of "divers English Gentlemen, in those Countries." These "Gentlemen" were two hundred English soldiers, along with other continentals, led by the "valiant Captaine Iohn Giffard," who had joined "Mulay Sidan" in his war against his brother. The author praised Giffard as "a Gentleman of a worthy spirit," whom Zaidan had honored with gifts and riches and even personal visits. R. C. confirmed that an English captain among the Muslims gained status and pay—25 shillings per diem to be exact, along with supplies. Furthermore, among the Muslims, all the needs of the English fighters were met by the ruler's bounty, which is why Giffard had had no difficulty assembling around him some of the finest English and continental soldiers: there was his kinsman, "one Maister Philip Giffard," "Captain Iaques a verie valiant souldier, captaine Smith one of the most esquisite enginers in Europe, captaine Baker an ancient Byzantine souldier, captaine Tailer, captaine Faukes, captaine Chambers, captaine Isack, men euerie way able to undergo their seuerall commaunds." [27] For R. C. these were glorious men who were earning good money. Each received twelve shillings a day, except the sea captains who earned four, while every common soldier earned twelve pence that was "truly payed them." R. C. wanted to assure his readers—particularly the common soldiers who were often left without pay and who subsequently had to plunder to survive—that there was regular pay among the Muslims and that Muslim rulers were prompt and generous.

Much as R. C. was advertising the good financial conditions of English soldiers among the Muslims, he continued to invoke the idea that English captains and soldiers were fighting with the Muslims not only for pay, but more importantly, for honor. They were men of courage and chivalry who not only lived by those ideals, but died by them too. As Mulay Zaidan was preparing to flee after the defeat of his Moorish soldiers he "sent th the [sic] English Captaines to be gone, and to captaine Giffard a good horse to saue him selfe. The English returned word, that they came not thither to run, but rather die an honourable death."[28] Again, as in the plays about Stukley, the English captain and his common soldiers would all die together in battle; they were noble and courageous Englishmen who upheld their honor among the Muslims. According to the French consul in the Netherlands, forty-five Englishmen, all of whom had manned the canons, died in the battle (22–25 February 1607).[29] The Britons were clearly playing an important military role in inter-Muslim feuding and warfare.

Many Britons (and other Christian Europeans) were trained in gunnery, and filled the technological gap in the Muslim military establishment. Obviously they joined the Muslims because they found satisfactory and reliable pay. Both the soldiers who joined of their own free will and the captives who were forced to serve at the cannons found reward among the Muslims. Because they were "nothing expert in Artillery," the Muslims either enticed or forced their captives into military service, as was the case with Richard Hasleton, who, after his capture in Algiers, was charged with "certain pieces of ordnance . . . which I refused not to do, trusting thereby to get some liberty."[30] It took a lot of commitment to his country, religion, and family for Hasleton to turn down the offers made to him by the Muslim ruler. As he recalled his captivity in the late 1580s, he listed what the "King of the Cabyles" promised him if he agreed to become a Muslim and to serve him as a gunner: "the King offered to give me 700 Doubles by the year, which amounteth to the sum of £ 50 of English money; and moreover to give me by the day, 30 Aspers, which are worth twelve pence English, to find me meat; and likewise to give me a house, and land sufficient to sow a hundred bushels of grain yearly, and two Plow of oxen furnished, to till the same; also to furnish me with horse, musket, sword, and other necessaries, such as they of that country use. And lastly he offered to give me a wife, which they esteemed the greatest matter."[31] The preciseness of the figures attests to Hasleton's recognition of the admiration such payments would evoke in his readers and unemployed countrymen.

In *Tamburlaine: Part One* (1590), Bajazeth the Turk boasted that he had as many "warlike bands of Christians renied, / As hath the ocean or the Terrene Sea / Small drops of water" (3.1.9–11). In 1596 an anonymous Englishman, "a Trumpeter," wrote Sir Thomas Glover, defected and betrayed the castle of Agria to the Turks.[32] In the *Letters from the great Turke lately sent vnto the holy Father the Pope* (1606), the Turkish leader boasted that his army had thirty thousand Christians who "are the founders of our artillerie, and other Instruments of warre" and all of whom are "Renegados" fighting "in defence of our lawe, and with vs to conquer your country." Not only would such a number have consisted of the Janizzaries (Christians who had been converted to Islam in their youth), but of Christian Europeans, too.[33] Sir Thomas Shirley, after denouncing "renegadoes" as "roagues, & the skumme of people, whyche beinge villanes and atheistes," added that many of them find themselves "vnable to liue in Christendomme, [and] are fledde to the Turke for succoure & releyffe." Conveniently, Thomas forgot about his brother, Anthony, who in 1606 was described as having "benn ymployed by the Emperour" of Morocco.[34] Thomas Coryat described the Grand Signior who, upon entering Istanbul, was followed by "French Souldiers, a company of fugitive Rogues, that to get a large pay somewhat more then they have, either in their owne Countrey, or could get in the Low Countries"—a view that was confirmed by Sir Thomas Roe who saw the "false French regiment, and their colonell" in December 1623.[35] In 1622 John Rawlins mentioned how the Algerians took for their gunners "two of our soldiers, one English and one Dutch Renegade" because they wanted to use them for their ordnance, while John Chamberlain lamented the following year that "seven or eight hundred of our mariners, among whom many gunners and men of best service at sea" had been captured and put to use by the rulers of Algiers and Tunis.[36] Sir Henry Blount, after repeating Shirley's condemnation that the "Renegadoes" were "Atheists," admitted that the converts "left our cause for the Turkish as the more thriving in the World, and fuller of preferment."[37] From the Elizabethan to the Stuart period, the Muslim dominions were attractive sources of military employment for both Britons and other Christians.[38]

The cooperation between Englishmen and Muslims continued well into the second half of the seventeenth century. "The captain" of a Tunisian ship that captured Edward Coxere in the 1650s "was an English renegade, as also was the gunner,"[39] and in 1664 "an English engineer...supplied the most cer-

tain advantages for the progress of the Ottoman arms."[40] "So eight
Englishmen told him [the Moroccan ruler] they knew what belonged to the
Guns, and they would go with him [to battle]," wrote Francis Brooks about
his experience as a captive in 1681.[41] That same year "William . . . Gunner
of ye Francis" ran into the castle of the bey of Tripoli in order to serve in the
bey's fleet.[42] In the 1690s Joseph Pitts, who had been captured in 1678 and
converted to Islam, fought alongside his master in Algeria, and in 1715
Thomas Pellow of Penryn converted to Islam and served as a soldier in the
army of Mulay Ismail.[43] To serve as a soldier/gunner among the Muslims
was viewed by Britons as a venue of military opportunity. It is no wonder
that a certain English "Gun-Smith" who was ransomed after his captivity,
"Reneg'd and chose rather to be a Mohammetan than to return to his own
Country." [44] He must have realized that among the Muslims he would play a
more prominent role and receive higher pay than among his countrymen.

Although some Britons reneged on their commitment to king and coun-
try to serve the Muslims, others were known to serve so well as intermedi-
aries that they were able to gain the confidence of both the Muslim and
Christian rulers. Jasper Tomson, whose family was closely associated with
Lord Cecil, participated in the campaign of Sultan Mohammad III against the
Spanish emperor and became, at the end of the 1590s, the confidant of Mulay
Ahmad al-Mansur of Morocco, whose grand design was to join his Muslim
army with Elizabeth's Protestant forces against Catholic Spain.[45] In 1627
John Harrison, the English agent, wrote to encourage King Charles I to send
two thousand soldiers to fight there.[46] Nine years later, while travelling in
the Levant, Sir Henry Blount was asked by the Ottoman sultan to join his
army; he declined the offer only because he had another engagement.[47] As
long as there was political cooperation between London and Marrakesh or
Istanbul, there was the possibility of military cooperation between the two
peoples. English travelers, traders, and foreign policy strategists were eager
to see their compatriots actively involved in the military affairs of Islam. And
Muslim rulers, aware of the growing technological gap between them and
Christendom, were eager to employ European soldiers.

Perhaps the most important event in the history of Renaissance Anglo-
Islamic military cooperation occurred in 1637. This was the first time an

English monarch actually approved his fleet's support for one faction of Muslims against another. There had been hundreds of English soldiers, gunners, and military personnel in North Africa for decades, but they had never been specifically sent by the monarch to carry out military action on the Muslim side. In 1637, King Charles authorized his fleet to assist Siddy Hamed al-Ayyashi of Old Salee against his rival in New Salee: "English gunners" were sent to the old town and "did fearful execution among the crowded defenders of New Sallee, battering the walls beyond repair."[48] By so doing the gunners helped reduce "Sally to the obedience of the [Moroccan] Emperor." Soon after, however, a rebellion broke out against the emperor, and eighteen English gunners were sent to fight on his side until victory, "and then with love and leave" returned to England.[49] For the first time since England had entered the Mediterranean, its fleet succeeded in altering the course of events among the Muslims—with royal approval.

There were military advantages for England in having its soldiers serve among Muslims since it could secure access to maritime bases on the Mediterranean. But there was another advantage for the soldiers themselves —heroism. One of the reasons service in the Muslim Empires was described in praiseworthy terms was the egalitarianism of heroism Britons were shown to share. Numerous Elizabethan and Jacobean plays emphasize the difference between the supposed heroism of captains and the cowardice of the common soldiers,[50] but in the literature set among the Muslims, both categories of the English shared in honor and military dedication. Among the Muslims, where a military meritocracy was known to prevail in sharp contrast to the elitism of the British military establishment, Britons shared with each other, across military rank and social status, in heroism and glory. That is why the Muslim Empires were repeatedly portrayed in English writings as places of military fulfillment; Britons (and other Christians) could go there to realize their dreams of battle.[51]

These descriptions of Britons among the Muslims tell more about Britons than Muslims; these plays, biographies, and historical accounts were produced amid the frustration redundant soldiers were experiencing in a monarchy that had adopted a less militaristic foreign policy than its Elizabethan predecessor. The focus of these writings was therefore on the

British soldier and his achievement among the forces of the Turks, the "present terror of the world." By placing the Britons among the Muslims, praising their military and diplomatic capability, and showing that they could work among non-Christians while retaining their commitment to their monarch and God, writers confirmed a heroic image of their compatriots and explicitly advertised the Muslim dominions to the unemployed, the unfulfilled, and the ambitious.

Pirates

Simultaneous with this idealized view of soldierly activity among the Muslims, and for another kind of British cooperation with Muslims, it is important to consider seamen and those who came to be described as pirates, either by their compatriots or the Muslims. In the period under study, as Fernand Braudel, A. Tenenti, and C. M. Senior have shown, British seamen played an important role in the Mediterranean, particularly in the Muslim dominions.[52] Captains and sailors established extensive contacts with Muslims by providing them with transportation. At times of high traffic, especially when Muslim pilgrims headed to Cairo on their way to Mecca, English and Scottish ships and their crew fulfilled a much needed service by providing them with safe transit across the North African coast. Often such services developed into personal friendships. In 1603 Henry Timberlake recalled how he had carried three hundred pilgrims from Algiers to Cairo (which was the North African hub of pilgrimage to Mecca) on his ship, the *Troyan*. Later, one of the passengers surprised Timberlake by remembering his name and offered to help him get into Jerusalem: "such kind care had the Infidel of me, as he would not leaue me unaccompanied in this strange Land."[53] The "Infidel" (whose name Timberlake seemed not to have remembered) stayed with him throughout his journey in the Holy Land. In 1614 William Davis recalled how the English ship on which he was serving, the *Francis*, carried "Turkish Goods by Turkes, and some Turks aboard with us."[54] Although such services were sometimes condemned by Britons, who were offended at their compatriots' collusion with the Muslims, English and Scottish ships were very active in the Mediterranean. As a result, many

Britons established friendly relations with Muslims—with great benefit to themselves. It was the letter sent by a Moorish sea merchant on behalf of Sir Henry Middleton to the basha that "saved my Life," recalled the Englishman after his captivity in the Arabian harbor of Mocha.[55]

While some sailors were able to establish amicable (and legal) relations with the Muslims, others turned to piracy. Ever since the Middle Ages, English monarchs, like their Western European counterparts, had issued letters of marque to legitimate the piracy of their subjects against their adversaries. But the line between royally legitimized plunder (privateering) and lawless piracy was never clear, and privateers did not always abide by the limitations set by the foreign policy of their monarchs. Although in the second half of the sixteenth century, English privateers such as Raleigh and Drake specifically targeted Spanish ships,[56] other Britons were not as discriminating; despite the amicable relations between their queen and the rulers of Turkey and Morocco, they attacked Muslim traders and travelers. In 1586, pirates from England attacked a Spanish ship in Moroccan waters, and as a result the Moroccan ruler imprisoned an English merchant. "I am here impryssoned amongeste a nomber of heathens," he wrote, adding that he would stay there until the pirates made proper restitution to the ruler.[57] In 1600, Sultan Mohammad III complained to the English agent in Istanbul about "injuryes and piracyes" committed by English pirates against Turkish ships; the queen was so embarrassed that she sent a letter, written "with her owne hand," to her agent offering her apologies to the Grand Signior.[58] Three years later, in 1603, the sultan complained to the French King Henri IV about English corsairs, and in 1607 the king in turn complained to the ruler of Morocco about the piratical depredations by Britons.[59] So outrageous and continuous were the piracies of the Britons that in 1626 Sultan Murad IV complained to King Charles in the following words:

certyn men of war apperteyning to yowr kyndomes had, contrarye to the capitulations, assalted the merchants, which with their goods returned from Indya, and fought and taken their ships; and it being made knowne to the sayd Fazeli bassa, that our merchants had beene damaged, to the valew of 600000 dollers...the sayd men of war, not conteyning themselues in due bounds, haue armed a-new seauen ships from your countrye, and haue come and assalted 14 ships of our merchants,

which from Indya were sayling to the scale of Ayman; and hauing taken the masters prisoners, haue made spoyle and depredation of all their facultye.[60]

Between 1580 and 1615, according to Alberto Tenenti, the English "showed themselves to be pirates more ruthless and dangerous than any others" in the Mediterranean.[61] It is no wonder that the Arabic and Turkish words for pirate or corsair, *qursan* and *corsar*, entered the two languages through Western Christendom.[62] In the same way that many Britons knew Muslims only as Barbary Corsairs, so did many Muslims know Britons only as infidel pirates.

Britons were involved not only in piracy, but in the slave trade too. Although they were more successful in their sub-Saharan African trade with the Americas (thus the "Gvinea" on the Virginia Company Chart p. 86 below), they did not hesitate to profit from North African slaves. In 1623, Sir Thomas Roe recorded the complaint of the Tunisians that English ships were capturing and selling Muslim "subiects and passengers";[63] a year later a "Mr. Madox, of London" captured a Salee ship and sold its crew of one hundred fifty Moors and Andalusians into slavery.[64] In October 1631, Harrison confirmed that Salee captives had been sold by the English to the Spaniards; and in June 1639, a "Mr. Marriot, master of the Blessing" sold eleven Turks in Spain and made over a hundred pounds in profit, which he offered to share with the King.[65] In 1658, the ruler of Algeria complained that English ships were selling "Mussulmans" as slaves to Venetians and other Christians;[66] in 1664, "Capt Chichley gave consent with the rest of the Capts that Tauries, a Turk, should be sold for 100 dollars to the Consul, Don Juan Vincent Raby"; by 1669 the enslavement and sale of Muslims was a common practice among English sea commanders.[67]

While some Britons attacked and captured Muslims, others settled in sea towns and served in Algerian, Tunisian or, Moroccan navies.[68] After James I criminalized piracy, and after he suspended his warfare against Spain and the Netherlands, hoards of seamen found themselves without employment—except as pirates (no longer could they claim to be privateers attacking England's Catholic enemy). Their search for harbors in which to dock and safely sell their loot coincided with the need of North African navies to learn maritime technology from the Europeans, and with the willingness of the North African rulers to accommodate the British (and other Christian) pirates in their harbors on condition of sharing with them in the profit. The result of this cooperation between Britons (and other Christians) on the one hand, and the Barbary Corsairs on the other, was the proliferation of piracy committed by Christians and Muslims together. In a 1611 deposition of some English sailors who were taken at Plymouth it was revealed that there were "40:sayle, and 2000: men, all English" and all pirates, who operated out of "Mamora in Barbarie."[69] Five years later Captain John Smith lamented that his countrymen were more eager to join Mediterranean piracy than to colonize New England: "our mindes" are so set "vpon spoile, piracie, and such villany, as to serue the Portugall, Spanyard, Dutch, French, or Turke (as to the cost of Europe too many dooe)."[70] Britons were more interested in the Mediterranean than in America, and more zealous to join "Turkish" pirates than to colonize Virginia. Over a century later, in 1731, J. Morgan was still recalling the denunciation by Sir William Monson in 1617 of "Englishmen" who were "too busy in trading with [Algerian] Pirates, and furnishing them with Powder and other Necessaries."[71]

These English, Welsh, Scottish, and Irish seamen learned the language of their hosts and clipped their beards as Muslims did rather than let them grow, as was the style in England. They ate their food, dressed in their clothes, and learned their games, especially backgammon, which they referred to as "tables"[72]—a translation from the Arabic (*tawla*). They also advanced the Muslims' knowledge of navigation, maritime technology, and shipbuilding. (The majority of navigational terms in Arabic and Turkish derive from European languages.) It is no wonder, then, that the combined capabilities of the North African Muslims and the Christian Britons produced one of the most successful periods in the history of piracy in the Mediterranean and the Channel. From the beginning of the Jacobean period until the Commonwealth era, the western Mediterranean was ruled by North African pirates and their converted and unconverted Christian supporters; the Atlantic coast of Europe and Africa, as far west as the Canary Islands, was also under the sway of the Barbary Corsairs. Between 1604 and 1640, British piracy, much of which was centered in Mamora and Tunis, reached its zenith. Between 1640 and 1660, Salee enjoyed its golden age of piracy. Importantly, the corsairs who manned the ships or financed the operations were not all Moors or Turks—they were also Britons and other Christians who had "Mahumetized" and "donned the turban." It is not surprising that the term *'allaj* (*'allooj* and *a'alaj* in the plural) was coined in Turko-Arabic to designate the *renegadoes*—the Europeans in the service of Muslims—and that in Arabic sixteenth and seventeenth-century sources about North Africa, references to these *a'alaj* are numerous.

In 1577 occurred one of the earliest demonstrations of English-Moorish maritime interactions. Francis Drake, intent on piracy in the Caribbean, arrived in December in Mogadore, on the west coast of Morocco. Soon thereafter a few Moors boarded his ship after being assured that the fleet was English (friendly) and not Portuguese (hostile). Drake and his crew entertained the Moors well, "courteously, with a daintie banquet, and such gifts as they seemed to be most glad of." The Britons even offered the Muslims some wine and learned that although Islam prohibits the drinking of alcohol, "by stealth it pleaseth them well to haue it abundantly." The relations were openly amicable, but on the following day the Moors kidnapped one of Drake's men, John Fry, in order to take him to their king, who wanted to be further assured that the fleet had no military designs on his kingdom. Although Fry was treated well and later released, he was unable to rejoin Drake, who had quickly sailed away. The Muslim ruler kidnapped Britons in order to learn about them in the same manner Drake kidnapped Indians to learn about them; Drake "discovered" the American Indians in the same way the Muslims of North Africa "discovered" the English.[73]

Four years later, in 1581, there was an incident of English-Turkish cooperation that could be characterized as piratical. Fifteen Turks boarded the English ship *Roe* and began a conversation with the captain, Peter Baker, who seemed to be "very great frende with them." Although the sailors wanted to attack the Turks, the captain was eager to entertain them and "sheyed them musicke and gave them a present."[74] So friendly did the captain appear toward the Turks that the Maltese suspected him of being a pirate operating under Muslim protection. In 1607 it was reported from Bayonne, in the French Bay of Biscay, that English pirates had carried off a ship into Barbary to sell the captives into slavery. Such was the notoriety of these English pirates operating out of Morocco that R. Cocks wrote that the English pirates were "mercyles . . . there is noe mercy yf they meete with an Englishman, and very littell yf they meete with a stranger."[75] That same year it was reported from Zante that a pirate ship from North Africa was carrying Englishmen, Turks, and Moors; and so was another pirate *bertone*, which carried ninety men made up "half of Englishmen and half of Turks from Tunis."[76] Again that same year France complained to the High Porte about English (and Dutch) pirates who were using North African sea towns to attack French ships.[77] Three years later, in 1610, "Anglo-Turkish pirates" operating out of Tunis attacked French and Italian ships; the following year a *bertone* reached Valona with sixty Turks and forty English and French pirates.[78] So numerous were English pirates among the Muslims that they came to be known as the "new pirates" of Barbary. Sir Henry Mainwaring recalled in his *Discourse on Pirates*, which he addressed to King James I around 1617 or 1618, his years of cooperation with the Tunisian and Algerian pirates. He had become so successful that "The Dey of Tunis eat bread and salt and swore by his head (which is the greatest asseveration they use) that if I would stay with him he would divide his estate equally with me, and never urge me to turn Turk, but give me leave to depart whensoever it should please your Majesty to be so gracious as to pardon me."[79]

Mainwaring had joined the Barbary Corsairs and become quite familiar with their culture. The reference to eating bread and salt signifies an Islamic assurance of safety. So, too, was the swearing by the head. Mainwaring lived, ate, drank, and cooperated with the Muslim rulers who favored him because of the success of his piratical depredations. In his subsequent exposé of the pirates, Mainwaring confirmed that numerous English pirates operated out of Algiers and Tunis: the Algerian pirate ships were "manned out by the Turks, after the proportion of 150 Turks to 20 English, yet the English in their persons are well used and duly paid their shares."[80] Lord Carew confirmed that "in the towne of Angire the Englishe are well enoughe intreated . . . [but] To assure themselves of renegados, the Turkes are so carefull as in every shippe there is three Turkes for one renegado."[81] Evidently there were many "renegados" from England and elsewhere in Christendom who were working on

Muslim ships. At Tetuan, Mainwaring added, much of the material pirates bought was brought over by the English and the Flemish. Mainwaring himself had overseen much of the activity of the pirates of Mamora, to the north of Salee, where he had established a kind of pirate "republic" for them.[82]

There were numerous pirates such as Mainwaring who must have acquired detailed cultural and military knowledge about the Muslims. Mainwaring returned to England, and after receiving a pardon from the king, rose in the naval hierarchy to become vice admiral. Similarly, a certain Captain Walsingham served in the Algerian navy, "(had ben a pirate)" as Chamberlain noted, was then pardoned by King James I, and served in the English fleet that attacked Algiers in 1621. Finding little reward in his position, however, Walsingham started "prattl[ing]" that he would leave England and return to the Algerians, a remark that resulted in his prompt dispatch to the Tower.[83] While he and Mainwaring returned to England, other pirates remained among the Muslims; John Ward, along with his accomplices, "James Procter of Southampton, and Iohn Fenth of Plimouth" and numerous other Britons were perhaps the most notorious figures in Renaissance English writings.[84] All were vilified in contemporary biographies while the play by Robert Daborne, *A Christian Turn'd Turke* (1612), specifically demonized Ward for enslaving many a "Brittaine." [85]

Little is historically known about Ward except that he settled in Tunis and acquired a large fleet. He shared his loot with Cara Osman, the agha of the Janizzaries, with whom he became such good friends that he called him "brother."[86] He lived in wealth and glory, quaffing wine instead of ale, and lording it over numerous compatriot "runnagates" such as Thomas Mitton, who was in Tunis for three years, William Graves and Toby Glanville,[87] and Anthony Johnson, who assisted Ward in the capture of *John the Baptist* in November 1606.[88] Ward's ships were often nearly completely manned by Britons, although sometimes there were Turks among them. Ward prospered as a result of his piracy, and by 1607 he had a huge ship manned by "an Anglo-Turkish crew of 400."[89]

Ward's name was frequently associated with the Dutch/Flemish pirate Simon Dansker (or Danser), whose crew included both Britons and Turks.[90] These two men became so famous that they were remembered by a Tunisian writer toward the end of the seventeenth century. In his *Kitab al-Munis fi Akhbar Ifriqiya wa Tunis,* Ibn Abi Dinar described the successful activity of the Tunisian fleet under Yousef Dey who succeeded Othman Dey, and he made the only reference in Arabic sources to Ward, whose Arabic name had been changed to Wardiyya ("of the rose"): "During his time [Yousef Dey], the corsair captains [ru'assa'] of the sea increased in number, and his ships became famous and fearful. Of the greatest corsair captains in his time were Captain Samsom and Captain Wardiyya: they were Christians, and sailed in his time while still Christians, but they turned Muslim later. They were famous at sea."[91] It is significant that the two men were remembered at all by the Tunisian writer; evidently they had left their mark on the Muslim population, and stories must have been told about them for decades after their deaths.

Another corsair pirate was Sir Francis Verney, who, like Ward, converted to Islam. Before his life of piracy Verney had joined Captain Giffard as a mercenary to Mulay Zaidan. After the latter was defeated (Verney, unlike his distant relative Giffard, preferred not to die heroically), he joined Ward and settled in Algiers, whereupon he attacked and captured a string of English trading vessels that were chiefly from Poole and Plymouth.[92] Another Briton who fraternized with Turkish corsairs in St. George's Channel was John Nutt.[93] According to Captain Plumleigh, who had been sent with a warrant to arrest him, Nutt was in command of "twenty seven Barbary vessels."[94] Meanwhile, a Cornishman named Ambrose Sayer was "a commander of a squadron of corsairs" operating out of Algiers.[95] In 1617, Sir William Monson feared that English pirates in Algiers might give their Algerian counterparts "Intelligence" about the plans to attack Algiers by the British fleet.[96] John Rawlins referred in 1622 to numerous Englishmen who had joined the "Pirates of Argier."[97] The English captains, Kelley and Sampson, served on Turkish ships and "tooke part with the Turks thus to rob and spoyle vppon the Ocean."[98] In 1625 the pilot of a Salee man-of-war, committing piracy near the coast of Devon, was "one Arthur Drake of Plymouth, that lyves amongst the Turkes a freeman." Later that year "one Bennett, a merchant of London," was captured with "a protection from the piratt Campaigne to all the picaroones of Salley."[99] Many were the Britons, lamented Henry Byam in 1628, who joined the Turks and turned their weapons against their countrymen and kindred.[100] The attraction of piracy out of Muslim waters was so high that it worried John Harrison, the English agent in Morocco. After observing the numerous English ships that arrived in Salee to trade, he wrote the following warning to King Charles in 1630: "the feare is some [of these ships] maie abuse their commissions and turne pirattes, and Englishmen goe out to sea in their shippes, the shippes of Sallye, and serve under them and turn renegadoes; so His Majestie looseth subjects and God so many soules."[101] In 1636 it was reported by a James Davie of Lyme Regis, who had been a captive in Salee, that the "870 English, Scots and Welshmen" who were captive there were planning to unite with the Turks and "come into the Channel . . . where they might carry away good store of people and booty." Although, he continued, the captives had desisted from so doing, they "vowed they will invite the Turks to do mischief in these western parts" unless they were ransomed.[102]

English, Scottish, Welsh, and Irish pirates flourished under Muslim flags. While many of them converted to Islam and settled in North Africa, others "worked" there until they made enough money to buy a pardon and return home. For them, settling among the Muslims was financially lucrative and professionally rewarding. Although these pirates operated chiefly in the Mediterranean, others were known to plunder from the Cape of Good Hope to China and Japan, including the Red Sea and the Persian Gulf. Throughout this period, piracy was a thriving profession and British pirates among the Muslims were very successful professionals.

Traders

Morocco was the most attractive and accessible location in the Muslim world for English soldiers, pirates, and traders. The country had amicable dealings with England, and Britons felt relatively safe there—and relatively free from English social control and law. Some Britons viewed Morocco as an easy place to commit a murder against a hated compatriot. Such was the case in 1585 when Elizabeth's envoy to Mulay Ahmed al-Mansur, Ralph Skydmoore, who had been in Morocco since 1579, was poisoned by an English merchant.

The murderer was later extradited to face "condigne punishmente."[103] Others saw it as a good place to escape to after a brush with the law at home. John Herman, an English rebel, fled England to Morocco in 1587, but was captured after the queen demanded his extradition.[104]

Most importantly, as T. S. Willan's *Studies in Elizabethan Foreign Trade* has shown in great detail,[105] Morocco was an excellent trading partner where numerous Britons resided for extended periods of time. In 1569, Mulay Abdallah al-Ghalib wrote to Queen Elizabeth assuring her that English traders would not be harmed in his realm; by 1572, there was already an English merchant, Thomas Owen, living and trading in Morocco (he would remain there until 1600), who, it was noted in a letter from a Moroccan customs officer, had mastered Arabic.[106] In 1574, Britons trying to establish a monopoly for trade with North Africa complained to the queen that "menye" Englishmen were already trading with Barbary, but not paying custom duties because they were using illegal harbors as points of departure and return.[107] No doubt before the incorporation of the Barbary Merchants (about which there were heated arguments for and against), numerous English traders and agents settled in North Africa without leaving any trace behind them. The "factour [long] resident" in Barbary, George Gyppes, is just one example.[108] In 1584, a trader described as "Artoos al-Ingleez" (perhaps translatable as Arthur the Englishman) delivered military hardware to "Dar al-Odda," the house of armament, in Morocco.[109] In 1589, Elizabeth's ambassador to Mulay Ahmad, Henry Roberts, reported that there were numerous English merchants living in the Moroccan kingdom, including "M. Richard Evans, Edward Salcot, and other English merchants." In 1591 there were numerous "merchantts" from London working in the "realme and domynions of Barbery . . . about fower yeares now last past." And in 1603, John Wakeman, an English merchant, was described as having had a "long residence in Barbarie."[110]

Alongside these merchants and factors were assorted Britons ranging from musicians to spies to women relatives who interacted with Muslims. In 1577, the Moroccan ruler Mulay Abdel Malek asked Edmund Hogan to send him a few English musicians to reside in his court; he promised to "let them live according to their law and conscience."[111] In 1579 in Morocco lived a

Thomas Cely of Bristol at the house of "Thomas Butleres, a Yngleshe man, and heer a dweller," whose function, in part, was to collect intelligence about the movements of the Spanish fleet in the Mediterranean.[112] In 1604 there were, according to Captain John Smith, many English "Gold-smiths, Plummers, Carvers, and Polishers of stone, and Watch-makers" living and working in Morocco. Each was being paid ten shillings a day, was given food and clothing by the king, and was allowed to import and export goods "custome-free."[113] In 1618 an Englishman succeeded in spending enough time in Algiers to be able to spy on Algerian military fortifications: "a certain individual . . . had been into Barbary to survey the fortress of Algiers, with the idea that by depriving the corsairs of that refuge the end would be in great measure obtained."[114] In 1620, Captain Gyles Penn was taken hostage by the Moors. After his release he remained a trader in Barbary for the next 20 years.[115] In 1623, Samuel Cade, who had "lived some time at the Court of Syder Ali, Prince of Barbary, and made friendship with him and his people," petitioned to take to Barbary "a ship laden with wares."[116] In 1631, Gertrude Lacon and Sara Bramforde were given passes to "goe into Barbara with a brother of theirs, being a marchant who liveth in those parts."[117] In 1638, Sir George Carteret met some "English Marchants" in Safi some of whom had lived "in ye Cuntry this 20 years."[118] And at Salee, the London merchants Henry St. John and Co. began trading in timber, wool, and military hardware in return for gold and saltpeter.[119]

It is clear, then, that the first Muslim country to which Englishmen were exposed was Morocco, and that as they moved outside their European parameter of commercial and financial interaction, the first people they encountered, traded with, and settled among, were the Moors. Other Englishmen traded with and resided in the Ottoman Empire. As early as 1560, William Dennis had been trading in Istanbul; so too were William Malim and Thomas Cotton.[120] In 1575 two merchants, John Wight and Joseph Clements, stayed a year and half in the Ottoman capital.[121] A few years later, in 1580, one of the agreements between Sultan Murad and Elizabeth stated the following: "14 Item, if any Englishman shall come hither [Turkish Empire] either to dwel or trafique, whether hee be married or unmarried, he shall pay no polle or head money."[122] Not only was the Muslim sultan eager to see the

English live and trade in his realm, but he was willing to make the necessary concessions that might encourage them to do so.

Again, as with Morocco, some Britons thought that the Ottoman Empire was a good place to conduct illegal activities. In July of 1599 a plot was discovered in London in which a number of men confessed to planning to counterfeit money in Turkey. Because neither the equipment nor the workers were available there, they were planning to make the "engine" in London and then smuggle it into Turkey.[123] A few decades later, Henry Robinson complained that religious instability and persecution in England were forcing numerous merchants "to goe and live in Turky"; ten years later Paul Haget confirmed that he had lived in "Turkey four years, and [was] acquainted with most of the officers of State in that port [Constantinople], and their inferior officers."[124] Between 1642 and 1660 there were small English communities in Istanbul and Izmir that were not only working for the Levant Company, but colluding with the exiled royalists against the Commonwealth.[125] In 1657, William Ellis caused a diplomatic near-crisis between Whitehall and the High Porte: having served as a shipmaster to the basha of Memphis in Egypt, he had absconded with some of the basha's property to Leghorn where he lived in luxury—until he was arrested after Cromwell sought help from the duke of Tuscany.[126] From the Atlantic coast to the Valley of the Nile, and from Istanbul to Salee, Britons lived and worked among the Muslims.

Merchants living in Morocco and elsewhere in the Muslim world were not always amicable to each other. They sometimes quarreled and sought justice in Muslim courts. In 1572 some Jewish merchants sued the English "Christian" merchant Richard Glassock for selling them poor quality cloth that was "burnt during dying and coarsely woven," but they later withdrew their suit.[127] Trade in cloth was very important to England, which exported the material to Morocco in return for sugar and saltpeter (and, in the 1590s, gold).[128] Queen Elizabeth frequently wrote to the Moroccan ruler requesting legal action on behalf of her subjects. Sometimes she wanted him to arbitrate among her merchants and at other times between her merchants and other European merchants and traders.[129] By the time King James succeeded to the throne, this English submission to Muslim law and court was so prevalent that it scandalized John Harrison who saw in it stark anti-Biblical behavior (he cited the prohibition of going to "unjust" courts in 1 Corinthians 6:1). Harrison ordered his compatriots to stop using Muslim courts and to seek justice in England. He also warned them against ignoring their Christian duties in the presence of Moors and Jews, "especially concerning the observation of the Saboth daie." Harrison started holding services for his compatriots, and was happy that they were willing to suspend business on Sunday to join in prayer. Only one merchant continued to trade, and when Harrison reprimanded him for his religious laxity the merchant claimed that the "common custome on the coaste of Barbarie [was] not to observe the Saboth daie."[130] Harrison suspected that that trader, along with other merchants, was counterfeiting money and passing it on to the Moors. Later, the deception was discovered by the Muslims, who spoke out against the English merchants and their nation. That is why Harrison decided to take "a mynister or twoo with me, bothe to preache to the merchaunts and make them observe better orders then formerlie they have don."[131] Especially in the dominion of the Muslims, Christianity was needed to reform the merchants.

Just as Harrison and the Barbary Company had recruited ministers, so did the Levant Company recognize the importance of ministers and sent many of them to reside in Aleppo and Istanbul. Some of these ministers who served in Arabic-speaking countries, such as Edward Pococke, learned Arabic and other oriental languages and, upon their return to England, proved instrumental in the development of Arabic studies. Harrison, however, who was a deeply religious man and always quoted the Scriptures, evidently feared—as Sir Thomas Shirley had feared—that Britons living among the Muslims, whether in Salee or in Istanbul, would quickly adopt the customs of the Muslims and forget their own.[132] That is why he felt there was a great need to keep a close religious watch over all who lived in the Muslim dominions. When in 1630 a treaty was signed between Charles I and Mulay al-Walid, the latter agreed not to force the English merchants to appear before the Muslim court on Sunday. If it was not possible to prevent Britons from submitting to Muslim law, it was possible at least to make them submit on days other than "their Saboth day."[133]

One of the areas in which an interesting exchange occurred between Britons and Muslims was in what might be described as industrial spying.[134] Throughout the period under study there was a sense of crisis surrounding the English cloth industry because of the decline in wool exports since the 1550s. The decline had exceeded a third of England's overall export, and had been caused by multiple factors. The traditional woolen material made in England was heavy and thick, while the Mediterranean markets demanded lighter textures. Furthermore, English traders sometimes cheated their customers.[135] As a result of this decline, cloth producing regions in England such as Kent and Suffolk suffered economically, and London merchants realized that they had to improve their products and services. They also had to learn how to accommodate the demands of the export markets in terms of design, color, and texture. Richard Hakluyt recognized the implications of the industry's decline and immediately set about to address it: he suggested that the only way Britons could improve their wool and dyeing production was to spy on the Muslims and learn their techniques. In 1579 the Privy Council advised London dyers to send two men "into Moscovia and Persia" "to learne and be instructed in a certaine perfecte arte of dyinge without woade used in thos countreyes."[136] That same year Richard Hakluyt wrote to "M. Morgan Hubblethorne Dier," who was on his way to Persia, telling him to learn all the Persian techniques used in dyeing.[137] Three years later Hakluyt gave his friend who was going to "Turkie" a list of things to look up and acquire (similar to the 1579 list of advice to the "Dier") that would help England's clothing and dying industry: "9. To note all kindes of clothing in Turkie, and all degrees of their labour in the same. 10. To endevour rather the vent of Kersies, then of other Clothes as a thing more beneficiall to our people . . . 12. To seeke out a vent for our Bonettos, a cap made for Barbarie, for that the poore people may reape great profite by the trade."[138]

In another dispatch that same year to the English agent in Istanbul, Hakluyt was quite open about the need to improve the quality of dyeing wool in England. It was essential, Hakluyt urged, that the English learn how the Turks dyed their wool and imitate them:

Forasmuch as it is reported that the Woollen clothes died in Turkie bee most excellently died, you shall send home into this realme certaine

Mowsters or pieces of Shew to be brought to the Diers hall, there to be shewed, partly to remoove out of their heads, the tootoo great opinion they have conceived of their owne cunning, and partly to moove them for shame to endeavour to learne more knowledge to the honour of their countrey of England, and to the universall benefit of the realme."[139]

Hakluyt continued by urging the agent to send to England the plants used by the Turks "by seed or by root in barrell of earth," and to observe closely the "order of the degrees of labour used in Turky." If the Turks did things better than the English, the agent should learn how things were done and bring that information home. Furthermore, added Hakluyt, the factor should locate a Turk who was expert in his "Art" and bring him to England so he would train Britons in the silk and woolen profession. Since it was difficult to get permission to send such a Turk to England, the agent should resort to bribing some "great Bassas" in order to expedite the matter.[140] By 1584, Hakluyt was hoping that the "Westerne discoveries lately attempted" would lead to improvements in England's trade with the "Moores in Barbarie and Affricke," particularly in the area of "wollen cappe," since ships on their way to America had to stop in Barbary and could use that opportunity to expand their trade. London and Hereford, Hakluyt believed, would especially benefit from this trade, which would provide "greate reliefe to oure poore people."[141]

Another area of engagement was in science and medicine. In 1582, a "Niqula," possibly Nicholas Cabry, Walsingham's apothecary, spent four years in Istanbul learning about drugs and remedies.[142] Islamic medicine was an important discipline for Europeans: all physicians in the medieval period studied the writings of Rahzes, Avicenna, and Averroes.[143] In 1593, Avicenna's *Canons* was published in Arabic and Latin in Rome to serve as a medical university textbook. Meanwhile there were technological innovations in Christendom that Britons were eager to sell to Muslims. In 1600, Edward Wright, a mathematician who was applying mathematical theory to navigation (and author of *Certaine Errors in Navigation*, 1599), was told by Thomas Bernhere, a resident of Morocco, that Mulay Ahmad would eagerly buy, at a good price, any "astrolabe that hath somewhat extraordinarie in it." Bernhere suggested that the astrolabe along with other instruments be made of either brass or silver, and that space be left so that "Arabique words and figures" could be inscribed.[144] Bernhere also told Wright to show the Moroccan ambassador in England some of his experiments with the "load-stone." Britons were to advertise their technology to the Muslims to impress them as well as to profit from possible sales. Bernhere recognized that scientific knowledge not only brought power, as Francis Bacon declared, but financial reward. Science and technology were part of trade.

Muslim rulers and their retinues eagerly sought to have English scientists and physicians reside in their courts to introduce the new sciences into their kingdoms. The study of *al-keemya'*, the changing of "lead into gold and copper into silver," as the Arab historian al-Wufrani defined it at the beginning of the eighteenth century, was quite popular (and controversial) in Morocco in the period under study. According to him, Mulay Abdallah was reputed to be scientifically adept,[145] and his successor, Mulay al-Mansur was "much delighted in the studie of Astronomie and Astrologie, and valueth Instruments serving for the course of the Sunne and Moone."[146] Not only was the latter interested in science but in the scientists too; in 1601, "one John Rolliffe, a mann of learning, and Richard Edwards, an apothecary" were sent by Queen Elizabeth to serve Mulay al-Mansur.[147] In an attempt to ensure good relations with Morocco after the Moroccan ambassador had visited England the year before, the queen authorized passes for the two men and urged payment of all their expenses.

Such scientific engagement continued well into the Stuart period. In 1637 occurred a curious episode between the king of Morocco and Edmund Bradshaw. It seems that after arriving in Morocco "without any money," as Robert Blake reported, Bradshaw had started dabbling in "chemistry" in front of the king and had "conversed with witches." Bradshaw retorted that he had with him a chemical powder that he had given to the "Queene of Morocco also being sick," which so relieved her that she sent "many thanks" and the king sent Bradshaw "a Barbary horse for ye powder hee had sent hym and after sent to him for more of the saide powder." Afterwards, Bradshaw indicated, some "of the most learned sorts of people of that country" went to him to confer about "the said powder & other experiments in chymicall art." Alchemy and chemistry had brought Britons and Muslims together.[148] Such interactions between Britons and Muslims show a wide and extensive range of mutual knowledge, familiarity, and engagement. They all show that the Muslim world, from Salee to Istanbul, provided the English and other Britons with opportunities to work, profit, and improve their social conditions. To many of the Barbary and Turkey traders, along with the soldiers and seamen, the Muslims were employers, partners, and sometimes accomplices. No other non-Christian dominions attracted more Britons to settle and work than Moorish North Africa and the "Turkish" Mediterranean.

Captives

Another dynamic relationship between Muslims and Britons on Muslim soil is portrayed in the important but as yet ignored writings of Englishmen who were captured and enslaved by Muslims, who lived and served among them, and then finally either escaped home or were ransomed by their compatriots. In this period, countless merchants and sailors, gunners and soldiers, cabin boys and preachers, lords and commoners, men and women, from England and the rest of the British Isles, were captured by pirates and taken to the slave markets in North Africa and the Atlantic coast of Morocco. These captives lived and worked among the Muslims, not as the mercenaries or traders that were needed and respected by Muslim potentates, but as prisoners and slaves at the beck and call of their Muslim owners. These men saw and wrote about the Muslim world from behind the galley oars or from within the *bagnios* (slave prisons), from the fields where they labored, or from the mansions in which they served. They experienced the Muslim world from below.

Between 1577 and 1704 there were twenty-two accounts written by Englishmen about captivity among the Muslims (see appendix A). In these accounts , former captives and editors were well aware of the many Britons who had renounced England and Christianity during their captivity, had converted to Islam, and had settled among the Muslims. Two of them, Joseph Pitts and Thomas Pellow (whose account appeared in 1739), had done exactly that. They along with the other captives knew that their home communities, which had heard a lot about *renegadoes* and *apostates*, were suspicious of them, and wondered how much captivity had changed them. In the majority of cases where a captive escaped and returned home, the community could only wonder whether he had apostatized and been physically marked by Islam. And short of stripping him naked to see whether he had been circumcised or not, which communities and sea captains sometimes did, there was no definite answer.

Such anxiety about the returning captive in seventeenth-century England suggests an identity insecurity. To have been among the Muslims did not necessarily mean that the English/British/Christian identity had been preserved. Rather, it had been tested, and there was no foregone certainty that it would have passed the test successfully. Long before the Stockholm syndrome was identified, communities worried that a captive would have started to identify with the captor—especially at a time when becoming Muslim might have led to advancement and financial gain. To have been among the Muslims was not just to have been a prisoner of war, but a prisoner of temptation too. And many of the prisoners reported on compatriots who had succumbed to Muslim allure and settled among the Muslims.

That is why in writing about themselves—or in submitting depositions and communicating with relatives—captives presented themselves as hardened Britons who had endured years of slavery and labor among the Muslims in order to preserve the integrity of their religious and national identity. Unable to present themselves as chivalrous Britons fulfilling their soldierly ideals amid Muslims, the writers transformed their accounts into intelligence reports about the military and strategic capabilities of the Muslims. Especially in letters they wrote to their relatives at home, they included military information hoping that the authorities would value them for their patriotism and reward them by paying their ransoms. In a letter to his sister about his captivity, Pethericke Honicombe included information about "thirtie saile of shipps att Sally now preparinge to come for the coastes of Englande in the begynninge of the sumer, and, if there were not speedy course taken to prevent itt, they would do much mischiefe."[149] The captives hoped to be viewed as spies for England among the Muslims. That is why many accounts, especially the later and lengthier ones in the seventeenth century, described the topography, the fauna and flora, the social customs, and the religious habits of the Muslim world. The writers presented to the English reader what no ambassador or traveler could have seen or known about the military preparedness, the movement of the fleet, and the number of soldiers among the Moors and Turks. Although the captives informed their writings with an agenda of Christian resistance and victory, they also provided important information about the peoples and dominions of Islam.

It is noteworthy that returning captives did not appear in dramatic and literary documents. While there are plays about British soldiers among the Muslims, only a few allusions to English captives among the Muslims that appear in the course of poems and plays. In a "A devise of a Maske for the right honorable Viscount Mountacute" (c. 1570s), George Gascoigne presented a fictional account of the captivity of an English youth, and in *A Challenge for Beautie* by Thomas Heywood, two Englishmen were captured by the Turks. When asked about their country of origin, one answered "England," to which the Turk replied "Y'ar Nobly Spirited," because he found him and his companion strong in their infirmity.[150] In *A Very Woman* (1636), Philip Massinger depicted an "English Slave" in Sicily who overcame a Turk. That same year the author of *A Brave Memorable and Dangerovs Sea-Fight* mentioned the "too too many" British ships and men that had "beene sunke, slaine, and taken."[151] In January of 1638, William D'Avenant wrote and Inigo Jones designed the masque *Britannia Triumphans* in celebration of the victory of the English fleet over Salee the year before. In the description of the "Border of the Scene" there is reference to "two nearly nude [male] captives, with their hands bound"; in another variation a woman was added to the captives.[152] This is the only occasion when the theme of captivity was broached in the masque. After all, it was not a happy topic since only rarely did the English monarch perform so heroically in ransoming his subjects.

Captivity did not appeal in England to the literary writers as it did in, for instance, France or Spain. There is no account in drama or fiction of capture, enslavement, and return similar to the one in Rabelais' *Pantagruel* or Cervantes' *Don Quixote*, *Life in Algiers* and *The Prisoners of Algiers*.[153] The reason for this absence could be that such a narrative would evoke a humiliation of which writers did not wish to remind their audiences—until the Interregnum period, British sailors were nearly helpless before the attacks of the corsairs. Another reason why writers might not have wanted to tackle the subject of returning captives was that the captives were creating a social problem; having been ransomed, captives were finding themselves not only in debt to their ransomers, but destitute as a result of having to start their lives anew after years of absence from their professions and their country. In the *Knight of Malta* (circa 1618), Beaumont and Fletcher showed how poor and destitute a released captive was after returning to his home. After Colonna explained that he had been a slave among the Turks he added that, having been freed, he found himself "a stranger, and my wants upon me . . . The hand of pity, that should give for Heaven sake, / And charitable hearts, are grown so cold."[154] For these and other reasons, captives and captivity were never explored psychologically or morally on the English stage or in English fiction. Throughout the period under study, no presentation of the social and historical context of captivity was offered, nor of the actual conditions of enslavement.[155]

Captives appeared more frequently in depositions than in fiction–usually in first person accounts, some of which were inevitably quite "dramatic" in their self-image and content. Once a captive returned to England, he had to submit a deposition to the authorities about his enslavement. The deposition did not so much describe the captive's personal experience as document the number and whereabouts of other captives, and provide information about the military and naval location of the corsairs. In the late Jacobean period two captives returned to England to report on fortifications in Algiers.[156] Numerous depositions have survived showing the carefulness with which the debriefings were conducted in the harbor towns where the captives had landed, and the precision with which information was documented and passed on to the Privy Council.[157] On 18 March 1635, the following report was submitted by the mayor of Plymouth to the Privy Council:

> **And my very good Lords. My duty in all humble manner: I saye lately arrived heere one Christopher Pige, a Marryner that hath liued long a captive in Argire, and speakes of diverse shipps now making readye there for the caost of England and Ireland, and likewise speakes of the strength of the Argerine, and Salye in shipping, and the number of his Ma[jes]ties Subiects that are prisoners there; this examinacon [was taken . . .] to make knowne to yor Honors, that some tymely course may be taken for theire redempcon, and soe rest.[158]**

In the mayor's view, the purpose of the deposition was to document information about the North African pirates and encourage some action on the part of the captives. After all, many of the captives came from harbor cities like the mayor's Plymouth. Attached to the mayor's cover note was Pige's deposition:

> **The saide Ex[aminant] saith that in or about five yeares [be]foure he was taken prisoner by twelue saile of Turkish men of warre—belonging to Argeere in a shipp called the Golden ffaulcon of London whereof was captayne one William Hokeridge and this Exam[inant] master of the said shipp and carryed to Argeere, and hath bin since continued a captiue there, duringe which tyme this Exam[inant] was often fforced to goe pylott in some of theire men of warre, And in december last this Exam[inant] was ransomed for nyntye three pounds; And this Exam[inant] further saith that [he saw] there sixe and thyrtye sayle of English Scottish and Irish shipps haue beene taken by men of warre of Argeare, And there are nowe fouer hundred captiues or there a bouts of English Scottes & Irish, And this Ex[aminant] further saith that there were tenn saile of shipps of Argeare which were to be made readye to come for the coast of England and Ireland this springe as he hearde, And this Exam[inant] further saith that in July last he was in Sally where he staied fiue weekes or thereabouts, and duringe his spring there there [sic] came in tenn saile of Sally men of warre which brought in three hundred Christians captives English Scotish Irish and French whoe had taken eight saile of English Scotish and Irish shippes, And then [the Examinant] further saith that he hath heared and beleeveth that there are one hundred and fiftye prisoners there in Sally of English Scotish and Irish, And further saith that there belonge sixe and thyrtye saile of men of warre to Sally, tenn saile to Tunnies, and fortye saile to Argeeare and most of them shippes of good force, And this Ex[aminant] further saith that Sally men of warre doe most of all frequent in sumer the English French & Irish coast, And that this last sumer some of them were as high as the Isle of Lundye in Scotland.[159]**

This deposition and others like it show that the captives were viewed as a much needed source of reliable information about Muslim military plans. Similarly, the long autobiographical accounts written by captives reveal the same goal: the captives wanted to show that they alone could describe the world of the Muslims accurately. Although many of the accounts (and the depositions) included a kind of adventure story of the captives and how they smartly or heroically or perseveringly escaped from among the "barbarous

Turks," there was always a religious/national purpose at the heart of the text—they were texts of confrontation between Christians and Muslims. In this respect, the captivity accounts are the first realistic documents in English that are situated within the conflict between Christendom and Islam.

The first account by an English captive who had been forced into the Turkish military was John Fox, a gunner.[160] After he escaped with 266 Christians (including three Englishmen) in 1577, he sought employment in Spain, where as a hardened soldier he received better pay than he would have in England. Although Fox did not have much information to convey about Turkish Egypt, his text was republished in 1608—under a different name— showing the need of English readers for any kind of information about the Muslim Mediterranean. That is perhaps why when Edward Webbe wrote his own account in 1590, *Edward Webbe, Cheif Master Gunner, His Trauailes*, he filled it with "information." He told, for instance, about the Turkish foray, in which he had taken part, into the territory of Prester John, where he saw a beast "hauing 4 heades, they are in shape like a wilde Cat, and are of the height of a great mastie Dog."[161] Webbe stated that after his capture his "skil in Artillery" led him to be pressed into the Turkish army as it went on the offensive through Persia, "Damasco," and then "the great Caer . . . the greatest Cittie in the world."[162] He had served as "chiefe maister Gunner in these Turkish warres," and participated in numerous battles not only against Muslim enemies of the Turks, but against the Catholics of Calabria. Although he had fought with the Muslims, Webbe intimated, he had been able to put that service to good English use since he had been able to acquire a lot of information about lands and territories that were unfamiliar to his compatriots.

The texts by Fox and Webbe are short and crude, written as they were by men who had been totally unprepared for the world of Islam. Neither knew anything about the culture or the religion of the Muslims—except that Islam was opposed to Christianity—and neither was able to enter into the lives of Muslims. Or if they did they did not bother to write about them. But both seemed to have been aware that their compatriots were going to meet with a new kind of experience in the Mediterranean, and both wanted to confirm a national commitment that was being challenged both by Catholicism and Islam. The Elizabethan English viewed the peoples of both these religions as enemies but they did not fear them equally; in a period when the Spanish, not the Turkish, armada threatened England, the Papist emerged as the more dangerous foe of the two. It is no wonder, then, that the English and other Britons felt safer among the Moors than the Spaniards, and soldiers were more willing to serve—or even be captured—by the former than by the latter. Richard Hasleton is a case in point: he was taken captive by Spaniards and tortured in order to convert him to Catholicism. In 1588 he managed to escape from Majorca and sailed in a self-made raft to the "Coast of Barbary." Hasleton knew how dangerous it was for a Christian to be there, since the only Christians who landed on the coast were Spaniards who abducted Muslims to sell as slaves. Hasleton, however, was fortunate in meeting an old farmer who took pity on him and offered him food and drink. Although Hasleton was later captured and imprisoned in Algiers, he was not tortured by rack and solitary confinement as he had been among the Spaniards.[163]

About half a century later, the attitude toward Islam and Muslims in captivity accounts had not changed much. In his account—published in 1670 but describing events in 1648 and after—a "Mr. T. S." told how he was enslaved after a sea battle and taken to Algiers, where he was forced into the army. T. S. confirmed what many of his readers knew—that English and continental soldiers who had converted to Islam constituted the main strength of the Algerian army, and that the "Infantry was made up of Renegado-Christians, whereof there are such number in that place, that they bear all the sway and command both by Sea and Land."[164] While Hasleton had preferred Muslims to Catholics, but still retained his allegiance to English Protestantism, others were choosing Islam over Christianity. The allure of the Muslim world and the challenge it posed to Christian identity and British nationalism had grown more powerful and more successful over the years.

T. S. assured his readers that he had not renounced his god or monarch, and that because of his military skills, he had fought in the battles of the Muslims, which took him over the vast and hitherto unknown expanse of the North African kingdoms. That is why his friends had urged him to write his account, as his editor stated; T. S. had information nobody else possessed. In his memoir, which was deemed so valuable that it was published posthumously, T. S. described the various campaigns in which he participated, the locations he visited, and the political rivalry of the numerous Muslim leaders. From the very start, T. S. emphasized his commitment to England by providing intelligence about Algerian military preparedness. He warned how the harbor in Algiers was very well protected against the "Attempts of any Christian Enemy" and reported on the weak places in the fortifications. He also told of the conflict between the Arabs and the Turks, and how much the former sought to remove the yoke of the "heretical" Turks.[165] Since the campaigns in which he was involved were directed against the Arabs and Moors, he provided an extensive portrait of the ideological and cultural differences between them and the Turks. His account was to be the document of a soldier who never reneged on his English values, never doubted his faith in the Christian God, and who presented a description of North Africa that no other Briton before him had offered to his country. It is interesting that T. S. became so involved in the battles and ambushes and fighting, and so committed to the cause his Turkish master was pursuing, that he started to refer to the Turkish authority as "Our Government."

Although many captives served as soldiers and seamen, others served inside their captors' household, where they entered into the intimacy of Muslim life. In this respect, their knowledge of the world of Islam was unparalleled in the early modern period of European geographical expansion. They were able to provide a view of the Muslims that no Muslim could provide of the Christians—no Muslim captive among the Christians left behind him an account of his enslavement as detailed and curious as those left by Europeans. Furthermore, and intentionally or not, the captives' accounts showed the Muslims as "round" characters, for some of the captives who stayed for long periods among the Muslims entered into interesting relationships with their captors. Although they were captives, they grew to like their captors and were not unwilling to recall the humor in cross-cultural misunderstanding between themselves and the Muslims. After his capture, T. S. reported, he was put to work as a cook for the ruler. Although he could cook well, when it came to preparing "other Meats less usual than in our Country," he ended up making such "mad Sauces, and such strange Ragoux, that every one took me for a Cook of the Antipodes." Soon after, the ruler was lamenting the death of his previous cook, whom T. S. had replaced. And when at a great feast T. S. mistakenly included a liver of a fish that "hath a most loathsom tast" but that he had never seen before, the result was a culinary disaster that so angered the ruler he had T. S. given "ten Bastonadoes" and then sold him out of the kitchen.[166] Later on, T. S. had many offers to stay among the Muslims. What made the Muslim allure powerful was the fact that T. S. had grown to admire the Muslims, having seen nothing "of that rudeness, which our People imagine to be in all Parts of Africa." "The Arabs," he continued, "all about Africa are People very polite, and well bred . . . they are affable, hospitable, courteous, kind, and very liberal."[167] The allure was difficult to reject, especially after a woman fell in love with him and offered him wealth and opportunities if he would convert to Islam and marry her.

While the years of captivity were difficult, they allowed Britons to enter into unprecedented relationships with Muslims. No traveler or ambassador had as curious an experience as that of Adam Elliot, who was taken captive in the early 1670s. Elliot became so free with his master, Hamed Lucas, that he joked with him about "serious" topics, telling him that French wine was so good that Lucas might want to "renounce Mahumetism to drink of it." Later Elliot reported that he sang to his master's company "the Mock-Astrologer, which was new when I left England; they [the company] were wonderfully affected with it, and were very desirous to have me translate ha ha ha, & c. into Spanish, which made me laugh more heartily than I sung."[168] That trendy London songs were being enjoyed by Muslim captor and Christian captive shows how familiarity could develop even under such hard conditions. Pitts remembered that his last master often called him "Ben ebn . . . My Son" and never suspected that Pitts would think of escaping; he had given the Exeter convert to Islam everything that a young man could want.[169]

Another area of engagement between English captives and their Muslim captors was religion. Very few traders or travelers entered into religious debates with Muslims—Thomas Coryat, Henry Marsh, and Sir Thomas Baines are among the few in the seventeenth century who did.[170] Captives, however, who lived inside Muslim homes could not help but find themselves discussing religion at some point in their cohabitation, especially since they would have grown to know and understand Islam better (without necessarily accepting it) than any other European Christian could. Many captives described Muslims as pious, obedient to their Qur'anic faith, and submitting in all tribulations to the unquestioned will of God. The world of Islam was not always portrayed as a place of infidelity and false "Mahometanism," and the Muslims were not always derided and denounced. Actually, Christians were shown by English writers of drama to pray for them: In *Soliman and Perseda* by Thomas Kyd (1588), the hero Erastus flees from Christendom and enters the service of the Turkish emperor "Soliman."[171] His beloved Perseda implores God for the Sultan: I will, she declares, "still solicite God for Soliman, / Whose minde hath proued so good and gratious" (4.1.201–202). Similarly, Sir Anthony Shirley assures the Persian "Sophie" in *The Travailes of the Three Brothers Shirley*, that during battle, Christians will pray for him: "Religious men shall weare their bended knees/ Even to the bone in ceaslesse prayers for you."[172] The Christian God could be invoked by Christians, both continentals and Britons, for the Muslim cause.

Some captives were challenged by the religious ethos of Islam and admitted that they had found themselves in the awkward position of having to demonstrate to their Muslim counterparts their commitment to their own Christian faith. In the early 1640s, the English cleric Devereux Spratt was captured and enslaved in Algiers. Finding there a group of Britons who were persevering in their faith, he was pleased that God had made him "an instrument" to preach to them. After a few weeks the reverend was about to be ransomed when "on a sudden I was sould and delivered to a Mussleman dwelling with his family in ye towne, upon which change and sudden disappointment I was very sad; my patron asked me to the reason, and withall uttered these comfortable words, 'God is great!' which took such impression as strengthened my faith in God, considering thus with myself, Shall this Turkish Mahumitan teach me, who ame a Christian, my duty of faith and dependence upon God."[173] For Spratt, the words of the "Mussleman" not only strengthened him but also humbled him. Spratt recognized in his master's words the vision of God that he himself sought to embody to the English captives: God as supreme over human life and ordering it in accordance with His mysterious will. What was humbling to Spratt was that he, as a Christian,

was preaching this theology to his fellow nationals but was obviously not recognizing its application to his own life. The "Turk" so showed him the sim-
plicity and effectiveness of this doctrine that Spratt was touched by the Turk's
words. After all, as a Christian clergyman Spratt could well have denounced
the statement as an utterance of an infidel; rather, he treated it as a statement
by a Muslim who recognized the power of God both in adversity as well as
in prosperity. It is significant that in his whole autobiography Spratt mentioned very little about his two years of captivity, and what he chose to
include—about preaching to other captives and being humbled by his master—highlights his response to Muslim captivity. Among the Muslims he had
had to come to brutal terms with his faith.

Captives related to Muslims in a unique manner because they met them
in different contexts—at prayer and at mealtime, in battle and in the ham-
mam, in the country and in the city, in happiness and in sorrow. The captives
learned that among the Muslims there was brutality as well as compassion,
that some Muslims were kind while others were vicious, that some captors
were men to be hated and despised while others, such as T. S.'s master, were
to be admired and served with devotion. The captives provided the English
reading public with precise, sometimes sympathetic, sometimes not so sympathetic, but most importantly, empirically derived information about the
Muslims. As a result of the popularity and wide circulation of the captivity
accounts a large sector of English society became familiar with the Muslims
and their world.

* * *

Englishmen and other Britons who went or were taken to the dominions of
Islam numbered in the thousands. Of those only a few wrote about their
experiences. Others were written about in literary and historical documents
and others still left depositions and impromptu accounts of their exposure
to the Muslims. How much information was transmitted orally to the local
communities as sailors, traders, captives, and pirates returned to their
homes with fictional and "factional" accounts of the Muslims and their world
cannot be known. But there is little doubt that the information about
Muslims that was available to Britons in the Age of Discovery provided them

with a window on an un-Christian but powerful empire with an unchallenged but challenging religion that was both unthreatened and threatening. It was not an empire England could possess, but one it had to watch and guard against. While Britons traveled and traded between London and Salee, or Plymouth and New England, or Bristol and Guinea, and as they expanded their "discovery" of the world, they were constantly aware of the Muslim Other, as buyer and seller, partner and pirate, captive and captor.

3

THE RENAISSANCE TRIANGLE: BRITONS, MUSLIMS, AND AMERICAN INDIANS

The Renaissance energy for exploration, along with the need for places to market goods propelled Britons to look eastward at the Turks and the Moors. It also directed them westward to America. In the half century between the establishment of the Turkey Company and the beginning of the Great Migration to North America, there were travelers and traders, pirates and adventurers, and migrants and emigrants within the triangle of England, the Muslim Mediterranean, and America.

Actually, during the Age of Discovery there were various triangles in the English experience. From the 1560s on there was the England-Newfoundland-Africa triangle in which Britons fished in Newfoundland, then sailed to the Christian and Muslim Mediterranean to sell their harvest, then returned home.[1] There was also the infamous slave triangle between Bristol, sub-Saharan Guinea, and the Caribbean. But in the period under study the most dominant triangle linked England to Moorish North Africa and North America. Surprisingly, this triangle has been ignored by historians. In his magisterial study of the Mediterranean, Fernand Braudel had little to say about England's North African/North American exposure while David Beers Quinn traced English travel between 1400 and 1600 from Iceland to the Caribbean but made no mention of the Mediterranean. These and other writers focused on the English westward venture.[2] By so doing they ignored the evidence demonstrating that in the Elizabethan and Jacobean periods, not only was the eastward venture a great rival to the westward one but it was actually more successful.

The Drake-Mellon world map, which traces Drake's itinerary on his "famous" voyage in 1577, shows the England-North Africa-North America triangle. On his way from England to America, Drake and his fleet stopped in Morocco; John White did the same in 1590.3 The Virginia Company Chart of the early 1600s confirms this triangle: it shows England along with its European rivals "Francia" and "Hispania;" it also shows "Barbaria" and "Gvinea" in Africa; and finally, it shows "Nova Francia," "Virginia," "Florida," and "Gviana" in America. This is a map of England's "new" commercial horizon in which America is as prominent as Barbary. Such prominence does not reduce the difference between England's colonial attitude to America and its commercial relations with North Africa. The Virginia charter of 1606 urged the adventurers and colonists to take possesion of the land and its resources; but it was over a decade later that an ideology of settlement was implemented. Indeed, as Mary C. Fuller has shown, the period between 1576 and 1624 witnessed the "failure of voyages" to America, which was "recuperated by rhetoric, a rhetoric which in some ways even predicted failure."4 Meanwhile, and as the previous chapter has shown, Britons "dwel[led]" among the Muslims as early as the 1580 Ottoman-English treaty. In the period which English history often dedicates to Roanoke, Virginia, the Somer Islands and Plymouth, there were more Britons going to North Africa and the Levant than to North America, and more Britons "dwel[ling]" there than in the coloniess of the New World.5

* * *

From the decade of the Roanoke debacle to the beginning of the Great Migration, the same complex impulses that motivated "vexed and troubled Englishmen" to cross the Atlantic motivated them to cross the Mediterranean too. Actually, the English had begun migrating to North Africa before they traveled to America. In 1577, William Harrison observed that "the wise and better-minded" English men and women were forsaking the realm "to live in other countries, as France, Germany, Barbary" and else-

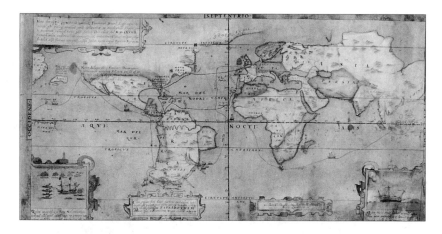

3. Manuscript world map on vellum showing Drake's route of Circumnavigation. Courtesy of the Yale Center for British Art.

where.[6] Later, an increase in England's population compelled some Britons to leave for Europe and North Africa. In 1609, Robert Johnson urged his countrymen to seek the riches of the West Indies rather than risk their lives and spill their blood "to reconquer Palestina from the Turkes and Sarazens"[7]; Britons were being encouraged to move westward rather than eastward. Evidently two years after the establishment of the Virginia colony in 1607, there were still more Britons exploring the Mediterranean than the Atlantic.

As has been shown earlier, large numbers of English and Scottish merchants and traders settled on the Muslim North African and Atlantic coasts. Meanwhile, others sailed to America, where in the early years of exploration the chief purpose of establishing outposts was to trade in fur and fish with the Indians—once it was realized that there was no gold—and to attack the Spanish treasure fleet. Many were actually more active in the latter than the former, much to the sorrow of Johnson, who lamented that John White's Roanoke colonists had turned from planting to "hunt after pillage upon the Spanish coaste."[8] Settlement had not yet attracted the first wayfarers in America. It was not until the 1620s that "English settlement actually took root in New England."[9] Earlier travelers had no plans to make America their home: "Of a merchantlike Trade," wrote the author of the *Discourse of the Old*

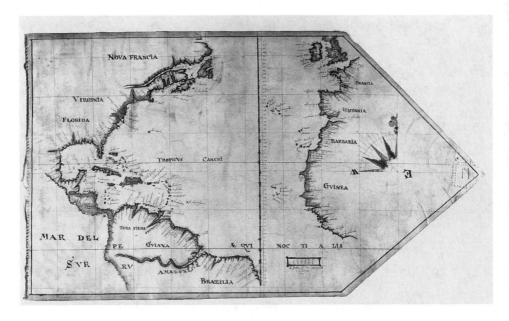

4. Virginia Company Chart. Courtesy of I. N. Phelps Stokes
Collection, Miriam and Ira D. Wallach Division of Arts, Prints and
Photographs, the New York Library, Astor, Lenox,
and Tilden Foundations.

Company in 1625, describing the plans for Virginia, "there was some probbil-
litie . . . but of a plantation there was none at all, neither in the course nor
in the intencons either of the Adventurers here [London] or the Colonie
there [Virginia]."[10] Rather, as with the first exclusively male Jamestown settlers, the goal of going to America was to grow rich by trade or pillage, and
then return home. In this respect, as Britons went to North America in quest
of opportunity and fast wealth, so did they seek North Africa.

In fact, the attraction of North Africa was stronger than that of North
America. There was more gold in the coffers of Mulay al-Mansur of
Morocco than in all the lands of Powhatan, and while the former had been

dubbed "the golden" after his seizure of gold-rich Sudan, the Indians of Virginia, and later of Massachusetts, cherished the trinkets the colonists gave them. In North Africa there was the certainty of gold (thus Morocco's choice of the gold casket in Shakespeare's *The Merchant of Venice*); in America, none had been found. It is no wonder that more Britons crossed the Mediterranean and stayed in North Africa than crossed the Atlantic to America. In 1605, James I issued a royal proclamation in which he called on his subjects who were in "the Service of divers forreine States, under the Title of men of Warre . . . [to] returne home into their owne Countrey, and leave all such forreine Services, and betake themselves to their Vocation in the lawfull course of Merchandize, and other orderly Navigation . . . [and not] otherwise employ themselves in any warlike Services of any forraine State upon the Sea."[11] Twenty years later, in Februay of 1623, another prolcamation repeated this call, condemning the "great numbers of Mariners and Sea-faring men, [who] contrary to their duety and allegeance, and against the Lawes of this Realme, have presumed without such licence to goe abroad, and serve other Princes and States in forraine parts."[12] If these proclamations are coupled with others denouncing British pirates "within the Mediterranean Seas," and the "protection which is given them in Tunis, Argiers, and the places adjoyning," a considerable English/British presence can be confirmed in the North African Mediterranean that was dependent on, and in deep cooperation with, the Muslim rulers: "so great a part of our strength," declared Robert Johnson, are "arming and serving with Turkes and Infidels."[13]

While "great numbers" of Britons served foreign princes in the Mediterranean, royal proclamations about overseas colonization show that James I viewed the American colonies as no better than convenient destinations for vagabonds and undesirables. One of his first proclamations issued just months after acceding to the throne urged that rogues might be banished to "some place beyond the Seas"; by 1617, after the colonization initiative had proved costly in both lives and funding, the place was specifically identified as "Virginia."[14] For King James, the Britons among the Muslims were useful while the men to be sent to Virginia were not. Muslim North Africa was a place from which Britons had to be lured back by pardons; Virginia was a place to which unwanted Britons were to be sent.

By 1617 only a few hundred Britons had survived sickness and famine in Virginia. The situation was so desperate that lotteries were introduced in London to help revive the transatlantic enterprise. In 1618 Wolstenhome Towne was built on the James River, but disappeared within a few years, while half of the 1620 Plymouth "pilgrims" died soon after landing. Meanwhile, there were "great numbers" in the Muslim Mediterranean not only consisting of pirates, but of traders and merchants who, in the first two decades of the seventeenth century increased England's commercial relations with the Levant and North Africa by one-third. [15] Traders, pirates, and even the king viewed North Africa as more promising than North America. And as many men, such as Captain John Smith, conquered, pillaged, burnt, and built in America, and then returned to a quiet retirement in England, so did many others do the same among the Muslims. William Mellon, who was denounced in one of the Jacobean royal proclamations as an Algiers-based pirate, returned to England and found a place for himself on the Admiralty Commission. [16] North America was a place, according to propagandists and colonists, in which Britons could work, explore, and then return home; and so was North Africa.

Britons may have had more reasons to seek North Africa than America. First, the journey across the Mediterranean and to the Muslim Levant was navigationally less dangerous than that across the Atlantic. There is a large number of references, especially in New England autobiographies and memoirs, about the terror of crossing the ocean. [17] While the Mediterranean was not without its hazards—since Britons had to sail in winter to avoid attacks by Spanish and Maltese (Catholic) pirates—it was not as forbidding as the "Ditch" and the "raginge floods" of the "Perillous Ocean." [18] Second, in America there were swamps and marshlands, mosquitos and typhoid-contaminated water, and, most terrifyingly, hurricanes the like of which do not exist in the Mediterranean. Sir Thomas Gates compared a hurricane in the Caribbean with the storms he had encountered in the Mediterranean: "Windes and Seas were as mad, as fury and rage could make them; for mine owne part, I had bin in some stormes before, as well upon the coast of

Barbary and Algeere, in the Levant . . . Yet all that I have ever suffered gathered together, might not hold comparison with this [hurricane]."[19] The Mediterranean was safer and more familiar than the Atlantic. Furthermore, the Muslim cities at which traders, captives, and sailors disembarked were clean and not unattractive. Muslim society was metropolitan; Algiers was nearly as big as London, and Sanaa (in Yemen) was "somwhat bigger than Bristol."[20] Meanwhile, the regions of America, as Respire objected in Richard Eburne's *A Plain Pathway to Salvation*, "are wilde and rude—no towns, no houses, no buildings there."[21] Until the 1630s there were no colonial towns in America, and colonists relied on London as their market. Although the American Indians had a complex culture, Britons did not bother to familiarize themselves with it and merely saw what they deemed "salvage" and uncivilized.[22]

Third, in the late sixteenth century and the first decade of the seventeenth century, numerous Britons returned from unsuccessful settlement adventures in America and propagandized against emigration. Many remembered the debacle at Sagadahoc in 1607. George Percy's account of the "Starving Times" of 1609–1610 in Jamestown drew such a frightful portrait of the plight of the colonists that it became familiar from England to Spain. In 1612, John Chamberlain described how "Sir Thomas Gates and Sir Thomas Dale are quite out of hart,"[23] and a decade later, news from Plymouth and Salem told of sickness and despair. Furthermore, the death rate in the colonies was very high: between 1606 and 1624 six colonists died for every one that lived in Jamestown, and of the women who were brought as wives in 1619, it is not clear if any survived ; between 1625 and 1640 the death rate was 50 percent.[24] That is why from the very beginning of Elizabethan travel to America, men such as John White, John Smith, Christopher Levett, and others, tried to refute the negative propaganda about America and to write glowingly about the fertility and attractiveness of the land; so too did some poets and masque writers who compared America with a terrestrial paradise.[25] But the last years of Elizabeth's reign and the first years of the Jacobean period witnessed so much suffering that "gloom . . . hung over the colonial prospect."[26] .Although the Great Migration in the 1630s made the English presence in America definite, colonists remained doubtful about settlements as thousands returned to England in the 1640s and 1650s.[27]

In the American colonies investors got good returns at the price of cheap or indentured or enslaved English, Scottish, and Irish labor. Among the Muslims, the "small men" with basic skills or with a willingness to convert to Islam were the ones to benefit. An indentured servant or dissatisfied colonist did not have much to hope for in America; among the Muslims, it was different. When William Okeley was about to escape from his captivity in Algiers in 1644, he paused to reflect on whether it was wise for him to do so since in Algiers he had work and income, while back in England he would find himself without employment and support at a time when civil war was ravaging the country.[28] Many of the captives in North Africa were free to roam the cities, start their own businesses, pursue their professions, and make money, part of which they gave to their masters and part of which they saved to buy their freedom. Okeley was hesitant to give up his Algerian captivity because he had seen others buy their freedom, convert to Islam, and settle in their new identities and careers among the Muslims.

Such opportunity was not as plentiful in the plantations. An indentured servant, even after winning his freedom, could not prosper without capital. In 1666, George Alsop wondered in a letter to his brother in England whether it was not better for him to remain indentured in Maryland than to become free. In words that are strikingly similar to Okeley's "dialogue" with himself before his escape, Alsop complained about his condition in New England: "Liberty without money," he wrote, "is like a man opprest with the Gout, every step he puts forward puts him to pain . . . What the futurality of my dayes will bring forth, I know not; For while I was linckt with the Chain of a restraining Servitude, I had all things cared for, and now I have all things to care for my self, which makes me almost to wish my self in for the other four years."[29] For Okeley, North Africa was more the land of security than North America was for Alsop.

As has been shown, from the Elizabethan until the Caroline periods thousands of Britons were captured and then made to work—some permanently to remain on Muslim soil. Between 1603 and 1615, 100 English and Scottish ships were taken by North African pirates. Between 1616 and 1620, the number is 150 ships; between 1622 and 1642 the number is 300. By the mid-1620s there were between 1200 and 1400 captives in Salee alone; between 1622 and 1642 over 8000 Britons were taken captive; between 1627 and 1640 there were 2828 British captives in Algiers alone.[30] Confirmation of such high numbers appears in the eyewitness accounts of captives: in 1640, Francis Knight used the word "innumerable" for the captives in Algiers alone, and in 1642 "An Act for the releife of the Captives taken by Turkish Moorish and other Pirates" mentioned "many thousands."[31] There would have been more references to the high number of captives had records other than those of seamen and traders been kept; the previous "thousands" do not include the British convicts who were captured by Muslims while being hauled to the American penal or slave colonies. Such people did not fall within the ransom budgets or record keeping of the trading companies or the monarchy. Many English youths either ran away to the Turks or were stolen or enticed by them, as a report in 1589 showed.[32] Of the thousands of Britons known to have been captured by or "emigrated" to the Muslims, the records that have survived listing their numbers and names show that "only a fraction, probably less than one-third,"[33] ever returned to England. And that "fraction" would be of captives only. The emigrants-turned-Muslim, the poor and indigent who were captured by the Barbary Corsairs, and the Britons who were sold to the Moors by their own countrymen remain numberless.

Finding themselves captured or enslaved by the Muslims, many such Britons "emigrated" to the Muslim dominions by conversion and acculturalization. Interestingly, the same "emigration" occurred to America. After all, only a few of the early merchant adventurers who crossed to America had investment capital and were able to acquire land and plantations. The rest, who were the majority, were the poor and destitute. Many of the "emigrants" to Virginia and other American colonies in the Jacobean and Caroline periods—and well into the eighteenth century—were spirited men, women, and children, zealous youths, helpless vagrants, and numberless orphans who were abducted or who, under the influence of drink or fanciful rhetoric, were made to sign agreements for transportation and then locked up to await shipping. From 1607 on, "thousands of poor children were shipped off to Virginia,"[34] while so many vagrants and vagabonds were viewed as naturally destined for the plantations. Francis Bacon complained in one of his essays that the plantations were being filled with "the scum of people, and wicked condemned men."[35] Furthermore, it was state policy in England to ship prisoners of war to the West Indian plantations, and after 1662 and the Act of Uniformity, to transport nonconformists and felons too.[36] "Scarce any" of those brought from England, complained one, "but are brought in as merchandise to make sale of."[37] Like their counterparts who were captured on the high seas by Muslim pirates, many Britons did not have a choice about their "emigration" to America. Nor did they end up in a better condition; as Muslim captors bought and sold British captives, so did colonial masters buy and sell Britons "at any time for any period of years."[38] It is no wonder that in 1620 "one Spark" reported from Plymouth "that the people are vsed wth more slavery then if they were vnder the Turke."[39] New England conditions were as bad if not worse than conditions in North Africa.

Although the number of British "emigrants" to America remains as imprecise as that of the "emigrants" to Islam, the existing evidence shows that from the first attempt at an English settlement in 1584 and 1585 in Virginia, until the accession of Charles I to the throne and the beginning of the Great Migrationt, the number of surviving colonists was small. It did not exceed five thousand, with "half of them in Virginia and the rest precariously scattered in New England, Bermuda, Barbados, and the Leeward Islands."[40] If this figure is correct, and if the figures about British captives in North Africa are correct, then it is possible to conclude that until the beginning of the Caroline period, the number of Britons in Muslim North Africa was higher than that in North America. Similarly, if the figures of three thousand captives in Algiers and fifteen hundred in Salee in May 1626 are correct, then it is safe to conclude that the number of congregated expatriate Britons in this period was higher than anywhere else in the world—Virginia included.[41] Unfortunately, it is not always possible to break down the numbers among the traders, settlers, pillagers, indentured servants, the kidnapped and captives. But it is clear that during the years Jamestown and Plymouth were being built, there were thousands of Britons among the Muslims—many more than in America.

Like their Muslim-bound counterparts, the America-bound emigrants hailed from the same areas in England and Wales, [42] that is, chiefly from the West country, London, and East Anglia. They also hailed from the same social groupings. Contrary to what Richard Slotkin has maintained, the first colonists in America were not "drawn largely from the rising Protestant middle classes."[43] Rather, as John White's list of names shows in 1587, members of the gentry were by far fewer than the "Households of the Common Folk." David B. Quinn has shown that the majority on White's list were actually "servants."[44] As long as America was seen as a place for "front-line operatives," as Cressy has called them, who worked for their masters in England, and were to return there after finishing their projects, the chief travelers were of the menial class. The list of names prepared by Edward Waterhouse in his account of the victims of the 1622 massacre confirms this view. Although there are some "esquires" and "masters" mentioned, there are many who are simply described as "his man" or "a boy" or whose full names were not known, attesting thereby to a menial status: "Collins his man;" "Robert Tyler a boy;" "— Atkins. — Weston;" "The Tinker," "Master Tho: Boise, & Mistris Boise his wife, & a sucking Childe. 4 of his men. A Maide. 2 Children . . .. 6 Men and Boyes."[45] That is why English propaganda for colonization repeatedly called for the emigration of men with professions and craft, the implication being that those who had *actually* been going there were not, but were instead, as the image of the first colonists of Virginia and Barbados remained until the end of the century, "loose vagrant people" intent on "whoreing, thieving or other debauchery."[46] The majority of Britons in America were of a low socio-economic class and/or of questionable moral background. In this respect they were not unlike many of the Britons among the Muslims who were of low moral and social status too—pirates and "renegadoes" and vagrants.

Actually, Britons were caught in the Renaissance triangle, much as they might not have wanted to be. Those who reached the American colonies hoped that the new land would be for them a haven not only from the Spanish Catholics, but from the "Turks" too. America, they hoped, would be safe in a way that Protestant Europe and the seas surrounding it were not. In 1621, Robert Cushman reflected on Europe in the grips of what would

become the Thirty Years War: "And if it should please God to punish his people in the Christian countries of Europe, for their coldness, carnality, wanton abuse of the Gospel, contention, &c., either by Turkish slavery, or by
popish tyranny, (which God forbid) . . . here is a way opened for such as have
wings to fly into this wilderness."[47] As Paul Baepler has noted, "from the
beginning of European colonization in America, settlers and North African
corsairs clashed."[48] In 1615, John Smith complained that the Turks had seized
a ship that had been sailing from Virginia to Spain, and in 1625, William
Bradford, the governor of Plymouth, recorded in his diary that Moroccan
pirates from Salee had captured ships on their way to England to trade in
beaver skins "almost within the sight of Plimoth."[49] There was no safety in
the waters of the British Isles; nor was there in the Atlantic. Although the
ocean did separate the colonists from Archbishop Laud and his "Popery," it
did not completely protect them against the "piratical Turkes." As Andrew
White crossed to Maryland in 1632, he was deeply afraid of an attack by the
Turks; and rightly so since in 1639, William Okeley, along with sixty other
Britons, was captured by Algerian pirates as he was crossing to Providence.
In 1640, the minutes of a court for Providence Island urged the sending of a
ship "with a magazine," since the *Mary* had already been captured by the
Turks. Again in that year, "several English ships on their way to Virginia" fell
into the hands of the "Barbary pirates."[50] Three years later John Winthrop
recorded that a ship sailing from New Haven to the Canaries was attacked by
Turkish pirates.[51] Until the end of the century, Britons on their way to New
England were captured by the Barbary Corsairs. Joshua Gee wrote an
account of a New Englander captured by the Muslims in the 1680s, and
Cotton Mather noted in his diary of May 1698 that "wee had many of our
poor Friends, fallen into the Hands of the Turks and Moors, and languishing
under an horrible Slavery in Zallea" (Salee).[52] In his sermon of 1700, *The
Goodness of God Celebrated*, he mentioned that "between Two and Three
Hundred" New Englanders had been imprisoned by the "Emperour of
Morocco."[53] Having prepared for a westward movement to New England,
these captives found themselves forced into an eastward trajectory toward
Islam.

Whether Britons were compelled to go to North Africa or North

America, or voluntarily chose to explore, trade with, or settle these lands, they found themselves exposed to a dynamic of relationships that tested the limits of their national identity. Confronted by the Muslim and the Indian Other, many Britons, chiefly the "small men," chose to superimpose Muslim on English or Indian on English: they converted to Islam and "turned Turk," or went "native." The Roanoke survivors, if any, may have gone native, as did Thomas Weston's band in the early 1620s. Later, Thomas Morton was accused of having transculturated into Indianness. According to historian Edmund S. Morgan, "some" Englishmen deserted Jamestown to join the Indians, while others were forced into transculturation after being captured by the Indians,[54] in the same way that many Britons were forced into conversion to Islam—or at least so they claimed.[55] During the Age of Discovery many Britons were willing to transform themselves, "fashion themselves," to use Stephen Greenblatt's term, into Indians or Muslims.

Voluntary self-fashioning, which was practiced by both Britons and other European Christians, shows that while the European aristocratic identity fashioned itself against the Other, as Greenblatt has argued, the commoner was willing to transform himself into the Other. Members of the lower classes who adopted Islam or Indianness saw no religious or cultural divide between them and the Other that they could not easily and willingly cross. And so many of them fashioned themselves into the Other that they caused deep anxiety in their home communities: for these "renegades" did not seek to destroy the Other, as Greenblatt claims in his analysis of the motivation for the invention of the Other;[56] rather they became so committed to their new communities that they gave up their Christian names and adopted Indian or Muslim names. Robert Marcum, who lived among the Indians, came to be known by his Indian name "Moutapass" in the same way that Richard Clarke, for instance, who joined the Muslims, was known as Jafar.[57]

Such men were very self-conscious about the fashioning of their identity. After all, admission into the Muslim *umma* (religious community), as into the Indian tribe, entailed rituals and processions that made both the adoptive community and the adoptee deeply aware of the "artful process" (according to Greenblatt) being employed to fashion the inductee into the Other, and to confirm his commitment to the Other. Such commitment proved quite strong since the "renegades" ended up teaching the non-Christian adversary a lot about European technology. For many Britons, the crossing of the boundary between London and Istanbul or Algiers proved tempting— although perhaps less difficult—than leaving Jamestown or Charlestown to the Indian hinterland. Crossing to the American Indians ensured survival at a time of famine in the colonies, and perhaps secured a consort in a community sorely lacking in women; crossing to the Muslims could produce wealth and power.

Britons and other Christians crossed over to Islam and to Indianness so much so that the term *renegadoe* or *runnugate*, which in 1599 represented to Hakluyt a convert to Islam, was soon applied to Britons who went native in America.[58] But more Britons converted to Islam than to Indianness because after 1622 the Indian was confirmed as a wild and violent creature. From then on, even those who were captured by the Indians, as Vaughan and Clark have shown, "successfully resisted efforts at assimilation by the French and Indians." The number of New Englanders who deserted their families and villages from the 1620s on to settle among the Indians was very small.[59] Only those who were captured as children or youths between the ages of seven and fifteen completely integrated into Indian life and rarely sought to "return" to their racial community.[60] Meanwhile, in every decade of the Elizabethan and Stuart periods there were Britons who embraced Islam.

It is clear that from the Elizabethan until the Caroline period, Britons found themselves in a triangular relationship between their own country, North Africa, and North America. In that age of English discovery, more Britons went to North Africa than to North Amercia, and more Britons crossed over to Islam than to American Indianness. Although America later superceded the Muslim Levant and North Africa in social and economic importance to England, in the age of Hakluyt and Purchas, the *Golden Hind* and the *Mayflower*, the Muslim world attracted more travelers, pirates, traders, and settlers than New England, Virginia, or the Caribbean.

For the majority of England's adventurers and seafarers, the Mediterranean and North America were the only locations where they could explore, fight, pillage, or live. Just as the age was one of discovering new geographical horizons, it was also one of expanding commercial markets, pursuing new careers, or exploring the different territories of the triangle. In the 1560s, Thomas Stukley decided to establish a kingdom in America to be independent of Queen Elizabeth, as he told her to her face. Over a decade later he died fighting with Moroccan forces against a Moroccan-Turkish-Spanish alliance in the battle of Alcazar. From England to the Americas to his final resting place in North Africa, Stukley lived and died in the new geographical triangle. Similarly, men such as the traveler George Sandys, the explorer William Strachey, the diplomat Sir Thomas Roe, the colonist Ralph Lane, the adventurer John Smith, the founder of New Jersey George Carteret, and others were in the Levant before they crossed to the Americas—in the case of Roe it was the other way round—again exploring the Age of Discovery's triangular options. Richard Hawkins, one of the foremost Elizabethan sea dogs, plundered the coast of South America before returning to England and serving against the Algerian pirates. In 1597, Sir Anthony Shirley came into possession of Jamaica, but left it, sailed home, and from there ventured to the Levant and Persia.[61] John Pory translated the work of Leo Africanus, one of the most influential and informative texts about North African Muslims in Renaissance England, and then went to Virginia and wrote about it; Sir Thomas Smythe was a founder of the Levant Company before becoming treasurer of the Virginia Company; four members of the Levant Company were also members of the Massachusetts Bay Company.[62] William Davis, a surgeon on the ship *London,* sailed in the Mediterranean until he was captured and enslaved by the duke of Florence and sent as a galley slave to South America. John Harrison was the English agent in Morocco before becoming governor of the Somer Islands in 1622— and three years later, King Charles's emissary to Morroco again. Captain John Smith's coat of arms, which appeared in his books about Virginia, showed the heads of three Turks he had killed, or claimed to have killed, in personal duels during his soldiering days against the Ottoman army in central Europe—much like the coat of arms of John Hawkins had shown "a demi-Moor" too.[63] In New England, before Cape Ann was known by that name it had been named by Smith "Cape Tragabigzanda . . . after his imaginary Turkish lady love," and across from Cape Cod he named three islands

"The three Turkes heads."[64] Even the topography of Indian America recalled the Muslim Levant. Sir Thomas Arundel, who financed George Weymouth's attempt to locate a Northwest passage, had fought the Turks and been named a count of the Holy Roman Empire in 1595; the father of Sir Ferdinando Gorges, Sir William Gorges, had fought the Turks in Hungary in the 1560s.[65] Before many of the early "adventurers" went to America, they or their kin had ventured eastward among the Muslims. Before John White drew Indians, he had drawn Turks and Levantines; before the *Mayflower* carried the so-called "pilgrims" to Plymouth, it had traded in the Muslim Mediterranean. By the 1620s, ships were carrying tobacco from the colonies "at easie rates into Turkie Barbarie," and in the 1650s, Andrew Marvell's colonists celebrated Bermuda with images of the Levant: "With cedars, chosen by his hand, / From Lebanon, [God] stores the land."[66] Colonists, trade, and ships linked North America to North Africa.

Finding themselves operating within the Europe–North Africa–North America triangle, the English turned to the example of Spaniards, who had pushed their *reconquista* of the fifteenth century into a holy war of occupation of North Africa in the sixteenth century, while pursuing the colonization of the Americas. As Britons thus launched their merchant adventurers they encountered the Spaniards as their chief European adversary and model; while Raleigh and Drake fought with them, Hakluyt included the works of some Spanish explorers of America in his *Navigations*. The Spaniards had partly defined their national identity through their encounter with the Moors and then the American natives. Because they had been well informed about the Muslims and their history, if only because they had been fighting them for centuries, once they began the conquest of America they applied their constructions of Muslim Otherness on the American Indians.[67] Although Amerigo Vespucci at the end of the fifteenth century was not inclined to compare the Indians with either the Jews or the Moors—they were far worse than these two groups—subsequent Spanish writers did not hesitate to link the "Moors" and the "Saracens" with the Americans, as can be seen in the writings of Da Verrazano, whose work was available to English readers in Hakluyt. Joseph d'Acosta compared the nomadic life of the Central Plains Indians with the "wilde Moores of Barbarie called Alarbes," while de Coronado repeatedly allied the Indian with the Turk in his account of his expedition of 1541 and 1542.[68]

Seeing that Spaniards superimposed Muslim on Indian, and recognizing in that superimposition a moral and epistemological function, Britons followed the Spaniards in the superimposition as well as in its inversion—Indian on Muslim. Such interchangeablity of models was possible for Britons because they "discovered" the American Indians at the same time they "discovered" the Muslims—real Muslims, that is, as opposed to Muslims in medieval romance and polemic. The encounter with and the "discovery" of the two peoples, whether in geographical books or on the ground, was simultaneous: the first English book on America by Richard Eden, thought to have been published in 1511, included information about "greate Indyen" and "Arabia." These references to Arabia were not fortuitous, for as Hakluyt reported at the end of the century, it was in that year England had begun sending its ships to trade in "Tripolis and Barrutti in Syria," thereby showing the "antiquity of the trade with English ships into the Levant."[69] The second English book on America, Eden's translation of Sebastian Munster, introduced the English audience to the Muslims of the East Indies and, rather interestingly, presented them in a more favorable light than Indians of the West Indies.[70] The third English book on America, Eden's translation of *The Decades* (1555), included "A breefe Description of Affrike" in which reference was made to "Tunnes, Bugia, Tripoli . . . Marrocko, Fes."[71] In Andrewe Thevet's *The New Found Worlde or Antarctike* (translated from French in 1568), allusions to the "Turkes" and "Moores," and to "Barbaria" and "Mahometists" are interspersed throughout the descriptions of "India America." In the next half century and beyond, Hakluyt's and Purchas's numerous editions of their geographical works brought the dominions of Islam—both in the Mediterranean and the Indian Ocean—into the English reading experience at the same time that the Americas were being introduced.

Historians have recognized that Hakluyt and his successor were responsible for creating the momentum for the westward migration, but those writers/compilers were also instrumental in providing information about the Muslim dominions in North Africa, central Asia, and the Far East. The expansion of the unit on the Muslim world between Hakluyt's first two editions of *The Principal Navigations* is noteworthy in that the first part of the 1589 *Navigations,* which covers the Asian and African domains of Islam, falls between pages 1 and 242; the third part, which covers America, falls between 506 and 825. The second volume in the second edition of 1599 and 1600 included two parts about the Muslim world—the first in 312 pages and the second part in 311 pages; the third volume focused on America in 866 pages.[72] Similarly, the expansion of the Muslim unit in Purchas's *Pilgrimage* (1613 and 1617 editions) and *Pilgrimes* (1625), the last significantly produced under the patronage of and with a subsidy from the East India Company, attests to an interest in the Levant that was as pervasive among English authors and readers as that in America.[73] North Africa and North America became part of English knowledge in the same decades and in the same texts.

Also in the same period, Britons began to meet physically with both the American Indians and the Muslims—not only in North America and North Africa respectively, but in each others' continents. They met American Indians in North Africa as slaves who had been carried across the Atlantic by the Spaniards and the New Englanders and sold into the Muslim markets; as late as 1691, Indians who had been captured during King Philip's War were "sent to be sold, in the Coasts lying not very remote from Egypt on the Mediterranean Sea."[74] Britons also met Levantines in the Mediterranean who were on their way to the Americas, as was the case with the first Arabic writer to leave an account of his sojourn in Spain's American empire in 1668, and who used an English ship to travel from the Levant to Spain in order to make the Atlantic crossing (see appendix B). Britons also met Moorish and Turkish captives of Spain in the Caribbean. In March of 1586 some Moors deserted to join Sir Francis Drake during the English attack on Cartegena, and later during the attack on Santo Domingo. In June of that year Drake captured hundreds of "Turks and Moors, who do menial service" in Havana.[75] Although the Moors the English encountered in the Caribbean were slaves who projected weakness and despair, they were subjects of rulers whom England's queen wanted to befriend, and whose assistance she sought against Spain. There must have been so many of these Moors in the American Spanish dominions that in 1617, Purchas mentioned that Islam had spread as far as America. Purchas was probably thinking of these captives, some of whom had been freed by their Spanish masters and were settled in the colonies.[76] (In 1658, William D'Avenant wrote *The Play-House to be Let,* in which he included a scene about "the Symerons," a Moorish people brought formerly to Peru by the Spaniards.)[77] Purchas could also have been think-ing of an ethnological theory that described the American Indians as descen-dants of the Moors of North Africa.[78] Clearly an English writer who was familiar with Muslims remembered and superimposed them on the American Indians while another who was familiar with American Indians remembered and superimposed them on the Muslims. Neither group was perceived autonomously—each was a predicate of the other, although they originated half a world away from each other.

Such superimpositions repeatedly appear in the writings of colonists and travelers. William Strachey recalled the "Turks" when he saw that the Indians drank water instead of beer, as the English did, and spread a mat at the entry of a distinguished guest. The Powhatan, noted Strachey, executed malefac-tors by having them "beaten with Cudgells as the Turks doe," and he married many wives he did not keep in the same house "as the Turke in one Saraglia or howse." The Indians danced in "frantique and disquieted Bacchanalls," resembling the "Daruises in their holy daunces in the Moschas vpon Wednesdayes and Frydayes in Turkey," and Indian men did not "haue those sensuall helpes (as the Turkes) to hold vp ymoderate desires."[79] For Strachey, understanding the Indians was partly predicated on his having observed the Turks. Similarly, John Smith compared what he saw among the Americans with the Tartars and the Turks, and linked together for his read-ers the two geographical and ethnographical directions of English enter-prise. In the table of contents of his *The True Travels, Adventvres, and Observations* (1630), he indicated that he would describe the religion and "Living" of the Turks, and immediately following, he offered "a continuation of his generall History of Virginia."[80] For John Smith the two worlds seemed complemen-tary, and although he advocated the Americas for colonization, he presented the world of Mediterranean Islam as a domain of adventure and exotic allure.

As a result, many of those who praised him or his work in dedicatory poems came to see the two worlds together. "In Climes vnknowne, Mongst Turks and Saluages," wrote his cousin N. Smith in 1616, Smith had labored "T'inlarge our bounds."[81] In 1624, a "Benefactor to Virginia" praised Smith:

By him the Infidels had due correction,
He blew the bellowes still of peace and plentie:
He made the Indians bow unto subiection,
And Planters ne're return'd to Albion empty."[82]

In the complimentary verses to *The True Travels, Adventures, and Observations*, Richard Meade, a friend, praised Smith for having combated "with three Turks in single du'le" and then "found a common weale / In faire America." Another friend, M. Cartner, praised him for having explored the "Westerne world" after having achieved "a Captaines dignity" among the Turks.[83] Even his epitaph alluded to his "service" in fighting the Turks and his "adventure" among the "Heathen" in America.[84] The two non-Christian angles of the Renaissance triangle were within the covers of the same English book. The vis-à-vis of the English reader was the Turk and the Indian.

* * *

Peter Hulme has correctly observed that as England began its imperial thrust into America, it used its repository of "images and analogies" from its classical knowledge of the Mediterranean, and applied them to America. "The discourses of the Mediterranean were . . . adequate for the experience of the Atlantic."[85] Such a statement must be broadened to include the discourse of the Muslim Mediterranean—particularly in the Elizabethan and the Jacobean periods—when Britons were still trying to come to terms with the Indians, and could do so only by comparing them with the other non-Christians close to home. While Herodotus may have informed English readers about the Persians and the Egyptians, and Homer and Virgil about the Graeco-Roman Mediterranean, as Hulme has argued, it was the Turks and Moors who provided the most immediate parallel to the Indians.

Hulme's statement must also be inverted: in the process of encountering the Muslims, English writers employed their categorization of the Indians to define the Muslims. This two-way superimposition can be seen in Shakespeare's *The Tempest*, where the island where the events take place serves, as Hulme has stated, as a "meeting place of the play's topographical dualism, Mediterranean and Atlantic."[86] But how could the Atlantic be superimposed on the Mediterranean? As Hulme continues, Caliban shows the superimposition of the American Indian imagery of a gullible, ugly, cannibalistic, treacherous man onto a Mediterranean "wild" man. This "wild" man, however, is not of the "pedigree that leads back to [Polyphemous in] the Odyssey," as Hulme explains. Rather, Caliban's pedigree is the "wild Arab" or the "wilde Moore" whom travelers and dramatists repeatedly described and denounced.[87] The Muslim and the Indian were hybrid products of two different cultural encounters that were forcefully yoked together.

This yoking was steeped in anxiety because English writers and strategists recognized, from the first establishment of the Turkey Company until the Great Migration and well into the rest of the seventeenth century, that their colonial ideology was winning against the Indians but losing against the Muslims; they were enslaving Indians while Muslims were enslaving them. In North America, Britons and other Europeans developed an ideology that placed them at the center of God's plan for history. They were to replace the old and the wild with the New and the English or British—thus "New England" and "Nova Britannia." But in the dominions of Islam they had an experience that turned their colonial projects upside down. It was devastating for a Briton, or any other European, on his way to America to find himself, perhaps along with his family, captured by the Muslims and brought to Algiers, Salee, or Tunis as a slave. Instead of fashioning the American "salvages" after his image, the English, Welsh, or Scottish captive found himself being fashioned after the Muslims—eating their food, learning their language, adjusting to their religious customs, and wearing their clothes and turban. In America Britons imposed themselves on the Indians, but among the Muslims they were forced to adjust and recognize the Muslims on their own "infidel" terms.

This adjustment appears in language. In America the colonists did not bother to learn the Indian language(s), unlike the many Britons who mastered, and knew they had better master, the language(s) of the Muslims. In America the colonists held a monologue with the Indians in which they talked to them and at them and recorded what they wanted to hear the Indians saying—or else they listened but did not understand what they believed was meaningless chatter. Initially, individuals were sent to live among the Indians to learn their language, as Edward Waterhouse reported in 1622 about "one Browne,"[88] while promoters such as Hakluyt, John Smith, William Strachey, and William Wood wrote lists of words with their English translations for the "delight" of the readers, "if they can get no profit."[89] But after the 1622 Indian attack, colonists gave up on learning Indian languages, which became the exclusive provenance of evangelists such as Roger Williams, or of dramatists who ridiculed the barbarity of the Indians' speech, as Philip Massinger did in *The City Madam*. Meanwhile, many Indians learned English in order to serve the colonists, and often so thoroughly adopted the English identity that they willingly fought against their fellow tribesmen; Wequash and Wuttackquiackommin, who led English colonists in their massacre of Pequot Indians, are examples.

In North Africa, however, or in other parts of the Muslim Empire, it was Britons who learned Arabic and Turkish—often, but not always, after converting to Islam. Furthermore, English ambassadors sometimes addressed the Muslim rulers in Arabic (Spanish and Portuguese were also used), while the rulers wrote in Arabic to the monarchs in London. A letter sent by the Moroccan ruler to Queen Elizabeth in 1579 included the following post scriptum: "Here goeth another letre of ours, written in our languish Arabiya the which copie is this; and if ther be any that can rede and entarpret, you may se what it doth declare; yt goeth in still and orderlie, which we usede on kynge to another."[90] Muslim rulers were punctilious about the proper use of language in royal communication. That is why interest in the study of Arabic grew in Stuart England, while the work of continental Arabists generated such enthusiasm that chairs of Arabic were established at Oxford and Cambridge in the 1630s.[91] It was not only punctiliousness, though, but accommodation that motivated Britons to learn the language(s) of the Muslims. Even Cromwell, who had the first navy that effectively confronted the Barbary Corsairs, realized that in peace-time he had to treat the Muslims on their own terms; he had to make appropriate concessions to a power he needed economically and did not want to antagonize militarily. Thus, in his correspondence with the North Africans, he used the Muslim calendar: "We received two letters from you," he wrote to Hamet Basha, "dated both on the third day of the second moon of Rabia, in the year 1066, according to your account."[92] When dealing with the Muslims, Britons followed Muslim rules; when dealing with the Indians, they followed and imposed their own. When they did not follow Muslim rules they found that they paid a heavy price: in 1662, the Dutch ambassador reported that the "English have been cheated in Lawson's treaty with Algiers and Tunis through ignorance of Turkish."[93] Britons knew they had to learn the languages of the Muslim Empire if they were to succeed in their trade and alliances, for there were no Muslim equivalents to Squanto or Samoset.

The English knew that they, along with the Venetians, the French, and the Dutch, were mere salesmen who, for purposes of improving trade and alliances, bribed and connived and endured all forms of humiliation. Although Britons developed extensive commercial dealings with the Levant and North Africa—chiefly but not solely in the form of investments, which by 1656 were reputed to be over four million pounds—these investments were not modes of economic control and leverage. They were not protected by armies and military superiority but were at the mercy of the Turks who, if provoked, could confiscate the money and ruin the traders.[94] In *The Glory of England* (1618), Thomas Gainsford described the humiliation of many English merchants and representatives by the Muslims: "our Consull at Alexandria," he wrote, was hanged; "diuerse" were imprisoned in the "blacke Tower" and "our slaues" were all committed to the "gallies without respect of persons."[95] In his letters to Sir Thomas Roe, George Lord Carew also described the violence that was committed against the English by the Turks, both by government officials and pirates. He concluded one of his intelligence reports by stating bluntly: "As for the harmes the Turkishe piratts do vnto our nation, no restitution or justice cane be had."[96]

No retaliation against the Muslims was possible in the manner it would have been carried out had the perpetrators been Indians. When the Pequot Indians defied the English colonists in 1637 they were massacred and subsequently disappeared from the Indian theater of action. Coincidentally, that same year, the English fleet attacked Salee and reduced the number of Muslim pirates there. A year later, pirates were back with a vengeance. It is no wonder that as soon as the American Indian was brought under control, Britons and other Europeans proceeded to invent him as the Noble Savage and the Edenic Indian; once he was domesticated or annihilated he could safely be imagined in a favorable manner.[97] No similar "innocent" invention of the Muslims occurred in Renaissance English writings; the Muslim ability to capture thousands of Britons and create an impact on English national politics in the Elizabethan and Caroline periods could not help but enforce an image of power.[98] Nor did English writers attempt to link Muslims, as they did the Indians, with the Lost Tribes of Israel and therefore bring them into the fold of biblical history. The Muslims could not be domesticated because Britons knew them for what they were—descendants of Ishmael, as the Book of Genesis had told them—and where they were. They shared with them the same European continent and the same Mediterranean, Atlantic, and Channel waters, and unlike the American Indians, they had reached the seas surrounding the British Isles.

Muslims were close to the Britons' home, and they were not "going away," as were the American Indians—at least those who survived the plagues, famines, and massacres—who surrendered to the English colonies and lived the rest of their lives in despair and starvation. Nor were the Muslims turning English, as the Irish and Welsh were being forced to do. No Turkish prince was like the Indian "Prince of Massaquessts" who "desired to learne and speake our Language, and loved to imitate us in our behaviour and apparell and began to hearken after our God and his wayes."[99] There was no equivalent to the Henrico College proposal in Virginiia, nor to Harvard College's charter to educate "English and Indian youth of this country in knowledge and godliness,"[100] simply because no Muslim youth wanted to become English.

As a result of their inability to bring the Muslims within their parameter of intellectual and colonial control, English writers turned to the discourse of superimposition, whereby they yoked the defeated Indian to the undefeated Muslim. Mitchell Robert Breitwieser has noted that puritan representation of the American Indians "was particularly adept at subduing fact with category."[101] Similarly, English—not just puritan—representation of the Muslims was adept at subduing facts to categories of polarization and antipathy. Only such a juxtaposition of representations can explain why Muslims were transformed into such an Other at a time when they were having extensive diplomatic, commercial, and intellectual engagements with

Britons. If "experience did not alter the Puritans' assessment" of the Indians,[102] then neither did it alter the English image of the Muslims. The stereotypes established by writers and tale tellers about both the Indians and the Muslims were not destroyed by the evidence advanced by trade, bilinguality, socialization, cohabitation, and even sexual familiarity. Evidence did not change constructions. Rather Britons classified the American Indians and the Muslims within devised categories—categories that were syncretic and interchangeable, and that totally disregarded geographical, ethnographical, and military differences. "If this be not barbarous," wrote the anonymous author of *Hic Mulier,* a 1620 tract protesting the rights of women, "make the rude Scythian, the untamed Moor, the naked Indian, or the wild Irish, Lords and Rulers of well-governed Cities."[103] By lumping the whole "uncivilized" world indiscriminately together, the author failed to understand the Other. But then this writer must have believed that this was the best way to deal with the Other.

With their assured sense of Christian election, English writers imposed a total separation from, and a moral sanction against, the uncivilized Other. The commerce, alliance, and cuisine that frequently marked the interaction between themselves and the Muslims and the Indians could not overcome Otherness—an Otherness that was repeatedly represented by reference to deviant sexuality, "sodomy," and defeat in a divinely legitimated war, a "Holy War." These were the two templates the Spaniards had used in their conquest of America. And they were the templates English writers adopted to justify their own conquest of the Indians. As the confrontation with Islam loomed, Britons recognized that there would be no conquest of the Muslims. But as writers between the 1570s and the 1620s "recuperated the [failed] voyages" to the New World in print (to use Mary C. Fuller's terms), so did they, in the same period, recuperate the confrontation with Islam in writing. With the two templates they had adopted from the Spaniards and with which they had justified their conquest of America, English writers turned to recuperate, in print, the conquest of Islam.

4

SODOMY AND CONQUEST

European writings about the American Indians make many allusions to homosexuality, or as it was referred to, sodomy. From the very beginnings of the encounter with the inhabitants of the New World, Western European Christians wrote about their shock at witnessing the unnatural lust of the "natives." Such denunciation, as Richard C. Trexler has shown in his detailed study, *Sex and Conquest*, was in the spirit of the denunciation that had been leveled at the Moors in North Africa and in pre-*conquista* Iberia. During the conquest of America, Spaniards and other Europeans were already familiar with reports about Africa and the Middle East describing "sexual practices . . . including of course homosexual practices."[1] Upon encountering the native Americans, whether inhabitants of the Caribbean or the mainland, the conquerors recalled the homosexuality they had seen in North Africa—and in various parts of Christendom as well. The term *berdache,* which the Spanish and later the English colonists applied to Indian homosexuals, was derived from Persian by way of Arabic.[2] Nothing was more convenient to the *conquistadores* than to see the pervert as the Moor or the Indian. In America the homosexuality of the natives conveniently rendered them immoral in the eyes of the conquerors, thereby legitimizing their destruction, conversion, or domination—whichever best served the conquerors. Sodomy became the devastating justification for conquest and possession; it served to distance, dehumanize, and ultimately render the Other illegitimate.

Oviedo was one of the earliest to denounce homosexuality among the American Indians and link it with Spanish domination and appropriation. "[M]any of these [Indian] men and women were sodomites, and it is known that many of them are [still]," he wrote in his *Historia*.[3] Oviedo continued by describing the gold with which the sodomites decorated themselves and how he had seized that gold. The denunciation of sodomy was a justification for taking away the possessions of the sodomites: " . . . in some parts of these Indies they wear a jewel made of gold, representing one man on top of another in that base and diabolical act of Sodom. I saw one of these jewels of the devil . . . [which was brought] to be smelted before me as a royal official and overseer of gold smelting."[4] Whether the Indians practiced sodomy, as Oviedo declared, or did not, as Las Casas refuted, is not the issue. The issue here is how sodomy is used both rhetorically and colonially; in Oviedo's words, sodomy legitimated for the Spaniard his conquest of Indian land and his theft of Indian gold. As Todorov has pointed out, pro-Spanish writers always praised the colonization of America because it civilized the Indians by eradicating sodomy from their midst[5]; on one level, the rhetoric of colonization became dependent on sodomy.

By simply describing the Indians as sodomites, Oviedo felt that the Indians' character was adequately defined and understood—the Indians were a group outside the cultural and moral acceptability of the audience, or at least outside the professed morality. Such a stereotypical definition of them, where one feature of their behavior supposedly represented their whole identity, subverted any questions that could be raised about the legitimacy of taking their gold or dominating them. For Oviedo, the "unnatural sexuality" of the inhabitants went hand in hand with their property and possessions. As he sought to punish them for their unchristian sin, so would he punish them by taking away their property.

This Spanish focus on sodomy as a stereotypical justification for the conquest of the Indians also appears in the writings of the English colonists in North America. For the colonists, "unnatural sexuality," as John Canup has shown,[6] not only broke the laws of the Bible, but also threatened the community at a deeper level—the level of the interior demons they felt that life among the Indians would unleash. In the wilds of America there was fear that the colonists would turn wild in their morality and sexuality. After all, and having been assured by Spanish texts that the Indians practiced sodomy, they feared that the unnatural behavior of the "Salvages" would infect them too. In 1642, William Bradford queried three of his ecclesiastical correspondents about "what sodomitical acts are to be punished by death."[7] The wilderness for him was a place where civilization was under threat, and where one of the articles of civilization was sexual conformity and an abhorrence of all that was Indian in its unnaturalness and deviance. Later, in the treaty the Massachusetts Indians signed with the Bay government in Boston in 1644, the English fear of sodomy was included in the terms to which the Indians had to submit; the Indians were made to pledge to "commit no unclean lust, as fornication, adultery, incest, rape, sodomy."[8] Political submission meant sexual conformity. Not only was the land of the Indians appropriated, but the privacy of the Indians' lives along with their sexual modes and perceptions. In 1648, John Cotton praised England's success in his *The Way of Congregational Churches Cleared* at weeding out from among the Indians all forms of "adultery and fornication, and unnatural lusts."[9]

The stereotype of the Indian sodomite helped the colonists in New England—just as it had earlier the Spaniards—to justify the dispossession and destruction of the Indians. The laws against sodomy that had been instituted in England by Henry VIII, and sustained throughout the Tudor and Stuart periods, had sanctioned dispossessing the sodomite of all his "goods, chattels, debts, lands, tenementes, and hereditaments."[10] As a result, the colonists in America treated the Indians as sodomites would have been legally treated in England. The Indians had broken English law and were therefore to be punished in accordance with that law. The Indians had also broken biblical law and would therefore be punished by God in accordance with that law. For the English colonists, the dispossession and destruction of the Indians was not a result of the colonists' superior technology or novel diseases, but of punishment inflicted on them in the manner of the inhabitants of Sodom among whom Abraham had found himself. John Winthrop made this point very clear. In discussing why the colonists had a "warrant" to seize the land of the Indians, he pointed out that just as Abraham was given permission by God to live "among the Sodomites," so had the colonists been authorized. [11] And just as God later destroyed the sodomites for their abuses, so would He destroy the Indians. The New Englanders were the new Abrahamic covenantors who applied on their enemies what God had applied on the biblical Sodom. Well into the second half of the seventeenth century, particularly after King Philip's War, this link between Abraham's conquest of the sodomites and the colonists' conquest of the Indians continued to appear in English texts. [12]

Given the repeated superimpositions of models, it is not surprising that the same stereotyping of the Muslims as sodomites appeared in English writings during the Renaissance period. As with the Indians, the Muslims were represented as a people who defied God, nature, and English law, and therefore deserved punishment. As plague, military defeat, and starvation assured the colonists that God's punishment was underway in America, writers about the Muslims hoped that the same punishment for sodomy would befall the "infidels." And just as God's punishment of the Indians had made possible the colonization of America, it was also hoped that His punishment of the Muslims would make possible the conquest of Islam. Leo Africanus assured his English readers (in John Pory's 1600 translation) that God had already begun punishing the Muslims for their sodomy. The Moors, he wrote, had lost the city of Azamur to the Christian Portuguese because of their sodomy: "Neither doe I thinke that God for any other cause brought this calamitie upon them, but onely for the horrible vice of Sodomie, whereunto the greatest part of the citizens were so notoriously addicted." [13] The Christian conquest of the Other, be the Other American Indian or Muslim, was divinely sanctioned because of the moral and sexual deviance of the Other.

In English writings about the Muslims of the Ottoman Empire and North Africa, both by English, Scottish and continental writers whose works were translated into English, there are many allusions to "sodomitry"—more so than in the discourse on America. Nearly every travel or captivity account includes references to Muslim sodomy and other sexual practices. As Winthrop C. Jordan has stated, whenever Africans were described, so was their sexuality. [14] And as Elliot H. Tokson has demonstrated, such interest in sexuality informed English drama—and travel literature too, as will be

shown later—throughout the sixteenth and seventeenth centuries: there is
" . . . hardly a black character created for the stage whose sexuality is not
made an important aspect of his relationships with others."[15] Given that the
North African Muslims had not been defeated as the Indians had, nor
enslaved *en masse* as sub-Saharan Africans had, the need to demonize and
alterize them became paramount. And what better proof of the Christian
Otherness from the Muslims than the widespread evidence of sodomy
among the latter? For writers, especially captives and theologians eager to
widen the gap between themselves and the Muslims, sodomy seemed to be
an incontestable dividing line. "These Turks," wrote William Davis in 1614
after having spent years in the Mediterranean, "are goodly people of parson,
and of a very faire complexion, but very villains in minde, for they are altogether Sodomites, and doe all things contrarie to a Christian."[16] Sodomy was
the dividing line between the Christian, civilized Briton and the Muslim
"barbarian." Belonging to the former group signified normalcy, civility, and
humanness, while sodomy signified barbarity. By predicating the barbarous
on the sodomite, English writers created the stereotype of the Turk and the
Moor.[17]

Numerous English writers used such a stereotype of the Muslims because
they sought to establish demarcation and polarization with them. "Sodomy"
was a topic about which there were very few historical writings in
Elizabethan, Jacobean, and Caroline England; it is not as if it were a topic
openly discussed and therefore at the forefront of social and rhetorical
polemic. Rather, as B. R. Burg has observed, homosexuality was ignored by
"ordinary citizens, officers of the church, the military, and by leaders of the
civil government," unless the denunciation of sodomy by none other than
King James I prevented the appearance of writings on such a topic.[18] But literary texts, especially those purporting to be translations or adaptations of
Greek and Latin sources, frequently presented both homoeroticism and
homosexuality.[19] This literature about an imaginary and distant past was the
only venue in which homosexuality was treated, since all surviving historical
data about English and Scottish homosexuality consist exclusively of records
of legislation and court decisions—both of which, as Alan Bray, Christopher
Hill, B. R. Burg, and others concur, are lacking in breadth and precision.[20]

They are also extremely few and do not provide enough bases on which to establish the early modern understanding of homosexuality in England.[21]

While homosexuality may have been either ignored by the general populace, or was so socially acceptable that it merited no mention by writers, it was repeatedly denounced in the Muslim context. Writers about the Muslim world felt they were expected to say something about Muslim sodomy in the same way it was expected of Muslims to be sodomites. The accounts therefore that describe Muslim sodomy are wide-ranging and appear in all genres—captivity accounts, drama, travel and, much less frequently and significantly, in government documents. Readers luxuriated in the degeneracy and deviance of the Muslims. The prurient interest in what was viewed as "Islamic sex" had appeared in the writings of medieval monks and would continue well into the early modern period, as with Lady Mary Montague. Now, in the period when for the very first time there were travelers, trading representatives, and captives among the Muslims, the claim about Muslim sodomy could be presented as verifiable and empirical.

In this context, the actual use of the word "sodomy" is important because it shows how Britons strongly linked it to Muslims. In medieval and Renaissance England there were varying meanings to the term "sodomie," but in documents pertaining to the Muslim world it was consistently used in a sexual context. Nicholas Nicolay vilified (in T. Washington's translation) converts from Christianity to Islam by listing the sins of the "Christians renied, or Mahumetised" as "whoredome, sodometrie, theft, and all other most detestable vices."[22] Sodomy sealed the fate of the sinful renegades. The preacher Meredith Hanmer, denouncing the theology of Islam in a sermon preached in 1586, could find no better image than that of "Mahometical Sodomits" to describe the Muslims in order to ensure their spiritual doom.[23] "[T]hose who have done buggery (as the most part of them [Muslims] do) and homicide, shall fall . . . to the profoundest pit in hell," wrote the Scottish traveler William Lithgow.[24] Sodomy was concomitant with homicide and both would lead the Muslims to eternal damnation. The Muslims, wrote Richard Knolles in his seminal *Generall Historie of the Turkes,* "are much inclined to Venery, and are for the most part all Sodomites."[25] Muslims, concurred J. B. Gramaye in Purchas's *Pilgrimes,* "expatiate . . . all

Lust, Sodomie and Adulterie" in their baths. Sodomy was Islamic and separated between the civilized and the uncivilized.[26]

In trying to explain why sodomy was so prevalent among the Muslims—
and of course absent in civilized Christendom—English and Scottish writers
appealed to what they viewed as the root of all evil in the Muslim world:
Islamic theology. None other than the religion of the Muslims was to blame
for legitimating homosexuality. Hanmer declared that for Muslims "the plea-
surs of the body hurt not nether hinder at all the foelicity of the life to come."
Because of this belief, he concluded, Muslims indulged in sodomy.[27] Edward
Grimeston, translating a 1626 French account of the Seraglio, believed that
Islamic theology did not condemn sodomy. Ignoring the death penalty prescribed for the sodomites in the traditions of Islamic jurisprudence, he stated
that "the Turkes doe not punish it" (sodomy) because they leave justice to
God. He then recounted a story about a boy who killed a man who had
sodomized him: "Mahomet their Prophet sent his Kinsmen to open his [slain
man's] Tombe, and see how many wounds he had; they came and saw no
body, but found in the place a blacke and smoakie stocke. Hence they say,
that seeing the diuine Iustice doth punish those that are culpable of this
offence, they must leaue the execution to him, and in the meane time suffer
this vnnaturall excesse to any."[28] The Qur'anic paradise, wrote Thomas
Calvert in 1648, promised Muslims pleasures of the flesh including "lusts of
Boyes."[29] Calvert had obviously not read the Qur'an, but in his view the
Muslims must be sodomites because the Qur'an must have condoned
sodomy. Since the Muslims had deviated from God by following the teachings of a "false" prophet, they could not but have become deviants in their
sexuality as in their beliefs.

The link between sodomy and "Islam" was deeply entrenched in English
minds despite the assertion by the widely read Purchas in his *Pilgrimage*
(1613) that Muslim law was "contrary" to that sin which is "most rife amongst
them, and that in the most filthie and vnnaturall kind of Sodomie."[30] Writers
declared that because there was sodomy among the Muslims, their religion
must necessarily permit it. But while there was sodomy among the Muslims,
as there was among other societies, it was not necessarily condoned by them.
The North African writer, al-Wufrani, recalled disapprovingly that the ruler

Abdel Malek had been accused of "being fond of youths" and that ash-Sheikh al-Ma'moon was "fond of fondling boys" ("al-'abath bisibyan"); in a dialogue with a Christian in Paris, the Morisco writer of the first half of the seventeenth century, Ahmad bin Qasim, strongly refuted the allegation that Islam condoned "luwat" (sodomy).[31] Still, English writers could not help but see sodomy as religiously sanctioned among Muslims.

In 1619 it was reported that the ship *Blessing* was captured by the Turks, and all its crew subsequently released except the cabin boy, who was retained for their "Sodomitical use."[32] Over half a century later, in 1680, it was reported in *The Case of many Hundreds of Poor English-Captives, in Algier* that a number of Quakers had been captured and sodomized—an incident that drove George Fox to denounce such behavior to the Algerian ruler.[33] In 1681 it was reported that Francis Cooley, a captive in Algiers, had been tortured by the Algerians in order to make him "comply with their Sodomittish Lusts."[34] Somehow only Muslims seemed to English writers to practice sodomy, although among pirates sodomy was not uncommon—whether in the Mediterranean or the Caribbean, by Muslims or by Christians.[35] Actually, sodomy was prevalent not only at sea, but also at home in England: homosexual practices were widely prevalent among the classes of vagrants and sailors, and in the first part of the century the realm was ruled by a homosexual king (James I) whose chancellor was also homosexual (Francis Bacon),[36] and whose Lord Admiral of the Fleet, George Villiers, was homosexual, or at least receptive to the king's homosexual desire. But no English writer thought of associating sodomy with Protestant Christianity, only with Islam. Simplification and stereotyping were the rules by which Britons represented Muslims. One behavioral deviance among some Muslims defined the whole Muslim population from Barbary to Cathay; there was no diversity among the Muslims.

Another association English travelers made with sodomy was that of class. Both in medieval and Renaissance England, as elsewhere in continental and Catholic Christendom, sodomy was viewed as a sin of the rich and associated in the public imagination with royalty and the court. Such an association had appeared in the Spanish writings emphasizing that it was Indian lords who practiced sodomy.[37] Similarly in the Muslim Empire, writers noted that given the expenses incurred in the procurement and the upkeep of "young Boyes," only the privileged and the elite among the Turks could practice sodomy. The basha and "the great Men of the Court," wrote Edward Grimeston, are given to this "abhominable vice."[38] J. B. Gramaye reported in Purchas's *Pilgrimes* that it was common practice among North African pirates who captured Christian children to "send them for Presents to the Turke or his Bassas" to satisfy their "Sodomiticall lusts to Boyes."[39] Paul Rycaut, English consul in Smyrna between 1667 and 1678, confirmed that "Persons of eminent degree in the Seraglio" as well as "the Grand Signiors themselves have also been slaves to this inordinate passion."[40] Ironically, the Grand Signiors sometimes relied on Christians to help them satisfy their desires. In the play *Tarugo's Wiles: or the Coffee-House* (1668) by Thomas St. Serfe, it is the "Dutch Ambassador in imitation of Algiers" who presented "the Grand-Signeur with a Covy of East-Freezland Boyes, fatten'd with black Beans and Butter-milk."[41] At a time of anti-Dutch sentiments in London, it was convenient to portray the Dutch as pimps to the sodomite Turks.

Writers emphasized that among the powerful elite of the Ottoman Empire, homosexual activity was not only acceptable but also inherent in the very nature of their sexual norms. Rulers talked about it without shame or anxiety, perhaps because social hierarchy had made a secure place for that "unnatural" activity. Britons asserted that among the Turks there was a niche carved by the ruler himself for "sodomy," and because the ruler was autocratic, not only could there be no criticism of his behavior, but the ruler might just be setting the example for the rest of the elite to emulate him. This link between the ruling authority and homosexual behavior among the Turks further confirmed for Christian writers their alterity with the Muslims. Not only had sodomy perverted morality, it had permeated the political institution as well. Not only was the religion of the Muslims depraved, but their political organization too. Since the ruler set the codes for his subjects, a corrupt and depraved ruler inevitably produced a depraved kingdom. As Edward Grimeston explained, "He that is the Head and commands them, doth furnish this pernicious example; for the Sultans Serrail is full of such Boyes, chosen out of the most beautifull of the East, and vowed to his vnnaturall pleasures: This doth countenance this disorder and corruption in the

Othoman Court: Such as the Prince is, such are most commonly the Courtiers which follow him."[42] The institutionalization of homosexuality started at the very top and cast its shadow over the whole society. Paul Rycaut spoke bluntly about Sultan Murad's infatuation with an Armenian boy, and at another time with a youth from "Galata."[43] The sexual orientation of the ruler was as unchallengeable as the ruler himself. It was not an aberrant whimsy of a few "eminent" men but, in the view of Grimeston and others, a stone in the edifice that held Muslim authority together.

So well established was the model of the "sodomitical Turk" in the European imagination that John Sanderson reported how a fellow traveler feared for his twenty-one year old "beardlesse" son because they were traveling through "Sodomitcall places."[44] The practice of sodomy was neither secretive nor clandestine but crudely public—much as it was in London, where Donne had satirized the "prostitute boy" (Satyre 1) and Shakespeare the "masculine whore" (*Troilus and Cressida*).[45] But for Britons engaged in consolidating the unbridgeable binary with the Muslims, sodomy was a practice of the non-Christian Other who had no moral or religious qualms about it. William Lithgow wrote that in summer, the city of Fez "openly licentiate three thousand common stews of sodomitical boys," and he confirmed that he had seen "at midday, in the very market places, the Moors buggering these filthy carrions, and without shame or punishment go freely away."[46] For Lithgow, sodomy was as obvious in the domain of Islam as the midday sun. Toward the end of the century, Thomas Baker confirmed in his journal entry of 30 June 1683 this openness of sodomy in the Barbary coast: "And this day alsoe the sonne of a Dutch Renegado a Brisk young Fellow of the Towne happened to goe into a Taverne, whither two Turks following him comitted a Rape of Buggery upon him Which (In regard it could not bee done without some bustle and noise) drew thither a great number of their dissolute fellow Souldiers, Thirty four of whom successively were as kind to him as the other Two Turks had been. And all this without ye least shame or feare of punishmt."[47] For Baker and Lithgow, Muslims openly indulged in sodomy because it was a structural deviance not only in the bedroom but also in the marketplace. Neither did the Jacobean traveler seem to know of King James's public dalliances with male companions, nor did the Restoration trade representative know about the Earl of Rochester's crude praise of sodomy in the play "Sodom." Sodomy was exclusively Islamic.

In 1682, Adam Elliot published an account of his captivity in Morocco in 1670 in which he included the only actual description of an attempted homosexual seduction of a Christian Briton by a Muslim owner. Elliot's language is hateful of the "Moor" who tried to sodomize him, but it is clear that his denunciation of the Moor was also intended as a denunciation of the notorious Titus Oates, who was known for his sodomy, and who had falsely accused Elliot of complicity in the Popish Plot. The deviance of the Moor made him doubly heinous in the eyes of the readers because he reminded them of the deviance of Oates: "While I was upon these thoughts, the Brute [Elliot's master] raises himself up a little, and mutters somewhat to me of not-to-be-mentioned Carnality, not only unworthy of Christian ears, but the bare mention whereof offers violence to the dictates of Nature, and which my charity would never suffer me to believe that it could enter into any mans mind, unless I had heard of the Citizens of Sodom, and a Doctor of Salamanca [Oates]."[48] Paul Hammond has shown in his discussion of the sodomy of Oates that "Englishness" was confirmed by linking the sexual deviance of Oates with the Turks.[49] By bringing sodomy, Turk, and Oates together, Elliot could not help but consolidate an unbridgeable alterity with the sodomist.

As much as the sodomy of the Muslims drew from Britons' anger and vituperation, it also perplexed them. As they observed the Muslims, whether from the angle of travelers or captives, they saw before them a powerful empire whose subjects and rulers practiced, brazenly, the sin that had brought God's destructive ire on Sodom. As Alan Bray has observed, nearly every allusion to homosexuality in Renaissance English sources mentions the biblical account of Sodom's doom.[50] Yet, to the confusion of English writers, the Ottoman Empire did not seem to be facing, nor indeed to be apprehensive of, that danger. Britons therefore could not invoke the biblical example of Sodom to threaten the "Sodomiticall Turkes" with dire punishment, nor could they proclaim, with the same assuredness they or their Iberian predecessors had proclaimed in America, that divine wrath and European conquest were close at hand. It is interesting that the discourse about Muslim sodomy rarely alluded to the destruction of Sodom, which in Genesis had provided Christendom with a divinely authoritative explanation of how homosexuality had originated and an assurance of damnation for homosexuals.

Deprived of this allusion, British travelers and captives found themselves having to explore theories about homosexuality that were outside the range of the biblical explanation, but that would apply exclusively to Turks and Moors. Some writers, therefore, proclaimed that sodomy was a sin generated by a hot climate. Although a link between geography and homosexuality is found among earlier Spanish and continental writers,[51] no contemporary writer in England or Scotland proposed it. But writers about the Ottoman Empire did. Francis Osborne wrote in his description of the seraglio that the reason the Turks institutionalized concubinage, as the Israelites had done before them, was to prevent "Sodomy, and Bestiality; sinnes infesting these hot Countrys."[52] For him, heat activated the blood into the sexual excess of sodomy. "A strange Fancy," wrote T. S., who was a captive in North Africa, "possesses the minds of all the Southern People; they burn with an unnatural Fire, which consumed Sodom and Gomorrah."[53] A hot climate, which England fortunately did not have, was the reason for sodomy.

Writers believed that England was fortunate not only in enjoying a cold climate, but also in not having built its civilization on the land and heritage of the Greeks. In the minds of some Britons, the source of Turkish sodomy lay in Greek sodomy: having conquered the land of the Greeks, and having absorbed the learning of the Greeks, the Muslim Turks had fallen under the spell of Greek unnatural lust, references to which abound in classical literature and philosophy. Both the Persians and the Turks, wrote Thomas Gainsford in *The Glory of England*, have adopted "that horrible corruption of the Grecians."[54] The Turks were continuing what the Greeks had started. Blame fell particularly on the Greeks because of the theory of Platonic love. Plato's *Symposium* had spoken clearly of the homosexual relationship, but in the revival of Platonism in Renaissance Christendom, particularly by the Florentine Neoplatonists, the homosexual element was dismissed, and Platonic love came to be seen as a purely spiritual relationship. Alan Bray has stated that there was no link in European history between Plato's theory and the actual practice of homosexuality.[55] Although early church fathers extrapolated from Plato a favorable view of homosexuals,[56] and although Michaelangelo's homosexuality may well have been associated with his Platonism,[57] Bray did not find any writer in Renaissance England who made the link between Platonic love and homosexuality. Nevertheless, English writers about the Muslims did; the most elaborate discussion of this link appears in that highly acclaimed and often reprinted work, *The Present State of the Ottoman Empire* (1668) by Paul Rycaut.

Rycaut invoked the theory of "Platonick love" to explain homosexuality among the Turks. In a book that proved to be seminal, Rycaut described every feature of the Turkish Empire, including the educational training of Turkish administrators. These future administrators, he wrote, started their lives as scholars in the seraglio where, they were made to follow a special curriculum that perfected their knowledge of Arabic, Persian, and Turkish. As a result of their extensive reading in literature they developed "a kind of Platonick love each to another, which is accompanied with a true friendship amongst some few, and with as much gallantry as is exercised in any part of the world."[58] Their reading in literature so refined their souls that it created spiritual amity among them.

This description of "love" between the Turkish scholars corresponds to the European theory of Neoplatonic love that writers such as Castiglione and others had described as a relationship of harmonious nonsexual male friendship.[59] Rycaut believed that this "love" among the Turkish youth was not unlike other "Platonic" loves elsewhere in the world. The Turks in this respect were in the mainstream of European Neoplatonism. Unfortunately, however, continued Rycaut, such exclusive male friendship—even at the highest level of spiritual purity—could only lead to imbalance. Sexual deprivation generated by the absence of women compelled men toward homosexuality, a homosexuality that was stated in the *Symposium* but not, in his view, intended by Plato to be taken literally. Eager to exonerate Plato of responsibility for Turkish sodomy, Rycaut proposed his own explanation of homosexuality based on psychological premises.

Because of sexual deprivation among this exclusively male group, wrote

Rycaut, homosexual activity inevitably developed. In what seems to be the first such theory by an English writer about homosexuality, Rycaut explained that as a result of the strict discipline of the scholars in the seraglio, and because female companionship was prohibited, they transferred their sexual desire for women toward each other. They "burn in lust one towards another, and the amorous disposition of youth wanting more natural objects of affection, is transported to a most passionate admiration of beauty wheresoever it finds it."[60] The source of homosexual desire was neither a depraved morality nor a hot climate but a harsh social system. Homosexuality was a result of repressed instinct.

In presenting this view of the youth of the seraglio, Rycaut had unwittingly portrayed, for the first time in English writings about the Muslims, what might accurately be described as a homoerotic relation. All previous allusions to homosexuality applied to sexual activity between an elder male and a forced youth who had been captured or enslaved. Here, in the middle of the seraglio, emotional and intellectual engagements led to sexual activity—exactly the same progression that Plato had proposed in the *Symposium*. Rycaut, however, believed that although the Turks' homoerotic love was "Platonick," it was really quite different from the Platonism that Christendom knew since Christian Platonism had no sexuality in it. In the next chapter, entitled "Of the Affection and Friendship the Pages in the Seraglio bear each other," Rycaut examined this issue further and repeated that the Turks strongly believed in "the Doctrine of Platonick love." This doctrine is about a "passion very laudable and virtuous, and a step to that perfect love of God." But the Turks had not understood Plato correctly since they had transformed this "spiritual" love that prevailed in the seraglio into physical desire. The Turks did so against Plato's teachings because of "their depraved inclinations." "In reality this love of theirs," concluded Rycaut, "is nothing but libidinous flames each to other, with which they burn so violently." What in Plato and among Christian Platonists was an avenue to God, among the Turks was an avenue to uncontrollable lust and unnatural desire.

These observations by Rycaut are important because they show how a well-traveled and well-read Englishmen in the second half of the seventeenth century actually believed that Platonic love was no different from

Neoplatonic love, and that homoerotic relationships were widely present among the Turks because of the influence of a misread *Symposium*. More important still is Rycaut's establishment of a link between sexual repression and homosexual desire—if men are deprived of women, they turn to each other, especially if they are men in literary and intellectual training who are apt to develop "Platonick love" for each other. The reason Christendom had not degraded Platonic love into sodomy, Rycaut implied, was that love occurred among married males—unlike in Islam where it occurred among unmarried men. Still, much as Rycaut recognized a psychological and cultural context for homosexuality, his final evaluation remained informed by the morality of his society: whatever its cause, homosexuality was "libidinous" and depraved and characterized the empire of the Mahometan Turks.

Rycaut's view on the origin of male homosexuality paved the way for examining lesbian sexual activity, a topic that was rarely linked in English popular thought with male homosexuality.[61] Rycaut applied his psychological analysis of male homosexuality to women and stated that Turkish women turned to lesbian love because they lacked male sexual partners. Sexual repression, in his view, was the cause of male and female homosexuality. "This passion likewise reigns in the Society of Women; they die with amorous affections one to the other."[62] Significantly, a similar view had been proposed in the French account translated by Grimeston: women in Turkey "grow passionately in loue one with another, and giue themselues to false and vnlawfull loue." They do so because they have enormous sexual appetites they cannot control, but also—and this view is in line with the psychological explanation advanced by Rycaut—because they seek to avenge themselves on their husbands for their husbands' "vnnaturall loue." For Grimeston, lesbian behavior was clearly a "disorder" that led women to "imbrace one another, and doe other actions which loue seekes, and modestie forbids to write."[63]

It is quite likely that Rycaut acquired his insights about homosexuality from his reading of Grimeston's very popular translation since he admitted that he had never been inside the harem[64] and therefore could not have based his views of lesbian sexuality on personal knowledge. He could have also learned about lesbian attraction from Purchas, who had mentioned how

Turks were given "in both sexes to vnnaturall lust (in these times) euen the women in publike Bathes."[65] In Pory's translation of Leo Africanus there too was a reference to Mauretanian women "who were afflicted of that wicked vice of using one another carnally."[66] Regardless of what source Rycaut used, it is significant that his and Grimeston's texts present an analysis of lesbian sexuality that does not occur anywhere else in English seventeenth-century sources. Theirs is the first interpretation of lesbianism in English sources that attempts to fit it into the framework of human sexual behavior.

At the turn of the century, the traveler George Sandys had surmised that there was lesbian activity among Turkish women because of punishments that had been subsequently imposed: "women with women; a thing vncredible, if former times had not giuen thereunto both detection and punishment."[67] Earlier in the sixteenth century Nicolay had described lesbian behavior in the Ottoman Empire: women in the Levant, he wrote, "sometimes become so feruently in loue the one of the other as if it were with men." They "handle & grope" each other in "luxuriousnes & feminine wantonnes." For Nicolay, however, the explanation of such behavior did not lie in repression but in geography: Levantine women, both Christian and Muslim, developed such tendencies because they were descendants of the "Tribades, of the nu[m]ber wherof was Sapho the Lesbia[n] which transferred the loue wherwith she pursued a 100 women or maidens vpon her only friend Phaon."[68] Lesbian activity came from Lesbos, and whether the inhabitants were ancient Greeks or modern day Turks, they were bound to fall under the spell of lesbian love because they shared the same geography with Sappho. For Nicolay, the Muslims were conditioned by their geography to adopt sexual deviance; for Rycaut a century later, the Muslims were conditioned by their social organization and political structure. For these as well as the other writers in between, sexual deviance among the Muslims was seen to be unavoidable: having observed the Muslims, but not their own societies, all the above writers declared that "sodomy" was a category of the Levant and not of Europe, of Mahometanism but not of Christendom.

In 1607, Thomas Shirley included the following statement in his treatise on the Turks: "Theyre [Turks] mannor of liuinge in priuate & in generalle is moste vnciuille & vicious; & firste, for theyre vices they are all pagans & infi-

delles, Sodomittes, liars, & drunkardes, & for theyre Sodommerye they vse
it soe publiquelye & impudentelye as an honest Christian woulde shame to
companye with his wyffe as they doe with theyre buggeringe boyes."[69] As the
rest of his treatise shows, Shirley did not like the Turks; he had, after all, been
captured and imprisoned in Istanbul. Was he therefore, like other English and
Scottish writers, referring to empirically verifiable evidence of homosexual
activity among the Turks, or were his references a product of theological and
political models of representation, of ideological assumptions that were
being developed in an atmosphere of anti-Islamic polemic? It is interesting
how uninhibited Shirley was in "naming" and explicitly mentioning the
words "sodomy" and "buggery." Was he trying to create a scenario wherein
the unfamiliar Other becomes familiar because of his deviance and difference?

In medieval Europe homosexuality was treated "primarily as a non-
Christian vice."[70] Britons did the same in the seventeenth century; sodomy
was the sin of the Other and therefore conveniently provided them with a
much awaited venue for exploring this taboo. If, as Jonathan Goldberg has
argued, homosexuality was an "open secret" in early modern England—a
known fact about which people did not talk or did not publish much[71]—
then the Muslims must have appeared as a gift from heaven for writers who
were not daring enough to examine that topic within their own society, but
who felt free to examine it among the "Mahometans." Furthermore, the possibility of discussing sodomy among the Muslims would have satisfied what
Winthrop Jordan has described as the "appetite for the 'wonderful' " that
"civilized Englishmen" showed, especially as they read reports about "cos-
metic mutilation, polygamy, infanticide, [and] ritual murder" that were practiced in North Africa and North America.[72] Sodomy can safely be added to
this list of "wonderful" topics that English readers would have wanted writers to describe. There is little doubt that as Renaissance readers turned to a
book about the Muslim world, they expected it to titillate them with information about the outrageous, the sensual, and the deviant so they could feel
secure in their moral and political spheres.

But the question remains: were the Britons who described Muslim
sodomy describing what they knew or were they describing what they heard
and perceived? Or was it that the word itself, sodomy, was so sufficiently

charged with evil, deviance, and barbarity that its association with the
Muslims was enough to demonize them beyond redemption? In 1600,
George Manwaring wrote an account about his journey with Anthony
Shirley to the Persian court. While traveling through the Ottoman domains,
Manwaring was beaten by a Turk—an episode that understandably caused
him to hate them. So once he turned to describing the Turks, he emphasized
that the Turks kept boys who are called "Bardashes, which they do use in their
beastly manner, instead of women."[73] A similar reference was made by his
companion William Parry, who along with the other English group had been
humiliated by the Turks in Cyprus. He denounced the Turks as "damned infidels and sodomitical Mahomets."[74] Both believed that by mentioning one
word, sodomy, they could win for their coreligionists the moral conflict with
the Muslims and the ontological conflict with Islam. But how precise was
their description? When their companion, a Frenchman by the name of Abel
Pincon, wrote an account of his journey, he did not mention sodomy at all.
Upon arriving among the Persians, the English group was well received, and
therefore, Manwaring asserted, while "it is allowed in the Turks' kingdom for
the men to have the use of boys, it is not so here, for the Persians do severely
punish that vice."[75] This pro-Persian assertion contradicts other reports
about male sexuality in Persia.[76] For a man such as Manwaring, who spoke
neither Turkish nor Persian, and who could never describe anything without
comparing it to England, and who presumed to describe what his friend
Parry indicated had been off limits to them—such as the inside of the
mosque court where ablution took place—it is evident that the allusions to
homosexuality stemmed not from direct observations but from the desire to
denigrate the religious adversary. And he was well aware that no other accusation needed less explanation or demonstration than sodomy. To mention it
was to confirm it and to condemn the perpetrator; sodomy was a self-
explanatory judgement, a cognitive keyword that proved that Muslims had
no family structure, no "natural" sexuality, and therefore no place in the civilized world.

There are no texts in seventeenth-century England that place homosexuality in English cultural history, while nearly every text on the Muslim
dominions does—even if it is anecdotal and brief. Between describing the

horses the Turks used and the market price of roosters, hens and pheasants, the traveler Thomas Coryat inserted the following words: "The Turkes are exceedingly given to Sodomie, and therefore divers keep prettie boyes to abuse them by preposterous venerie."[76] To describe sodomy among the Muslims was, for Coryat, as commonplace as talking about hens and market prices; sodomy was not just part of Muslim immorality, it was part of everyday life. By repeating the reference to sodomy in every context associated with the Muslims, by reminding English readers in every text about the Levant of the depravity of the "Mahometans," and by relentlessly exposing the Christian to the Otherness of the Moors and Turks, English writers transformed sodomy into a structural transgressiveness that defined the character, religion, and dominions of the Muslims. The sodomite was the Muslim writ large.

Just as sodomy had functioned ideologically in the conflict with the Indians, it was also made to function in the conflict with the Muslims. Britons developed an analogy that was logical but not empirical: since their existence among the Indians was an existence among the sodomites, who were destroyed, their existence among the Muslims was also an existence among the sodomites, who would also be destroyed. The alleged prevalence of sodomy among the Indians and Muslims presaged their moral and subsequent military decline before the sinless Christians of England. In the discourse about the American Indians there was, as the cultural historian Djelal Kadir has pointed out, a collusion of deed and language—"action and rhetorical infrastructure."[78] The rhetorical infrastructure of the discourse about the Indians emphasized their moral and sexual illegitimacy—thus the "action" of domination and conquest. A similar collusion can be seen to have operated in the English discourse about Muslim homosexuality: just as the Indians were demonized in English writings by being associated with the heinous sin of sodomy, so were the "Turks." Sodomy served to legitimate Christian/European moral superiority and to prepare for holy war.

5

Holy Land, Holy War

The image of Muslims and American Indians as sodomites created one of the strongest forces for polarization between Christians and non-Christians. The reaction of the Briton to the heinous people who committed such heinous sins, whether in America or in North Africa and the Levant, was similar to that of the Spaniards—demonization and destruction. And the Briton, like his Iberian counterpart, was justified in so doing because of his Christian ideology of holy war.

For a war to be holy the land over which it was fought had to be holy. That is why Britons justified the conquest of the sodomites' lands by turning to the most uncriticized imperialism in Judeo-Christian history—the conquest of Canaan and the creation of the "holy land." To justify destruction there was a need for the holy.

Holy Land

On the eve of Columbus's landfall in America, Christendom's crusade against the Muslims was proving unsuccessful. Neither had the Holy Land in Palestine been re-Christianized nor had the unholy Muslims, along with the Eastern Christians, been annihilated. Rather, Islam had reemerged under the Ottoman sultans as one of the strongest powers in Europe, and over a quarter of a century later the military and cultural leadership of Suleyman the Magnificent proved both awe-inspiring and terrifying. Spain was the exception in its encounter with Islam and, much earlier, Portugal. By 1492 the Spaniards had succeeded in defeating the last Moors of Granada, and by 1571 they had defeated, with support from the Papacy, the Turkish fleet at Lepanto. As they began their conquest of the Americas they transported their anti-Muslim ideology of religious war across the Atlantic and applied it to the American Indians. Christopher Columbus viewed the capture of the Indies as part of the holy war against Muslims for the liberation of Jerusalem. A few decades later Richard Eden confirmed the link between "The warres of kynge Ferdinando ageynst the Sarasens" and "the conqueste of the Indies."[1] The Spaniards had treated the Muslim infidel as an object of polarization and holy destruction, and they began viewing the American Indian in the same light.[2]

Similarly, English colonists and adventurers interchanged discourses and prejudices as they crisscrossed between the Muslims in the Mediterranean and the Indians in America. Drawing on their eschatological and military fears of the Turks and Moors, and on the writings of anti-Muslim and anti-Indian Spaniards, English colonists applied the imagery they had designated for the Muslims on the Indians. In the same way that the Mahumetans were "beasts," "wilde," and "bloody and cruelle," the Indians became "doleful creatures . . . the veriest ruins of mankind," the "devil-worshippers" and "flying serpents."[3] It is significant that Thomas Brightman (1562–1607), one of the two most influential eschatologists in seventeenth-century Britain, denounced the Muslims and threatened them with divine destruction, but since he was writing before the English colonial venture to America had taken shape, he made no mention of the Indians. In the writings of Joseph Mead (1586–1638), however, the other influential eschatologist, the Indians were depicted as worshippers of the devil who, like the Muslims, would lead the satanic attack on Christendom, but would ultimately be defeated. Beginning in the 1630s when Mead's writings were published, therefore, the Indians were joined to the Muslims as enemies of Christ and categorized as "infidels" and "heathens"—exactly as the Muslims had been categorized for centuries.[4]

Such a categorization of the people entailed a categorization of the lands the people inhabited. That is why the Britons, like the Spaniards, the French, and other European colonizers, renamed the American territories they "discovered." Lands that were "waste" and "wild" were transformed into villages and cities that recalled the homelands of the "discoverers." This transformation into the "New" established not only the power to possess but also the annihilation of the old Indian; what had been was without meaning or history or value. Meanwhile, what was new was both a continuity of the Christian/European old and a re-creation and redefinition of what was to become different, better, and higher: "New."

The renaming that took place at the outset of the North American conquest served not only to eradicate the old Indian, but also to eradicate other "Christian" claims. It was an act of finalizing Indian destruction and marking exclusive national beginnings. Europeans were seizing lands not only from the Indians but also from each other. To the Britons, renaming was to be a form of anglicization—of giving Jamestown an English name rather than allowing the Dutch to name it "Iacobopolis."[5] Britons were apprehensive of rival colonizers and traders who were naming places New France, New Spain, New Holland, and New Sweden: "the Dutch plantations, now by them called the Netherlands, have not been commonly so called and known, until of very late years, but was better known and commonly called by them the New Virginia, as a place dependent upon or a relative to the Old Virginia. And as there is in that an acknowledgement of English right, so I conceive it to be true, which is commonly reported, that by the permission of king James they had granted from him to their states only a certain island, called therefore by them States Island, as a watery place for their West Indies fleet; although as they have incroached upon, so they have given it a new Dutch name . . . wiping out the old English names in those parts in America in their old sea-charts, and have now Dutchified them."[6]

While Britons conquered and renamed what was or had been American Indian, they could not duplicate that process in the Muslim Mediterranean, where they had to adjust to place names already in use. While in America they were conquerors who could reconstruct and redefine, in the Mediterranean they were traders who were following other Europeans, Levantines, and North Africans into territories and zones to which only they were new: "1620, May 13. The Master, Wardens, and Assistants of the Trinity

House certify that the Mediterranean Sea begins at the Straights of Gibralter or Moraco, and extendeth itself to Mallaga, Allicant, the Isle of Mayeyorke, Minyorke, and Candy, Cyprise, Scanderowne, Trypoly, Alexandria, and is called the Levant Sea, and hath ever bene so accompted and called by all navigators of those countries."[7] This statement by Trinity House, a government office that had been established by Henry VIII to oversee maritime affairs, shows how the House officials were coming to terms with the lands and borders of the Mediterranean, and preparing English and other British sailors and pilots to work within a given geography. There was no English renaming of islands and sea routes that had either been navigated earlier by other Christians or were dominated by the powerful empire of the Turks and Moors.

Only in the case of Palestine did Britons feel the "power" to challenge the existing names and duplicate in the Levant what they were doing in America. In the Palestinian Levant, they believed they were bringing back and reclaiming the biblical lands that had been lost to the Muslims. Their approach to Palestine was not topographical but textual: in the same manner that Columbus, as he first named the territories in America, still believed himself to be in the lands of Marco Polo's text, English and other Christian travelers in Palestine insisted on seeing themselves in the geography of the Pentateuch, and on using the Old Testament and the Christian (actually Greco-Roman) names of the places that had come under the sway of Islam. By using names such as "Land of Canaan" or "Land of Jury," English writers signified the unchangeableness of the land since its conquest by Joshua. Curiously, they saw no anachronism or incongruity in referring to "the present Fertility of Canaan," or to the Jews who "now [1655] live in Canaan."[8] Although the Arabs and Turks had transliterated and continued to use the name Filisteen,[9] English travelers and cartographers viewed the land as frozen in a second millennium name—Palestine was still Canaan. They superimposed faith on political geography to produce a name that was both unchanging and divinely confirmed.

Not surprisingly, a similar faith informed the politics of renaming America. In a process that is psychologically complex but imperialistically understandable, the English who came from Boston or Plymouth in England

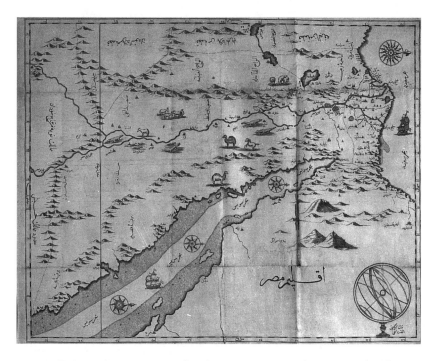

5. "Iqleem Misr." Courtesy of Professor E. Birnbaum (copyright holder),
University of Toronto.

and created a new Boston and a new Plymouth in New England, also saw
themselves as actually coming from Canaan or Salem and turning those biblical concepts into American colonies. They were building "Ierusalem in virginia."[10] By identifying themselves as the new Israelites, these adventurers
typologized their migration; it became a quest, as with Joshua's Israelites, to
the American land that "would Flowe with milke and honey,"[11] and a return,
as with the eschatological Jews, to the "land of promise." Numerous preachers who served as promoters of the "western plantation" appealed to this
image. Sir George Peckham asserted that America, like the biblical land of
Canaan, had been given to God's peculiar people, the English colonists.[12]
For Peckham, America was actually "parallel" to Palestine in that it had a tem-
perate climate, "even of that in which Adam, Abraham, with the Prophets and
Apostles were bred in, and received as an Earthly priviledge."[13]

America was the Canaan or Palestine of the Western hemisphere. This "Canaan theme," as Alfred A. Cave has called it,[14] was so frequently invoked by colonists in the seventeenth century that it defined their ideological representation of America. In 1609, Robert Johnson assured the colonists that they would possess the new land in the same way that Caleb and Joshua had conquered the old Canaan. The colonists, preached Robert Gray in 1609, were to "conquer and cast out those Idolatrous Cananites, & to plant themselues in their places." They were like the "ancient patriarchs," wrote Robert Cushman in 1621, for whom it was "lawful now to take a land which none useth."[15] More than the French or the Spaniards, the English colonists viewed the American lands as the holy land that had been promised to the Israelites in Genesis. By turning the conquest of the land into a holy conquest that fulfilled typologically the Old Testament model in which the Canaanites had been made to disappear, they legitimated for themselves the marginalization and destruction of the Indians.

Inherent in the English discourse about the Indians, as well as the Muslims, were arguments that English thinkers either borrowed from the Spanish *conquistadores* or arrived at independently. The first argument centered on the fact that the lands of the Indians and the Muslims were devoid of people. Some travelers to North America and to North Africa and the Levant confirmed that the lands they traversed were "empty"—so much so that later writers who had never left their English or Scottish libraries agreed. Other travelers explained that the small population of those lands was idle and lazy, and did not cultivate the land. Because the land was empty and the people useless and uninterested in industry—in a treaty between the Massachusetts Indians and the bay colonists, the Indians agreed not to be "idle"[16]—it was legitimate for European Christians to conquer the idle population and possess the empty land. Because the land was a *vacuum domicilium*, and because the natives did not "enclose" their property, John Cotton concluded, as had numerous advocates of colonization from the 1620s on, that "where there is a vacant place, there is liberty for the son of Adam or Noah to come and inhabit."[17] Armed with this reasoning, it was not difficult for puritan writers to make a logical leap from a vacant land to a land made vacant by the agents of God, who were commissioned by God to drive the indolent natives out or destroy them altogether. "Thus," wrote John Mason after massacring the Pequots in 1637, "the Lord was pleased to smite our Enemies in the hinder Parts, and to give us their Land for an Inheritance."[18] God gave the new Canaan to the English in the same way He had given the old Canaan to the Israelites.

This argument for justifying the appropriation of native American lands was repeated in the context of Muslim lands. The same motifs that appeared in the description of the American Indians appeared in the description of the Muslims. Like the Indians, the Muslims were seen to leave their lands wild and unattended. In 1601 an anonymous writer proclaimed that in the Ottoman dominions, "all things [are] laid waste, few cities well peopled." The Turks, concurred Thomas Gainsford in 1618, using the same imagery that was used for the "salvages" of America, "liue sluttishly on roots, fruit, garlicke, onions, gourds and such like."[19] Even a captive such as T. S., who had become quite familiar with the North African Muslims during his years of captivity, could not resist the comparison between the Indians and the Muslims in terms of their agricultural underdevelopment: "The Earth of it self abhors Idleness; when therefore it is neglected by reason of the small Number of Inhabitants, or when it hath been long without employing its innate productive virtue, it then breaks forth into Trees & Woods, as in the West-Indies is sufficiently known."[20] T. S. was describing a wild forest in the hinterland of Algeria. However, in what he believed was the unwillingness of the Muslims to cultivate their land, he recalled the notorious unwillingness of the Indians. Both peoples, whether in North Africa or in North America, were alike in their lack of industry. The fact that Indians produced enough food to feed both themselves and the early colonists, and the fact that North Africa produced the sugar supplies that early English merchants so much desired—along with an abundance of fruit and vegetables—were completely ignored by English writers.

In the same way that colonists in America failed to "see" the complex level of social and political order in the Indian community, neither did English writers "see" the Muslim cities in the Levant. Instead, they saw the cities of biblical history. While Aleppo was one of the busiest and most important cities on the silk route linking the Mediterranean to China—so important that the Levant Company set its headquarters in it—and while Sidon and Jerusalem were thriving hubs, Gainsford insisted on the opposite: "Shall I come backe againe and tell you of Ierusalem, Tyrus, and Sidon? alas, they are but names, and all the plagues denounced by the Prophets haue broken their bones in sunder . . . Aleppo, which would faine be old Antioch, yea dare from the mouth of some Authors publish, the antiquities of Niniuie."[21] Similarly, when Purchas reflected on Constantinople/Istanbul, he saw not a vast and powerful metropolis but "Mahometople" after its "bottomlesse hellish downefall."[22] Meanwhile, a traveler such as Fynes Moryson described the Holy Land in biblical terms, and only rarely referred to the Arabs and Turks there. The Eastern and Levant worlds Britons had studied in their Bibles or their classical history textbooks had changed. But that change was superficial, since under Istanbul or Mahometople still lay a retrievable Constantinople. In the Muslim dominions, the Old was real and the New superficial; in America, the New was real and the Old was savage, unnecessary, and eradicable, just as Patuxet had been eradicated to give way to Plymouth.

Britons specifically applied the discourse of the Indian *vacuum domicilium* to the Holy Land. Men such as George Sandys, who traveled in the Levant before going off to the Americas, insisted that the land was empty of any "real" inhabitants other than the Arab and Muslim "theeues." There was no "true" population in the Holy Land, no people who really belonged to that geography: "Those rich lands at this present remaine wast and ouergrowne with bushes, receptacles of wild beasts, of theeues, and murderers; large territories dispeopled, or thinly inhabited; goodly cities made desolate."[23] For Sandys, the land was God's, and because the Saracens opposed the Christian God they were made to disappear from the land of Christ. Their disappearance had already begun as the land, in Sandys' view, was already "dispeopled." (Peckham had earlier used the same word, "dispeopled," in his description of the "New World.")[24] The land was vacant and those Muslim "theeues" who were there were indolent and lacked industry. Sandys employed in Palestine what the Puritans employed in colonial New England—"a structural model based upon the opposition between God and the devil." While for the Puritans the devil was manifested by his Indian followers, for Sandys he was manifested by the Muslims. With this model Sandys was able to justify "distancing [and] depersonalizing" the population,[25] so that the Muslims would be destroyed just like the Indians.

This attitude of "distancing" the inhabitants of the Holy Land was a legacy Britons and other Europeans had inherited from the Crusades. Ever since those medieval wars the peoples of the Levant had been illegitimated in European eyes. The Crusaders had viewed the Christian and Muslim Arabs of Syria and Palestine as extraneous intruders who were to be expelled in order to fulfil the messianic purpose of the Holy War. This ideal of an eschatological empire of Western Christians in the land of Jesus remained entrenched in European thought well after the Crusades had failed. Even peaceful friars believed in the illegitimacy of the Arab presence. In the late fifteenth century Fra Francesco Suriano praised the land of Palestine and "all things contained therein and appertaining to it—I mention not the Saracens who do not belong to it."[26] Such an attitude continued into the early modern period to such an extent that both theologians and travelers concurred that the "Saracens" had no geographical or historical legitimacy in the Levant, and had it not been for their "robberyes" of the land and the bloodiness of their swords, the Saracens would not have been in the Levant in the first place.[27]

In North Africa the presence of the Moors was similarly decried as the glory of Carthage and Rome was recalled. Not only was the land not theirs, but there were still claimants to that land—Carthaginians and Romans, as the introductory poem to a treatise published as early as 1546 purported to show, and as did a poem published over a century and a half later in 1680; in 1728, Daniel Defoe was still lamenting the demise of Carthage.[28] While Britons, Spaniards, and other Europeans enjoyed divine legitimacy in colonizing the Americas and other places, the Arabs were "theeues," although they had settled on the North African coast over eight hundred years earlier.

The second English "holy" argument for seizing the land was formulated in terms of a religious goal. Only by conquering the lands of the Muslims and the American Indians would it become possible to bring to these infidels the knowledge and religion of Christ and eradicate the religion of "Mahound" and the Indian worship of the devil. While this goal seemed possible, although not always desirable among the Indians, it was impracticable among the Muslims. And while some advocates of the Virginia enterprise hoped for the conversion of the Indians, others knew that no such conversion was imminent among the Muslims. Still, there were writers who insisted on believing, as many American colonists insisted on believing about the American Indians, that the Muslims in North Africa, chiefly Morocco, were awaiting Christian salvation. John Harrison was even convinced that the Morisco émigrés in Morocco were deeply "desirous" of Christian books, "of Calvin and other bookes of our religion . . . Yea, both, Moores, Jewes and all, [are] listeninge after nothinge but wares against Spaine, and peace and friendship with England, with generall disposicion and inclination both towardes our nation, and even to Christian religion."[29]

Although similar Christianization-cum-colonization was widely prevalent in Spanish writings about America, the English writings went further in linking conversion to a political and military goal. The English proclaimed their intention to *protestantize* the American Indians, not only to save their souls but also to prevent them from being converted to the idolatry of Catholicism.[30] In America the demographic and military adversary of the British colonist was the American Indian, but the ideological and religious adversary was the Catholic from Spain or France. The conquest of America was seen to kill two birds with one stone—convert the Indians and subvert the Catholics. Actually, for ardent anti-Papists such as Cotton Mather, the latter project was even more important than the former. That is why the Bible was translated into Algonquian by John Eliot in 1663. What was believed to be the ultimate Protestant weapon against Catholicism was to be placed in the hands of the Indians: that is why a Society for the Propagation of the Gospel among the Indians had been established in 1649.[31] Similarly, Henry Roberts hoped to convert the Moors in Morocco to Christianity, not only to win them over to the Anglican Church, but also to prevent them from coming under Spanish Catholic authority. The concern for saving the souls of the "savages" and the Moors was clearly rooted in the imperial enterprise: evangelization ensured colonization.

Holy War

Since the lands to be conquered and colonized were holy, then the war against the Indians or the Muslims was holy too.

The term "holy war" has received extensive scrutiny since the magisterial studies by Carl Erdmann, Roland Bainton, Michael Walzer, David Stannard, James Turner Johnson, and others.[32] Although these historians have approached the holy war from different angles, sometimes equating it to and at other times distinguishing it from, "crusade," "just war," or "religious war," and although David Stannard has convincingly shown how the American holocaust of the Indians was motivated by holy war ideology, no historian has applied the term to the war between England and the Muslim Empire in the Renaissance—not even James Turner Johnson who, in his *Ideology, Reason and the Limitation of War: Religious and Secular Concepts, 1200–1740*, examined the rationale for the holy war in English seventeenth-century thought.[33] Many Renaissance Britons used the terms "holy war," "just war," and "crusade" while describing the conflict with Muslims, but while twentieth-century theoreticians recognize significant differences between these terms, Renaissance writers did not discriminate sharply.

For English writers, any battle with the Muslims was a "Holy warre" simply because the Muslims were seen to oppose the Christian God and to have usurped the Christian land of Palestine. Thus when Roland Bainton specifically described the crusade as a war (but not a holy war) "on God's behalf . . . [for] a divine cause" fought "under the authority of God," he could well have agreed with Henry Marsh's call for a holy war in 1633; for Marsh there was no difference between a "Holy warre," a war fought on behalf of God—a crusade—and a war fought with God's assistance.[34] If a holy war, as Carl Erdmann maintained, required that Christians fight under the banner of Christ,[35] then the sea battles that were enacted in Jacobean pageants depicted a holy war by Erdmann's definition because the combatants actually fought under banners of St. George and the Crescent. If the "just war" is, as Bainton stated, "secular and restrained," then the "Holy War" about which Francis Bacon wrote in 1622 complies with this definition, exactly as David Little stated in his criticism of Bainton.[36] If the need to protect the English shipping industry required fighting the Turkish navy in a "Holy Warre," as the Anglican minister Nathaniel Knott suggested in the early 1630s, then he was using the term in the way David Little explained it[37]—a war for national security-cum-religion. Finally, if the attack on Salee in 1637 is similar to the war against the Amalekites, as Edmund Waller suggested in his poem celebrating the English fleet's victory, then it resembles the "Yahweh war," a term coined by Peter C. Craigie to replace "Holy War."[38]

Although seventeenth-century English writers viewed the fighting with Muslims as part of a holy war reminiscent of the medieval Crusades, recent historians have argued that by the late Elizabethan period, England's holy war ideology had come to an end. In *Piracy and the Decline of Venice, 1580–1615*, Alberto Tenenti stated that by the early seventeenth century, England and the rest of Europe no longer sustained the ideals of the anti-Muslim Crusade.[39] Christopher Tyerman also argued in *England and the Crusades 1095–1588* that by the beginning of the seventeenth century, England had lost its crusading ideal and military zeal. Although the "memory of crusading lingered in academic, literary, and antiquarian circles . . . the resonances grew faint" by the end of the Elizabethan period; "the end of the story of England and the crusades," concluded Tyerman, occurred in the "reign of Elizabeth I."[40]

Johnson has shown that theoretical interest in holy war remained in England throughout the Protestant-Catholic conflict.[41] Meanwhile, throughout the English conquest of America, holy war theorizing (which included the Canaan theme) and practice underpinned the conflict with the Indians: "Austen hath allowed it, for a lawful offensiue warre."[42] Such an ideology of conquest was repeated after the 1622 Indian attack on colonists in Virginia. Edward Waterhouse, the first London preacher to give an account of the Indian attack, confirmed that God's "justice" would surely "correct" the Indians. He assured his merchant and adventurer audience that "by right of Warre, and law of Nations," it was now legitimate to "inuade the Country, and destroy them [the Indians] who sought to destroy vs: whereby wee shall enjoy their cultiuated places."[43] Although Waterhouse did not use religious language in his document, he confirmed that all English action against the Indians was justified by the God the English worshipped.

A decade and a half later this ideology was triumphant after the English victory over the Pequot Indians in 1637. John Mason, commander of the colonists' forces, declared the war against the Indians "Just" because God, who had "brought [the colonists] to Canaan at last," made the Indian "Enemies of his People . . . as a fiery Oven . . . Thus did the Lord judge among the Heathen, filling the Place with dead Bodies."[44] William Bradford confirmed that it was God who "fried" the Indians and gave the colonists "so speedy a victory over so proud and insulting an enemy."[45] Captain Underhill confirmed that the "sword of the Lord" destroyed the Indians and "drove [them] out of their country," and that it was the Scripture that declared "women and children must perish."[46] The poet Michael Wigglesworth recalled in 1662 the war against the Indians as a war of "Great Jehovah" against the "curst Amalekites."[47] Increase Mather opened his description of the 1675 King Philip's War with words that leave no doubt about his Yahweh-inspired holy war: "That the Heathen People amongst whom we live, and whose Land the Lord God of our Fathers hath given to us for a rightfull Possession, have at sundry times been plotting mischievous devices against that part of the English Israel which is seated in these goings down of the Sun."[48] Two decades later, his son, Cotton Mather, confirmed that the Indians were monsters, Scythians, "Myrmidons," "Loup-Garou," "Barbarous Canibals," "Blood-Hounds," "Tygers," and "Dragons."[49] For both father and son it was clear why God supported the English in their religiously inspired and justified war of annihilation.

Meanwhile, from across the Atlantic, Joseph Hall, bishop of Norwich, included in his *Resolutions and Decisions of Divers Practical Cases* a discussion of war in the context of America and the "uninhabited" islands of the Caribbean. Was it lawful, he asked, "for Christians, where they find a country possessed by savage pagans and infidels, to drive out the native inhabitants, and to seize and enjoy their lands upon any pretence"?[50] His answer was in the negative ("Infidelity cannot forfeit their [Indians'] inheritance" to their land) except when colonists and traders came under attack and had to resort to war in self-defense. Interestingly, Hall compared the war against the Indians to the medieval holy war that had been launched by Pope Gregory against the Muslims: "Justum sanctumque esse bellum, & c. ("That is a just and holy war which is by Christians made against infidels, that they, being brought under subjection, the gospel of Christ might be preached unto them; lest that if they should not be subjected, they might be an hinderance to preaching, and to the conversion of those that would believe")." Hall rejected the principle of war for the cause of Christ, and therefore denounced Gregory's goal as becoming more "a successor of Romulus than of Peter." In the same breath he denounced the bull of Pope Alexander VI that had legitimized the "expedition against the barbarous Indians" in 1493, and the subsequent defense the Spanish writer Sepulveda proposed for the "holy invasion" of America. For Hall, neither the war against the Muslims in the eleventh century nor the war against the Indians in the sixteenth and seventeenth centuries could be holy because there could be no legitimacy for war in the cause of Christ: "It is for Mahometans to profess planting religion by the sword; it is not for Christians." The "true way of Christian conquests" (presumably of the Indians), lay in preaching and amicable cohabitation. But neither in the medieval period nor during the Renaissance should Christians use the ideology of holy war to justify the invasion and colonization of the non-Christian Other.

Despite Hall's refutation of holy war, numerous English writers appealed to that ideology, especially in their writings about Muslims. This anti-Muslim holy war jingoism had been echoed in English religious and political culture even during the Elizabethan period when the queen had had amicable relations with the Muslims. In 1575 the translator of the *Notable History of the Saracens*, Thomas Newton, called for a crusade against the Muslims and cooperation with other Christian countries against "this arrogant and bragging hell-hound."[51] In 1594, Thomas Heywood wrote a play about the Crusades, *The Foure Prentises of London* (republished in 1615), in which he told of four Britons who had joined the Crusaders and marched against a combined force of Turks and Persians.[52] The polarization between the English and the infidels is shown to be exclusively religious; the Muslim "Soldan" taunts the Christians on religious grounds: "by your Crosses on your brests / Yee're markt for death, and base destruction." Meanwhile, one of the four apprentices describes "The Soldan, [as] the grand enemy to CHRIST, / The deuils Lieutenant, Vice-roy vnder him!"[53] The Muslims are "pagans," bombastic and cruel; the Christians, as one of the apprentices states, "are the best brood of martial spirits," because they come from England

> Whose wals the Ocean washeth white as snow,
> For which you strangers call it Albion:
> From France, a Nation both renown'd and fear'd
> From Scotland, Wales, euen to the Irish Coast,
> Beyond the pillars great Alcides rear'd,
> At Gades in Spaine vnto the Pyrene hils,
> Haue we assembled men of dauntlesse spirits,
> To scourge you hence ye damned Infidels.[54]

That same year, 1594, appeared in England the translation of the first five cantos of the most influential Renaissance poem about the Crusades, Tasso's *Jerusalem Delivered,* by Richard Carew.[55] Six years later appeared the full translation by Edward Fairfax: *Godfrey of Bulloigne: Or The Recouerie of Iervsalem. Done into English Heroicall verse by Edward Fairefax.* The poem wielded a strong influence on King James I who valued it above all other poems, on Charles I who read it during his imprisonment half a century later, and on many English writers.[56]

With the accession of James I to the throne in 1603, the initiative toward a religious war against Islam and Muslims moved from literature to realpolitik, if not exactly to the battlefield. James reversed his predecessor's amicable policy toward the Turks and confirmed the conflict with the Muslims as a religious one. In his poem on *Lepanto,* written in 1585 (first published in 1591 and then republished in the year of his accession), he defined the conflict as one "Betwixt the baptiz'd race, / And circumsised Turband Turkes" (lines 10–11). Significantly, these references to "baptiz'd" and "circumsised Turband," which at its opening, give the poem a religious polarization, were not in the original Scottish version but only in the English "translation" that was prepared for the English press. At his accession the king wanted to emphasize his anti-Muslim stance—and his anti-Catholicism too since the poem concluded with an attack on the "Antichristian sect" (line 1025).[57] So widely known was his anti-Muslim position that the English representative in Morocco, Henry Roberts, hastened to urge him in April of that year to undertake a war against that country because its conquest would be "godly and christianlike . . . to subdue the same from Mahomet to the knowledge of Christ."[58] Roberts was well aware of Morocco's extensive trade with Central Africa, which England would seize. He also believed that the resistance of the Moroccan army would be weakened if the king promised that whoever turned Christian "shall not only enjouy all their owne goodes, but your Matie will give them that they and theirs shall live ever heerafter very well." Although Roberts suspected that his proposal would be rejected by many in the king's service, he urged the king to pursue the project in order to "wynne many thowsand soules to God."[59] There was wealth, empire, and religion in the conquest of Morocco; a war against the Moroccans was both holy and lucrative.

James did not attack Morocco, but signaling his change of Mediterranean policy in 1604, he signed a peace treaty with Spain and turned against the Ottoman Empire. In the treaty, Spain and England agreed to a common resistance of the Turk, the common enemy of Christendom.[60] Soon after in that same year the Turks attacked some English ships in Alexandria. As a result the king threatened to retaliate,[61] thus heralding the piracy and sea-fights as well as the capturing of hostages and pillaging of coastal cities that would become the chief mode of confrontation between Jacobean, Caroline, and Interregnum England and North Africa, and between the two religious civilizations of the Mediterranean.

Inspired by the anti-Muslim zeal of their king, and perhaps embarrassed that England had not produced an anti-Muslim hero on the scale of Prester John (who was either in Ethiopia or in Central Asia), or Scanderberg in Hungary,[62] or Tasso's Italian warriors, or Camoes' Portuguese navigators, Jacobean writers recognized the need for presenting to the English reader and pageant-goer some models of native English heroism in the holy war against the Muslims. While continental Europe had produced epics about anti-Muslim national heroes and produced actual warriors who had fought and conquered in the lands of Islam, England had not. A few pageants produced in celebration of royal events during the first half of the Jacobean period served to fill this anti-Muslim gap. If these pageants had a public function other than to entertain and to drain the public coffers, it was to raise the spirit of the viewers and provide them with illusions of victory over the undefeated Turks and Moors. At a time in the early seventeenth century when Algerian and Moroccan attacks on English and Scottish shipping were increasing and resulting in the dramatic capture and/or sinking of countless ships, as well as the enslavement of hundreds and (later thousands) of Britons, there emerged in England, specifically in cities such as London and Bristol, which had a large seafaring population, an audience not unwilling to accept works of pure fabrication in which writers and stage designers, politicians and historians, literally "made up" episodes of Christian victory and Muslim humiliation. Ignoring the actual situation at sea or in the slave markets of Algiers and elsewhere, the fabricators portrayed heroic Britons who defeated and enslaved both Turks and Moors. Relying on a suspension of disbelief in their audience, entertainers presented a military spectacle of Britain at sea in which British Christianity prevailed over Mediterranean infidelity.

These pageants, it is important to note, were not closet shows for the exclusive eyes of the court. They had an audience that included royalty, nobility, foreign ambassadors, and the London crowds. They were a kind of mass entertainment, a product of popular culture that aimed not at complexity but at appealing to the audience's sentiments and anxieties. These pageants, therefore, defined and sharpened the national identity; they united subjects and ruler in a common cause and served as powerful modes of state propaganda—not least of which was religious propaganda against the infidels. They also served to send an international message to Britain's friends and foes by exhibiting the power, wealth, and military might of the monarchy. That is why the language in these pageants was dominated by religion. The conflict between the Britons and the Turks was not presented as a conflict over trade or shipping or pillage; rather it was an inherent conflict between good Christian merchants and bad Muslims. This was a conflict of gods, not of men, and it was not merely over London or Algiers but over the land of God, the Holy Land. Although Britons did not conquer the Holy Land in these pageants, they were shown to fight the Turks in the spirit of the medieval holy warriors who had conquered that land.

In May of 1610, "London's Love to the Royal Prince Henrie" was presented on the Thames, "with a Worthie Fleete of her Citizens." The celebrations started on Thursday and ended on the following Wednesday with a "water-fight" between a "Turkish pirate" and "two merchant's shippes."[63] While actual encounters between Britons and Turks in the 1610s often resulted in the capture of English ships and their crews, this encounter showed the heroic valor of the English seamen and merchants who together defeated the Turks: "In conclusion, the merchants and men of warre, after a long and well-fought skirmish, prooved too strong for the pirate, they spoylde bothe him and blewe up the castle, ending the whole batterie with verie rare and admirable fire-workes, as also a worthie peale of chambers."[64] There is no evidence in the early Jacobean period that the English fleet had attacked a "Turkish" outpost and destroyed it. But truth was not the function of this or other pageants; a fabricated victory over the Muslims was the main purpose for which the "no meane multitude of people" assembled.

A more sober description of the Christian encounter with the North African Muslims appeared three years later in John Taylor's "Heaven's Blessings and Earth's Joy; or, A True Relation of the Supposed Sea-Fights and Fire-Workes" (1613), which described the celebration of the marriage of King James's daughter Elizabeth to Duke Frederick—a marriage that was seen as a confirmation of Protestant unity against the Catholic Habsburgs on the continent. For the Water Poet, and as King James himself would also have hoped, the marriage was also to establish a military alliance against the Ottoman armies in Central Europe. Taylor described a celebration that was far more impressive than the 1610 one; in this "Sea-fight," there were ''16 ships, 16 gallies, and six friggots; of the which Navy the ships were Christians and the gallies were supposed Turkes, all being artificially rigged and trimmed, well manned and furnished with great ordinance and musquet-tiers."[65] The Christian ships, which in this case were specified as Venetian, were to confront "Turkish gallies . . . belonging to a supposed Turkish or Barbarian Castle of Tunis, Algiers, or some other Mahometan fortification." The Mediterranean war was between Christians and Muslims. That is why this celebration recalled the greatest of sea battles against the Muslims—"the happy and famous battell of Lepanto."[66]

Aware, however, of the true nature of the conflict on the Mediterranean, and the disastrous impact it had on Christian shipping, and despite the sense of Christian pride at the victory of Lepanto and English pride at the victory over the Spanish Armada, Taylor presented a battle that lasted for three hours but ended evenly: "the victorie inclyning to the nether side, all being opposed foes and combined friends; all victors, all triumphers, none to be vanquished, and therefore no conquerors."[67] The Muslims were not defeated and the Christians were not victorious. Perhaps because of this ambivalence Taylor seized the opportunity at the end of his account to praise his king as a Briton who could rouse the English/British nation "to the terrour of all malignant opposers of his Royall state and dignity."[68] Of course there could have been nothing further from the truth than the description of James as a warrior king. But again, the purpose of the celebration and the text was to provide the "pertubatious multitudes" with entertainment and national polarization against the "Turks."[69] This was a national, not merely a metropolitan event, and its theme was international not local—the war between the Christians and the Muslims.

For Taylor, pageantry prevailed over Mediterranean reality. After all, the preparations for the pageant had been "extraordinarie," as Chamberlain noted in one of his letters.[70] Three castles had been "built upon eight western barges, and one great castle upon the land over against the court." The vast expenses that had gone into this project, along with the extensive planning and the multitude of designers and builders, participants, and overseers demonstrated that the pageant had an important and relevant subject. The expenses for this pageant were by far higher than those of court masques or royal celebrations. As Chamberlain continued in a letter to Sir Ralph Winwood, a "troupe of three or five hundred musketts [was] made redy by the citie to gard the court during these triumphes . . . The preparations for fire workes and fights upon the water are very great and have alredy consumed 6000[ll] which a man wold easilie believe that sees the provison of sixe and thirty sayle of pinnesses, gallies, galeasses, carraques and other vessells so trimmed, furnished and painted, that I beleve there was never such a fleet seen above the bridge, besides fowre floting castles with fire workes, and the representation of the towne, fort and haven of Argier upon the land."[71] Such extensive preparations could only have impressed on the audience, as they did on Chamberlain and his addressees, the anxiety in the public mind associated with Algiers.

Another account of this pageant described a different set of events—or indeed elaborated on the events in order to magnify English might. Its title was "The Magnificent Marriage of the two Great Princes Frederick Count Palatine, & c. and the Lady Elizabeth . . . Now the second time imprinted, with many additions of the same Tryumphes" (1613). These additions were clearly aimed at evoking English pride, and contrary to what David Bergeron has maintained, at presenting a strong "dramatic theme."[72] The pageant begins with Venetian ships being taken as "booty and prize" to the Castle of Argeir. Soon after, a Spanish "argosay" is also taken. Clearly the Catholic enemies of England were no match for the mighty Turks. But then the "English navie" appeared on the scene, "with their red-crost streamers most gallantly waving in the ayre, to the great delight of all the beholders." Soon, a mighty sea battle took place between the English navy on the one hand, and the Turkish/Algerian fleet and the castle on the other. It ended in the surrender of both the castle and the gallies to the "English Admirall, who fiered many of the said gallies, sacked the Castle, and tooke prisoner the Turke's Admirall, with divers Bashawes and other great Turkes, and also recovered the Venetian and Spanish shippes before taken by the gallies. After the performance of all these aforesaid, the English Admirall, in a most tryumphant manner, carried as prisoner the Admirall of the gallies, attired in a red jacket with blue sleeves, according to the Turkish fashion, with the Bahsawes and the other Turkes, guarded, to his Highness' Privie-stairs at Whitehall, where his Grace, Prince Palsegrave, and his Lady remained, which prisoners were led by Sir Robert Mansfield [Mansel] to the Lord Admiral's, and by him they were conveyed to the King's Majestie as a representation of pleasure, which to his Highness moved delight, and highly pleased all there present."[73]

Unfortunately there could not have been less assuring evidence of England's superiority over the Muslims than the actual outcome of the pageant. Numerous mishaps occurred during the mock shooting scenes that resulted in the blinding and disabling of actors: "one man lost both his hands, another both his eyes, and a host of others were burned and maimed."[74] It was a fiasco that, aside from the expenses and the casualties, did not entertain the king. While the Levant merchants and traders were worried about Algerian and other North African attacks, and the disastrous impact those attacks had on their financial activity, the king was more concerned about events in Central Europe. And while sailors and soldiers, who were the ones to be captured by pirates, worried about the lack of naval security in the Mediterranean and fantasized about English victory and Muslim defeat, it would take the king eight more years before he authorized the English fleet to attack the "Algerines." Although the official account indicated how much the king had enjoyed the pageant, the unofficial reality was that he had been so bored that rather than allowing the show to resume a few days later, he ordered the dismantling of the fortress and the disbanding of the companies.

Although the show had failed to entertain the king, the ideal of fighting the Muslims remained strong. A few months later Queen Anne took a visit to Bristol, a city whose sailors and ships had been widely exposed to North African attacks. In the "Royall, Magnificent, and Sumptuous Entertainment" that was presented to the queen, a "Water-fight" between Turks and "worthy Brutes" was presented. In the verse rendition by Robert Naile that described the show, an overview of British / Christian-Muslim relations was offered. Aware that he was addressing the consort of the monarch who held naval power in his hands, and perhaps hopeful that the king would initiate some action against the pirates, Naile emphasized the "barbarous cruelty" of the Turks who had captured "many a Christian Marchantman" and turned them into "gally-slaves condemn'd, / There bound in chaines for to remaine till death their lives doth end." Naile further emphasized that Christian rulers had failed to join forces to fight off the Turks, and he openly urged them to launch a new crusade against the infidels:

> Ye Christian Kings and Potentates, joyne both your hearts and hands,
> To chase this off-scumme Scithian brood from you and all your lands;
> Unite your forces Christian-like from Europe to expell
> Proud Ottoman, too dangerous a neighbour neare to dwell.[75]

After his anti-Muslim opening Naile turned to the description of the combat between an English ship brandishing "the Bloudy Crosse" and two Turkish Gallies with their "moony standerds."[76] A fierce battle ensued in which the Britons won over the Turks, not only because of their superior courage and swordsmanship, but because God, the Christian God, was on their side: "For God, which bounds the raging Seas, hath bounded their [Turks] desire,/ And turns to smoke their proud attempts whereto their thoughts aspire."[77] Once the show was over the queen returned to Court, but not before she stopped for a moment to view the "Turks" who had been captured by the English sailors. The victory of the Christian God in this water combat showed both queen and audience ("many a thowsand") that only by God-inspired fighting could the Turks be defeated and the Britons attain glory in the holy war against Islam.

Holy war imagery and fanfare were popular in Jacobean England. The last pageant, it was reported by Chamberlain to Sir Ralph Winwood, had been attended by ''30,000 persons."[78] It is against the backdrop of these anti-Muslim crusading sentiments that one of the clearest calls for a real—not imaginary or staged—holy war during the Jacobean period was made. Francis Bacon cannot be accused of harboring "romantic" views of a crusade; he was a man who knew King James well, had served him for over a decade, and was, at the time of initiating his call in 1622, in disgrace. Bacon was quite aware of how devastating the attacks of the North African corsairs on English and Scottish shipping had been. In 1617 he had drawn up a memorandum urging the use of the English fleet against the Algerian pirates. Later, as England entered into marriage negotiations with Spain, Bacon hoped that an Anglo-Spanish alliance could work well "to extinguish and extirpate pirates, which are the common enemies of mankind, and do so much infest Europe at this time."[79]

Whether it was because Bacon advised the move—he was involved in the planning of the campaign that was later launched—or whether it was a result of the trading companies' pressure, in 1621, King James initiated a naval attack on Algiers for the purpose of ending Muslim piracy, and regaining for the English fleet the seamen who had been captured and who were desperately needed at home. This campaign against Algiers was not viewed in England as a "holy war" but as a confrontation with an adversary who was destabilizing commercial activity in the Mediterranean. The accounts in the minutes of the Privy Council reveal no religious language and speak only of security needs. But the attack on Algiers was the only military campaign against the Muslims James I authorized during his whole reign, and it was the first time an English fleet entered the Muslim side of the Mediterranean with military intent.

The attack was unsuccessful and resulted in retaliation against English trading vessels by the corsairs. As Thomas Roe, the English ambassador in Istanbul, complained that year, "the estate of the poore merchant is most miserable, and, I will be bold to say, much the worse since our late unhappy and unperfect attempt; for they [Algerians] are enraged doggs, and protest a bloudy revenge upon our nation . . . no head-land, no place from Sicily as high as the North Cape free of them."[80] The failure of the campaign was embarrassing to the king, especially since many Englishmen suspected that the prime cause of the failure was the Spanish ambassador, Count Gondomar.[81] Soon after the Algiers fleet returned to England, therefore, a description of the campaign was published anonymously praising both seamen and king for confronting the Muslims. As in the pageants, in this propagandist account there was need for lying about a Christian-English victory over the Turks. While one accurate account of the campaign complained that the seamen "had feasted and banqueted in the harbour instead of scowering,"[82] the reader of the questionably official account was asked to imagine "the Canon playing, and Turkes by hundreds tumbling into the Seas, our owne stretching out hands to saue a miserable number of poore Christians made slaues to the barbarous Turke & crafty Moore, but deliuered from that seruitude by vs, God assisting our labours."[83] In this account, as in both drama and pageant, the conflict between Christianity and Islam, between honest Christian traders and infidel pirates, was at the heart of England's dealings with North Africa. It did not matter to the English reader that because the attack had been unsuccessful, the frustrated English seamen who had not plundered sufficiently later fell on a Christian French bark, and then on another ship carrying a Christian Dutch envoy traveling from Leghorn to Algiers—in short, that the English fleet had turned to piracy against fellow Christians. The description of the attack on Muslim Algiers was conveniently couched for the skeptical reader in the language of a religious victory over the infidel Moors.[84]

It was Francis Bacon who turned this "secular" military campaign against

Algiers into a holy war. Writing a little less than a year after the House of
Lords had sentenced him for accepting bribery, and hoping to ingratiate himself with the king through Lancelot Andrewes, "counsellor of Estate to His
Majesty"—who in 1599 had preached a sermon on the justness and lawfulness of war—Bacon composed "An Advertisement Touching An Holy
War."[85] The subject was not, as J. Max Patrick has stated, an "unlikely" one
to write about [86]; the attack on Algiers was still fresh in the peoples' and the
king's minds, and while the English were deeply anxious about relations with
Spain and the prospect of an English-Spanish marriage alliance, Bacon sought
to remind them that the true enemy of England and the rest of Christendom
was the "Turk." The "Advertisement" was not an attempt by Bacon to seduce
King James "with a fiction into a war of the Cross against the Crescent." It
was a vindication of the unsuccessful attack on Algiers on the ground that the
attack had been part of King James's holy war against the infidels. Bacon may
have recognized a role for himself in redeeming if not the outcome of the
expedition, at least its supposed ideals. The word "Advertisement" for Bacon
did not simply mean information and notice, but explanation (*O. E. D.*)—
explanation of the real purpose behind the unsuccessful attack. Bacon
wanted to explain the expedition as a holy episode; this would show the king
as an anti-Muslim leader, and divert people's attention from the negotiations
with Spain to the danger of the unholy Turks.

Bacon did not finish his treatise and therefore did not present a conclusion on the legitimacy or illegitimacy of "Holy War." But in the long speech
of Zebedaeus, the "Romish Catholic Zelant," he presented a justification of
holy war against the Muslims: "a war against the Turk is lawful, both by the
laws of nature and nations."[87] Significantly, as Zebedaeus was testing his theory of a holy war against specific examples, he mentioned war against the
Algerian pirates, "the pirates now being, have a receptacle and mansion in
Algiers."[88] For him, war against pirates was holy because pirates were "com-
munes humani generis hostes," and there was a "natural and tacit confedera-
tion amongst all men against the common enemy of human society." All
potentates should fight them, he continued, not only those who live adjacent
to them, but "any nation never so far off."[89] Although these references are
identifiable with England's recent attack on Algiers, Zebedaeus was careful

not to mention that attack openly. The attack had been a failure and could not compare with the three holy wars against the Muslims that Martius had earlier praised: Lepanto, the Portuguese attack by Sebastian, and the "incursions of Sigismund the Transylvanian prince."[90] Still, Zebedaeus succeeded in situating the attack on the pirates of Algiers within the context of these three battles against the Muslims—something that would have been deeply appreciated by his readers since the speaker was a Catholic "Zelant." Bacon put the praise of war against pirates in the mouth of an enemy of Protestantism to show that even Catholics admired the holy enterprise against the Muslims that England's king had launched. War for religious reasons, as the war against the Muslims was seen by him, was justifiable and "Holy."[91]

In his treatise Bacon urged the Protestants to wage a holy war against the Muslims in which they would either destroy the Muslims or convert them. In justifying this "holy war," it is quite likely that Bacon was deliberately echoing the same arguments that had been advanced to justify war against the Indians in America. In the treatise by Sir George Peckham previously mentioned, the argument had been forcefully made, and echoed by later colonists, that if the Indians resisted trade with the English or attacked them, they would violate "the mutual society and fellowship between man and man prescribed by the law of nations," and they should be punished. Bacon appealed to the same argument in emphasizing that war was holy against the "Turks" because they had violated the laws of humanity. Any attack on the English anywhere in the world, regardless of what the English were doing, was a crime against the law of nations. In the Mediterranean as in New England, the English were fighting a holy war in defense of God's English Zion.

English holy war zeal was fanned by the Turkish attack on Poland in 1621. Because the "whole face of Christendome" was "troubled," and because "soe many swords [were] drawne," declared a member of the Commons, it was "very inconvenient his Majesties should be sheathed."[92] Three years later, in 1624, Fairfax's translation of Tasso's *Jerusalem* was republished. In this edition the portrait of Godfrey faced the title page with the following words under it: "This is that Godfrey by whose valiant hand / God freed from Saracens, the Holie Land." There was also a dedication in which John Bill praised

Godfrey, who had redeemed "one countrey to the honour of Christ," and he expressed hope that the Crusaders' spirit would "in this latter age inflame all Christian Princes to the like designe, that the Theater of Mars might be erected in the gates of Hierusalem and Constantinople." Bill recalled the battle of Lepanto, and although he regretted that England had not taken part in it, he praised Charles I's father for his poem on that battle in which Don Juan had followed the "example of Godfrey."[93] Of further interest to Fairfax was that the Christian-Muslim encounter during the Crusades had not only had a historical meaning, but an allegorical one too. In "The Allegorie of the Poem" he explained that the Christian armies represented "Man," Godfrey was "Vnderstanding," Jerusalem was "Ciuill happinesse," and the "Turks" were the unsubdued passions. The Crusade for Fairfax was not only a historical or military episode; it represented the perennial conflict between the rational man and the barbarian, the civilized and the uncivilized, the Christian crusader and the Muslim infidel.[94]

While holy war was seen as a Muslim-Christian confrontation by the majority of English writers, other writers saw it as a Protestant-Catholic conflict. In the same year of Fairfax's translation, Alexander Leighton showed in *Speculum Belli Sacri: or the Looking glasse of the Holy War* (1624) that a holy war meant a confrontation with Catholic Spain and not with Islam. Two years earlier, it had been reported from Aleppo that there was talk of a French, English, Dutch, and Turkish alliance against Spain.[95] Clearly for some Britons, particularly those with strong anti-Catholic feelings, a war of religion could well be against the Catholic enemy of Anglicanism. In 1627, John Harrison, King Charles's representative in Morocco, described in biblical language the confrontation between English ships and the Spaniards: God "sent his angell beforhand to strike a terrour into their hearts, as he did in the daies of Josuah. Were there anie Josuahs in these our daies to fight the Lords battayles, which fayling, he will choose to himsellff foolish and weake things, vile and dispicable things, yea, things which are not to bring to naught things that are inclynning the hearts of the verie Moores and infidels to fulfill his will. I say this is the Lords doing."[96] Three years later, in October 1630, Harrison wrote to King Charles about a "Designe against Mamora in Barbary." Harrison urged the king to attack the Spanish outpost in North

Africa because the Spaniards were "the professed enemies both of our nation and religion," and because the king would receive assistance from the "Moores." Harrison added that should the king wage such a war against the Catholics, the Moors, who "affect . . . the English above all other nations" would join him and "turne from their lawe."[97] Charles would win the Muslim Moors over to Christianity if he fought against the Spanish Catholics. A war was holy even if it was directed against fellow—although false— Christians and succeeded in converting the Muslims to Christianity.

Despite this anti-Catholic stance, in the minds of Britons who were exposed to Muslim attacks, both at sea and on the mainland, the idea of a holy war continued to target Muslims. In a sermon given upon the return of an English captive from Algiers in 1628, the preacher Edmund Kellet recalled the glorious days of the medieval Crusades and expressed his hope that such wars would be waged again against the Muslims, not only those in North Africa, but those who still "occupied" Jerusalem: "There was one [in margin "Luther. vid. ub: supra] who sometime said. We might not wage warres against the Turkes, and that it was no Christian warrfare: Aliquid humanie passus est. He was a Man and so he spake. O might I liue to see the time when our Roberts, Godfreies, Baldwins would set foote in stirrop againe! and might I be one of the meanest Trumpettors in such an holy expedition."[98]

Along with such nostalgia for the Crusades there were concrete proposals for a new holy war against the Muslims. In 1633 Henry Marsh published *A New Survey of the Turkish Empire History and Government Compleated,* in which he turned to "The Interest of all the Princes in Christendom upon the accompt of Policy and Religion in a War with the Turk."[99] Marsh believed that the Turks were intent on establishing a "universal Monarchy" that included Europe. And since the laws and traditions of Europe were "enter-woven with Christian religion," the Turks would inevitably destroy Christendom. Marsh therefore delineated the advantages of a holy war, recalling Bacon's argument about the "earthly honour" that would result for Christians from this war, the unity that it would effect in Christendom, and the conversionist impact it would have on the defeated Muslims. A war against the Turks would also reduce the population in a Europe "now sur-feited with people."

Marsh turned then to the debate about whether religion legitimated war, whether there could be a war motivated and justified by the Christian God: "Object. But is it Lawful to make a War for Religion, to inforce that which should be perswaded, to make our Christian Saviour an Heathen Idol, in sacrificing the blood of men to him, and whilst we would let the world see we are Christians, to forget the rest of the world are men? Answ. We allow not War to plant Religion, though we allow Religion to make advantages, of war for its Plantation, beasts may till the ground, though men sow the seed."[100] The "beasts" that fought prepared the way for Christian "men" to improve the conditions of Muslim lands. Marsh appealed to the often repeated argument among Spaniards and Britons that in the case of an inferior people with an inferior political and social culture, Christians had the right, "a just cause," to conquer them, to change and impel them "to a better Government amongst them." With this ideology safely adopted, Marsh pushed the Ottoman Turks into this polarity. Ignoring, or ignorant of, the cultural and military history of Ottoman civilization, he declared that the Turks were "confessedly a rout and shole of people, so ignorant, and so barbarous that they are uncapable of government, their constitutions are so unnaturall as that of slaves governing freemen." It was therefore necessary that a war be launched against them in order to "reduce beasts to men." For Marsh, a holy war was not only to be religiously but rationally sanctioned; once the war was over and Islam— although not all the Muslims—destroyed, the Christian "principles of reason" would be sufficient to "perswade those men" (those who had survived and had been transformed from beasts) "to be Christians."[101]

In writing about a religious war Marsh was not reflecting on an imaginary scheme. For him, "Holy warre"[102] was a realizable prospect that needed preparation and organization. He thus turned to specify the number of men who would be drawn from England, France, Spain, Germany, Italy, and the "Northern Kingdomes." The war was to be a European Christian campaign that would be modeled on the medieval Crusade, and there was no doubt in Marsh's mind that the Christians would win because they had "experience" on their side. Not only were Christian soldiers "serviceable and valiant, not a heap of Barbarians,"[103] but their leaders and kings still possessed the strategy of attack on the Holy Land that had been used over half a millennium earlier. To impress on the reader the congruity between the First Crusade and the one he was proposing, Marsh presented a brief history of the Crusades, not only to remind his readers of what many of them had doubtlessly forgotten, but to assure them that the same itinerary Godfrey of Bulloigns had taken to the "Land of Promise" could still be used.[104] Marsh believed that by reminding Christians of the glory of their ancestors, they would become better and more motivated fighters.[105] The medieval "Holy War" could be duplicated in a seventeenth century war against the Muslims.

Marsh's text presented the most open and clear call for a holy war against the Muslims in the Caroline period. The war was to be launched against the Holy Land, which was inhabited by unholy people. The result would be a victory for Christ through the conversion or destruction of the Muslims. Marsh's ideal in 1633 was not different from that proclaimed by Pope Urban II over half a millennium earlier. Not only was the goal the same, but even the route the Christian armies were to take was the same. For Marsh, the war with Islam over the Holy Land had not ended. A year after Marsh's work appeared, circa 1634, a certain Nathaniel Knott, an Anglican minister, wrote a treatise on "Advise of a Sea-man touchinge the expidition intended against the Turkish Pirates," in which he, too, showed that the war had not ended. Knott was eager to see an improvement in the quality of English seamen, whose reputation had fallen in the "eastern partes"; he urged those preparing to join the expedition to "consider what enterprize thei haue in hand" because it was part of the "holy warrs . . . against these Infidells." He chided English seamen for not being like the "Hollanders" and the "Infidells" who endured "longe voyages." "If you will not learne of Christians," he exclaimed, "learne of Turkey."[106] The Muslims had to be fought for religious reasons, just as they had been fought during the holy wars of the Crusades. Meanwhile, there was much to learn from them in the art of warfare.

Talk about a holy war against Muslims continued in England in the 1630s, especially after the English attack on Salee in 1637. Although the attack was not described in the minutes of the Privy Council as a holy war against the Muslims, it was perceived as such by no less than the Moroccan king himself, whose faction Charles had supported. In a letter sent to King Charles I by way of his ambassador, al-Jaurar bin Abdallah, Mulay Mohammad Esheikh urged the king to support him in the future against Algeria and Tunisia "and other places (Dens and Receptacles for the Inhumane Villanies of those who abhor rule and Government)." The Moroccan king did not hesitate to use the language of religious war to describe what was to be a joint Christian-Muslim campaign against the Ottoman-held regencies. By launching the attack, he wrote, "we interrupt the Corruption of malignant Spirits of the World, [and] we shall glorifie the Great God, and perform a Duty, that will shine as glorious as the Sun and Moon . . . This Action I here willingly present to You, whose Piety and Vertues equal the Greatness of Your Power, that we who are Vicegerents to the Great and Mighty God, may hand in hand Triumph in the Glory which the Action presents unto us."[107] What is of particular interest in the letter is the view Mulay seems to have had of England. While he saw himself as a man of peace, he viewed the English as deeply involved in religious war. After all, "the Great Prophet CHRIST JESUS was the Lion of the Tribe of Judah, as well as the Lord and Giver of Peace, which may signifie unto You [Charles I], That He which is a Lover and Maintainer of Peace, must always appear with the terror of his Sword; and wading through Seas of Blood, must arrive to Tranquillity."[108] For Mulay, Charles's military design showed him to be a follower of Christ his Master. It is no wonder that in another letter the Moroccan praised King Charles in the highest Arabic rhetoric: "To the King who possesses, among the kings of the Nazarenes and the sects of Christians, a power of exalted authority, and an eminent position, firm in foundation, and enduring in office, the Sultan of the English, and Brittany, and England, and Scotland, and France, and Ireland and all their regions, quarters, capitals, and lands, the Sultan Carlos son of the great sultans who possess over the kings of their people a fame that is elevated and far-reaching in all the lands and for all times and ages."[109]

Despite this praise, King Charles did not send his troops to help the Moroccan king against Algeria and Tunisia. Meanwhile, in London the king was praised for the successful attack on Salee, and although the attack had been motivated by English commercial expediency, Edmund Waller described it in his poem "Of Salley" in quasi-religious terms. It seems that no conflict with Muslims could be far from a war between the God of the English Israelites and the Muslim Amalekites. After comparing the English expedition with classical heroic campaigns such as the ones led by Jason, Theseus, and Hero, Waller turned to the Old Testament and to Yahweh's war against his enemies:

> The Prophet once to cruel Agag said,
> As thy fierce sword has mothers childless made:
> So shall the sword make thine; and with that word
> He hew'd the man in peece with his sword:
> Just Charles like measure has return'd to these,
> Whose Pagan hands had stain'd the troubled Seas.[110]

For Waller, the war in which God's people defeated the infidels was between the Israelite/English and the "Pagan"/Muslim. Waller conveniently forgot that the English fleet had succeeded in battle only because it had been co-opted by the pro-imperial Saleans, who used the English—and the English were not unwilling to be used—for what were to be mutually beneficial political and trading goals.[111]

A year after the Salee expedition, the first of the Bishops' Wars broke out. It is significant that the war between the English monarchy and the Scottish Covenanters was seen in England, at least by Archbishop Laud, as a "holy war," and that it was he who gave the war that ecclesiastical title. The Anglican bishops had been driven out of Scotland, and an English victory, Laud hoped, would serve to reinstate those bishops in their sees and achieve victory for the truly holy Anglican Church.[112] Laud may also have viewed the conflict as holy because of the writings of Thomas Brightman, who had attacked the Church of England and "prophetically" identified the enemy for the emerging saints of Puritanism, and for the Ironsides, as a combination of the Anglican Laodicean Church, the Papal Anti-Christ, and the Turks. Both English and Scottish opponents of the king and the Book of Common Prayer were inspired by the writings of Brightman, and the "Protestant [Puritan] warrior," as Michael Walzer has commented, became "not very far from a crusading fanatic."[113] It is quite possible too, as Arlette Marie Zinck has suggested, that the numerous treatises on "psychomachy," which had been widely popular in England, changed the soul's "holy war" against Satan into a real war on the battlefield.[114]

As Thomas Fuller, prebendary of Sarum, surveyed the English religious and political horizon at the end of the 1630s, he could not have helped but see the rising tide of religious polarization in Britain and the imminent approach of Laud's "holy war" between the Anglican Church and its Presbyterian opponents. He also looked south and saw the continued attacks against English shipping and trade by "the Pirates of Tunis and Algier."[115] Like other observers of Ottoman policy, he knew that the sultan used these pirates to his own advantage. He supported them when it was expedient and denounced them when his Christian allies, on whom they preyed, "complain to him of the wrongs those searobbers have done them." The corsairs of these two regencies were quite active in the late 1630s; although England had signed a peace treaty with Morocco, it had remained at war with Algeria, Tunisia, and the less powerful Tripoli. In a country full of holy war emotions, the corsair attacks and the realization that the Muslims still possessed the Holy Land must have revived the anti-Muslim ideology. Whether against Muslims, Scottish Covenanters, or Laudian Anglicans, Britons were thinking of religious war.

It is in such a context that in 1639 Fuller published his history of the Crusades, including an assessment of the ideology of the Holy War. Fuller's work proved so popular that it went into numerous reprints. In the frontispiece Fuller bluntly refuted the Holy War: the "Holy Warre" that had been launched by the Papacy was a "counsel of men," not of God and therefore it came "to nought," as Fuller cited from Acts 5:38. The two figures at the top of the frontispiece represent a Christian and a Muslim potentate; both also represent the Christian/Catholic and the Islamic ideologies of religious war, and both are undermined by the words that surround them. In the case of the Christian, whose ethos should be, like that of Christ, suffering and humility, Fuller introduced the reprimand: "No crown of gold where Christ was crowned with thorns." No Christian should seek military glory or worldly power in the land where Jesus died. In the case of Saladin, the words also emphasize the futility of his war: "This black shirt is all Saladine conqueror of the East hath to his Grave." Where Fuller derived this reference to the black shirt is unclear, unless he was confusing it with the famous shirt of the third Caliph Othman, but it is clear that for the Muslim leader too, there was no glory in war.

In "A declaration of the Frontispice" Fuller explained the "Page" (of the frontispiece) in rhymed verses. The armies of the Crusaders left rich ("We went out full") and those who returned did so poor ("But return empty"). They had gone out in great numbers, of kings, prelates, friars, warriors, ladies, infants, and invalids "collected out of Hospitals / And Spittles," but returned few after being struck down by the three destroyers: the Angel of God, the "grand Signor," and human frailty, "th' Anatomie." Fuller recognized the religious sincerity of the Crusaders and sang the praises of the "prelates":

> Since all their mild perswasions could not work
> Upon th' obdurate Antichristian Turk,
> They will at length (if nought prevent their plot)
> Confute his Alcoran with sword and shot.

Despite the strength of their Christian commitment, the holy warriors had ended in grief and misery, and most disastrously, in national poverty: "the poore Purse is emptie of relief." For Fuller, the Crusades had been noble in intention but devastating in consequence—not for the infidels but for the Christians.

This emphasis on the financial and human disaster of a war, any war, even a war with religious legitimacy, constituted the theme of the rest of Fuller's treatise. Fuller gave a lengthy and detailed account of the Crusades, but his Crusades were not the heroic wars of Tasso; rather, with his critical eye, he described the violence committed by both the Muslims and the Christians. For a man of Fuller's irenical sensitivity, war was horrible because it produced unjustifiable violence. That is why, at the beginning of the treatise, in chapter nine, he introduced a discussion of the theory of religious war entitled "Arguments for the lawfulnesse of the Holy war." In the next, "Reasons against the Holy warre," he presented his views on the illegitimacy of such a war. First and foremost, he stated, there was no holy land to fight for; since the expulsion of the Jews, Palestine was no longer "Gods land by any peculiar appropriation."[116] And since the Saracens and the Turks had been in Palestine for the past five centuries, he concluded, God obviously must have approved their presence, "so long peaceably to enjoy it." That is why there could never be a holy war to recover Jerusalem: "We may safely conclude, that the regaining of Jerusalem and the Holy land from the Turks, may better be placed amongst our desires then our hopes; as improbable ever to come to passe: except the Platonick yeare, turning the wheel of all actions round about, bring the spoke of this Holy warre back again."[117] Fuller further rejected as papistically "superstitious" the argument that Christians needed the Holy Land in order to go on pilgrimages and, in chapter 11 he expounded on what he saw as the real motives of the Holy War: "The private ends and profits of the Pope, which he is charged by authors to have had in this Holy Warre." Although he did not reject the principle of fighting the infidels, he viewed the Crusades as having been motivated more by greed than God: "Yet must we not here forget, that such as at this time went to Jerusalem (whether ridiculously or blasphemously, or both, let others judge) did carry a goose before them, pretending it to be the holy Ghost."[118]

With an eye toward the approaching wars in England and Scotland, wars that were holy both in the view of the Anglicans and the Presbyterians, Fuller sought to warn his compatriots of the folly of military theology. He was also well aware of the ongoing religious war on the Continent between Catholics and Protestants. Fuller therefore condemned Catholicism's Crusades against the Muslims because he was apprehensive that its ideology was already being proclaimed against opposing Christian factions, from London pulpits to Edinburgh kirks. In this respect he sought to undermine the theoretical justifications of holy war, including the Crusades, because he wanted to undermine such a justification at home.[119] Although Fuller wrote to refute the holy war ideology of medieval Catholicism, he did so precisely at the beginning of what religious zealots viewed as the impending holy wars of Britain. Both as a theologian and a historian, Fuller condemned the medieval Crusades and the theoretical justification of holy war that was being revived among his compatriots.

Although Fuller's denunciation of the anti-Muslim Catholic crusade should have sealed the fate of any future calls in England for a holy war against the Muslims, writers still found the idea attractive. In 1645, Edmund

Waller called for a crusade against the Muslims in order to "wrest" the Holy Land. Putting his hope in Charles I and "Gallia's Dauphin," he invoked them to "discharge these wars" against the Turks and emulate the Crusader heroes of medieval romance, "Young Rinaldo and Tancredo." Why Waller should have thought that King Charles would be interested in an anti-Muslim crusade at a time when Civil War was already underway in England is not clear. Waller, however, was adamant about holy war: in another poem written "To His Worthy Friend, Sir Thos. Higgons," he used some of the same verses from the previously cited poem, hoping that Christians would "discharge these wars" against the Turks to "wrest/ From Pagan hands, and triumph o'er the East."[120] Again it is unclear why Sir Thomas was being invoked to regain the holy land. Perhaps the repetition signified not only Waller's lack of poetical inventiveness, but also the fact that the call for a holy war was a stock image in England.

In 1645, as the Ottoman armies besieged Crete, a treatise was published in England about the "Blasphemous Manifestation of the Grand Seignior of Constantinople, against the Christians; of his entrance into Christendome, and the Particulars of his Great ARMIE."[121] The treatise described the preparations of Mediterranean Christian armies against the Muslims, and although the author/translator did not allude to a holy war, his anti-Islamic tone was clearly intended to remind his English readers that the war going on in Europe and the Mediterranean was between Christ and the "Turkes." A similar reminder of the religious conflict appeared in the "Caveat" that Alexander Ross added to his translation of the Qur'an in 1649. Explaining why he had undertaken the translation of a blasphemous book, he wrote that the origins "and the grounds of this war" between Christians and Muslims could be found only in the "Alcoran." Only by reading the text would Christians fully realize that the "Mahometans" were implacable "enemies of the Cross of Christ," and therefore that "Christian Princes" were "bound to oppose the enemies thereof." For Ross, the translation of the Qur'an was part of the war of the Cross against the Crescent; the Islamic text clearly showed Christians that the conflict between themselves and the Muslims was nothing if not religious.[122]

In 1655, Sir Richard Fanshawe published his translation of *The Lusiads*,

which, after Tasso's, is one of the most anti-Muslim epics in the national literature of Renaissance Europe. In it Camoes had lambasted the English for
failing to sustain their crusading ideals. It is not unlikely that Fanshawe, an
ardent royalist, was pleased to have an opportunity to attack Cromwell as a
false "Monarch" who was more involved in inter-Christian fighting than in
fighting the Muslims out of the Holy Land:

> See England's Monarch, styling himself yit
> For deeds long past KING of the HOLY TOWNE,
> The filthy ISMAELITE POSSESSING IT
> (What a reproaching Title to a CROWNE!),
> How in his frozen Confines he doth sit,
> Feeding on empty smoake of old Renown;
> Or gets him new, on Christian Foes alone,
> Not by recov'ring what was once his own![123]

Nine years later, soon after the fall of Crete to the Ottomans following a long
siege, a poem was published in London in which the Muslims were compared with the Papists. The author opened *Rome for the Great TURKE* with a
quotation from the book of Kings in which the war between "Juda" and
"Assyria" was described. He called on all Christians, Britons included, to join
against the Turks/Assyrians and bring Constantinople back to the Christian
fold.[124]

   In spite of these calls for Christian war against the Muslims, by the middle of the seventeenth century an all-out war against the Ottomans and their
satellites was looking very improbable to Britons. Appeals to Christian soli-
darity were no longer as resounding as they might have been a century earlier: "Christendom" had given way to European national boundaries and
interests, and while English poets and theologians may have lamented the
loss of a unified and peaceful (imaginary) Christendom, as Thomas Traherne
and Henry More did,[125] politicians were oblivious to such an outmoded
goal. Meanwhile, the language and the justification of war were changing in
England, as can be seen in the difference in tone and imagery between the
letters and journals of Robert Blake and Sir Thomas Allin. While Blake, who
served under Cromwell, prefaced his military strategy and initiatives with

"(the Lord willing)," and frequently interjected divine assurances and hopes, Allin, who served under Charles II, had no place for godly invocation and intervention. [126] The idea of a war that was holy was giving way to a war that was part of realpolitik. It is no wonder that when John Bunyan published his treatise on *The Holy War, made by Shaddai upon Diabolus, for the regaining of the metropolis of the World* in 1682, he portrayed the holy war not as a conflict between Muslims and Christians, but between sin and the soul. [127] Holy war had become a metaphor that no longer recalled the anti-Muslim crusade. Why Bunyan called his war-in-the-soul a "holy war," thereby recalling the Christian-Muslim polarization, is not difficult to find: in Fairfax's introduction to his translation of Tasso, the holy war between the Christians and the Muslims had been described in terms of a war inside the soul of man. Bunyan had adopted Fairfax's psychology but had discarded the military history behind the poem on which Fairfax was commenting. For Bunyan, holy war was against sin in the same way that for Fairfax it was against sin as embodied by the Turks.

* * *

Curiously, as the language of holy war declined in England it flourished in New England, where writers clamored for a war against the "Mahometans" in which Jesus would serve as general to the Christian soldiers and bring about victory over the infidels. Such anti-Muslim zeal may have been inspired by anxiety over the possibility that "Turks" had actually landed in America—that the Atlantic had not completely protected the colonists from their Muslim nemesis. On 5 August 1636, it was reported that "the French and Turks have surprised all the English in New England." [128] Did the "Turks" really reach North America, perhaps as pirates cooperating with French pirates? Unfortunately, there is no further clarification of the statement. Another interesting statement appears in John Josselyn's account of *Two Voyages to New England*. In June 1660, he wrote, "a damnable cheat like to have been put upon England by a brief for New-England, which as it appeared was produced before the King came in, but not printed (by Mr. Leach in Shoe-Lane) till June, pretending that 18 Turks-men of War the 24 January 1659/60 landed at a Town, called Kingsword (alluding to Charles-town) three miles from Boston, kill'd 40, took Mr. Sims minister prisoner, wounded him, kil-l'd his wife and three of his little children, carried him away with 57 more, burnt the Town, carried them to Argier, their loss amounting to 12000 pound, the Turk demanding 8000 pound ransom to be paid within 7 mon-eths. Signed by Thomas Margets, Edward Calamy, William Jenkin, William Vincent, George Wild, Joseph Caryl, John Menord, William Cooper, Thomas Manton Ministers."[129] Although it is not clear whether the "Cheat" was about Muslims or not, it is sufficient that "Turks" were believed by the writer and other colonists to be within reach of America. The terror of the Turks, if not the Turks themselves, had crossed the ocean.

Such terror, associated with anti-Muslim biblical imagery, resulted in holy war declamations. In 1651, Edward Johnson assured the churches that the times were ripe for war since "Christs wrath is kindled, who can stand before/His anger." He then called on the saints to "Destroy his [Mohammad's] seed 'mongst Persians, Turkes and Moores" in order to "ope the Prison doors" for the "poor Christians" who had been conquered by the "brood of Mahumetts."[130] Writing at a time when there was anxiety in New England about the fate of the colonies and their colonists, one way in which Johnson tried to revive his readers' divine errand into the wilderness was to remind them of their universal mission; as they continued in their Christ-led and just wars against the heathen Indians, they still had to fight the infidel Turks. Zion was not only in America, but in the Holy Land. Zion was the kingdom of God on all of the earth, an earth cleansed of Indians, Papists, and Mahometans in a way that is godly and holy. Similarly, Samuel Sewall wrote in his diary in January of 1686 about a sermon he had heard in which the preacher "Spake of the inverted Rainbow, God shooting at sombody. And that our Times better than the former, and expected better still, Turks going down, a sign on't."[131] Later in the century Cotton Mather prayed for the destruction of the Turks on the same page that he invoked God to "procure speedy and wondrous Rebukes . . . upon our Indian Salvages."[132] In New England the war of God against the Indians was still underway and so, he hoped, was the war against the Muslims. The holy war was still in progress in both "Canaan" and the "New Canaan."

* * *

The Age of Discovery was also the age of holy war. As some English writers praised the holy war against the Indians in America, others revived the idea against the Muslims. Much as the Age of Discovery was an age of innovation and exploration, of defining and mapping new worlds, it still contained within it a medieval core that consisted of a warring and exclusionary God whose chief concern in the world was to oversee the holy destruction of the Indians and, it was hoped by English writers on both sides of the Atlantic, the destruction of the Muslims too.

BRITONS, MUSLIMS, AND THE SHADOW
OF THE AMERICAN INDIANS

When Joseph Pitts was captured by Algerian pirates in 1678, his first fear was that they might eat him: "I being but Young the Enemy seem'd to me as monstrous ravenous Creatures, which made me cry out, O Master! I am afraid they will kill us, and eat us."[1] In the mind of this terrified youth from Exeter, the "Moors" and the "cannibals" had become interchangeable in savagery and violence. Pitts' reference to Muslim cannibalism, however, is curious in that it had never appeared before in anti-Muslim writings. Rather, it had appeared in Muslim anti-Christian invective during the Crusades when Christian *taffurs,* as the Muslims called them, ate the bodies of the Saracens. Meanwhile, from the beginning of the conquest of America, cannibalism had been associated with the Indians. For Pitts, the literature he had read or the stories he had heard about the Indians had now come to define the Muslims. North Africa, sub-Saharan Africa, and North America were all the territory of the cannibalistic and savage Other. It is no wonder that when Thomas Phelps, a captive in Morocco in the 1680s, tried to describe the savagery of the Moroccan ruler Mulay Ismail, he could find no analogy more suitable than that of the American Indians: "I have been several times in the West-Indies, and have seen and heard of divers Inhumanities and cruelties practised there . . . but indeed I forget them all, they are not to be named in comparison with this Monster of Africk."[2]

By the end of the seventeenth century the Muslim "savage" and the Indian "savage" became completely superimposable in English thought and ideology. But it was only in the eighteenth century that this superimposition was transferred into the colonial discourse; in that century a colonial discourse against Islam in the full sense of the term evolved. After over two centuries of conquering, dominating, and enslaving Americans and sub-Saharan Africans, Britons found that their discourse of empire had become fully articulated and fully transferable anywhere in the world. They had begun to conceive of a new imperial world order to be ruled by Britannia. And in this new order the Mediterranean was ready for Britannic domination.

This transferability of discourses can be traced in the works of Daniel Defoe. In 1728, about a hundred years after the beginning of the Great Migration to America, Defoe reflected on the history of English commerce and the prospects for its future. He was deeply satisfied by the extent of British trade when he viewed the vast territories that were colonized by his compatriots or serviced by their merchant ships. Defoe, however, was aware of competition, and hoped that England would expand its markets by integrating the natives of many parts of the world into the commercial cycle. For, he noted, while the Portuguese and the Spaniards had made the native populations of South America and Africa "subservient to Trade as well as to Government," England had failed to do so in her American colonies, and had not integrated the native populations into the commercial and political infrastructure. Rather, Britons had developed an ideology of excluding natives and relying completely on themselves both as producers and consumers. They had failed to create markets among the native populations, although the natives offered an "Ocean of Commerce" that would reward both exploration and exploitation.[3]

Aside from this failure the only thorn in Defoe's English side was that of the "Turks or Moors of Tunis, Tripoli, Algier, and Sallee." These Muslims were delaying and sometimes threatening the fulfillment of Defoe's imperial dreams of trade by attacking British ships in the Mediterranean and the Atlantic. And for Defoe there could be no evil greater than a people who were not eager to pursue trade. For him the world was divided between nations who traded and nations who did not—the two "cities" of modern capitalism. As he reflected on the North African states that did not trade he recalled Carthage, which had been a great trading city, and lamented that it had been overrun by the non-trading Vandals, and then "some Ages after them the Saracens, Arabians, and Mahomitans, came in over the Heads of the Vandals."[4] The Muslims in North Africa inherited the legacy not of commercially enterprising Carthage, but of the pillaging Vandals. And that, to Defoe, was an unforgivable flaw in their character: "These Mahometans, as I have said of the Turks, have very little Inclination to Trade, they have no Gust to it, no Taste of it, or of the Advantages of it; but dwelling on the Sea-coast, and being a rapacious, cruel, violent, and tyrannical People, void of all Industry or Application, neglecting all Culture and Improvement, it made them Thieves and Robbers, as naturally as Idleness makes Beggars: They disdain'd all Industry and Labour."[5] For Defoe, the Muslims were indolent nontraders, and the only way to confront them was for France, England, Spain, and Holland to unite their forces and "fall upon them [North African Moors] in separate Bodies, and in several Places at the same Time."[6] Just as a century before, the apologists for the colonization of America had advocated a "falling upon" the Indians, Defoe advocated attacking the North Africans for the same commercial and imperialist reasons.

This way of resolving the conflict with North Africa was not, of course, new. Over a century earlier, Sir Francis Bacon, Sir Thomas Roe, and others had hoped for a similar united European front against the Barbary Corsairs. That hoped-for unity never materialized. Now, however, after centuries of European colonization, Defoe was certain about how the conflict with the Barbary states would be conducted; it was not going to be simply a battle or a war in which the enemy would be defeated and subdued. Rather, it was to be a reenactment of the American experience of conquest and colonization. The Muslim "natives" were to be pushed southward—as the American Indians had been pushed westward—emptying the land, whereupon "Multitudes of [European] People would be encouraged by the Advantages of the Place, to go over and settle upon it." The "Barbarians" would be removed from the "Cities and Provinces of Algier, Tunis, Tripoli & c."—note the etcetera—so that the cities would be "peopled with a new Nation, or new Nations made rich by Commerce." Such an act of ethnic cleansing would surely, concluded Defoe, "bring more Glory to the Christian Name."[7]

Defoe's call for the colonization of Muslim territory was not motivated by Christian zeal despite his repeated allusions to Christianity. At no point in the text did Defoe mention the hope of converting the Moors by such an invasion, even if mentioning it were to be, as it had been with other imperialists, a camouflage for conquest. Rather, Defoe's was a studied call for domination and possession based on market needs, not on God's will—on greed, not religion. Defoe's proposal is important because it marks the transition of the conflict between Christian Europe and Muslim North Africa and the Levant from the religious to the commercial, from a holy war to a trade war, from battle to invasion. It further demonstrates how the model of the conquest of the American Indians was continuing to inspire British imagination and ideology.

The conquest of America had set the pace for the conquest of the rest of the world. Just as the English and other Europeans had conquered America by displacing and annihilating its "idle" and "sodomitical" population of Indians, they were also to conquer the non-trading and lascivious Moors and Turks. Given that the Moors and the Indians and the other ethnic groups all appeared the same to the enterprising Briton—they were either consumers or natives to be dominated or removed—there was no obstacle to duplicating and triplicating the American process elsewhere. The world was ready to be refashioned by Britain.

* * *

Defoe reveals how British ideology against the American Indians was superimposed on the Muslims. In the same way that the Indians had been "removed" and their lands repeopled by new nations, North Africa, too, was to be repeopled and divided into "several and separate Allotments of Territory upon the Coast, and in the Country adjacent."[8] In advocating this goal, Defoe confirmed the British rather than the Spanish model for dealing with the Indian/Muslim Other. Throughout the fifteenth- and sixteenth-century conquests the Spaniards had tried, and succeeded, in Christianizing and hispanicizing the conquered, whether by force or by conviction, whether Moors in reconquered Iberia or native Americans. The Spaniards sought to integrate rather than to exclude. Britons, on the other hand, did not try to anglicize the colonized. Although there were missionaries who wanted to Christianize the American Indians, the overwhelming attitude of the colonists was simply to ostracize them—even the converted and anglicized ones. For the colonists, particularly in New England, the Indians were not only culturally inferior, but racially too; their skin color doomed them to "evil" Otherness.[9] And this is exactly the attitude that developed in England and Scotland toward Muslims in the early modern period. Britons simply did not want to be near the "Turks," even if they were converts to Christianity. As Indians, relegated to praying villages in northeastern America, were mocked and ostracized, so would the Muslims.

Consistent with Britain's ideology to want land rather than people, the desire to possess more than to proselytize is reflected in the account that was published at the end of the eighteenth century. In 1797 the first autobiographical account by a Muslim convert to Christianity in England was published. The Muslim was Ishmael Bashaw, a Turk, who had settled in England and fallen into such poverty that he dictated his life story so it could be published and sold: "Printed for the Benefit of I. Bashaw and his Family, and sold by him" (title page). This was the first English text describing a Muslim's experience in England in the Muslim's own voice—or at least as close to his own voice and sentiment as was possible.[10] Bashaw had been born in Constantinople in 1735, had been married, had been lustful and brutal in his youth—as the English readers expected Muslims to be—had joined a merchant ship that was captured by Spanish pirates, had been imprisoned and had escaped, and then had hidden in the house of the English Consul in Lisbon for three years, after which he fled to England. In London, still dressed in his Turkish clothes and turban, he "met with much abuse from the common people, carters, porters, & c. some of whom pulled me by my whiskers, and others threw me down."[11] He was attacked and robbed, after which he left the metropolis and started wandering from village to village, living on the roads, sleeping on "butchers' shambles,"[12] sometimes receiving money from church collections that were made for him, and at other times simply enduring abuse and disgrace. He could not speak English and communicated only with those who spoke French or Italian, one of whom was the duke of Buccleugh at Durkeith, in Scotland. The duke preached Christianity to him in French and Latin, whereupon Bashaw was convinced of the truth of Christianity and the falsehood of "Mahometanism" and asked to be baptized. But the duke refused and "advised me to exercise patience."[13] Upon leaving the duke Bashaw met again with thieves who robbed him and "abused me as a Turk."[14] To be a Turk in England or Scotland, he discovered, was to be an object of Christian ridicule, persecution, and violence.

In Richmond, Yorkshire, Bashaw met a woman named Elizabeth Formes, fell in love with her—conversing with her in Spanish—and married her. How a Muslim could marry a Christian without being converted and baptized is not explained, but, strangely, Bashaw, who always described the difficulties he encountered, did not seem to have faced any problem marrying a Christian in church. The Edinburgh minister who performed the ceremony tried to dissuade the woman from such a marriage, not for religious or theological reasons, but for cultural ones. He alerted her to the different treatment women received in Turkey. Again, it is interesting that no theological argument was presented by the minister against the marriage between a Muslim man and a British Christian woman.

After the marriage the couple wandered from place to place, sometimes eking out a living, at other times, relying on the charity and kindness of people, especially the Quakers. Bashaw meanwhile was pleading to be baptized, but as one minister in Norwich retorted to him: " 'Do you think I will baptize a Turk who cannot say the Lord's prayer?"[15] Christianity, for the minister, was a religion of and for the English. Later in Lynn, Bashaw met with similar refusal: "I applied for Christian baptism, but was refused on account of the trouble of preparing me for it."[16] Six weeks later he met with another refusal. No Briton would accept a turban-wearing, non-English-speaking "Turk" in the Christian fold; Christianity had linguistic, cultural, and national requirements, which Bashaw did not meet.

In his despair, while in the village of Spalding, in Lincolnshire, Bashaw went to a church. The congregation gazed at him in surprise, and when he sat down the sexton approached and "offered to take off my turban, which I refused."[17] Bashaw soon realized that he was in the right place, for the minister was the first to agree to baptize him. And in order for him to learn the

"Lord's prayer, the creed, and the ten commandments," the minister gave
him a "book containing instructions to the Indians"[18]; Christianizing a
Muslim was the same as Christianizing an Indian. As the minister looked at
the "Turk," he could think only of the heathen Indians. And as the Indians had
been baptized after reading the book, so would this "infidel." The fact that
Bashaw, as a Muslim, was a monotheist while the Indians were pagans, did
not seem to make any difference to the zealous minister.

The baptism of Bashaw entailed the same cultural and personal changes
that were required in the baptism of Indians. Just as Pocahontas had had to
become English in her apparel, habits, and looks, so did Bashaw. He was told
that he could not be baptized with his whiskers, so the bishop conducting the
baptism turned barber and clipped them. He then removed Bashaw's Turkish
clothing and brought him new ones. "Now Ishmael," the bishop said, "you
look like an Englishman and a Christian."[19] He then gave him the English
name James, just as Pocahontas had been given an English name. To become
a Christian was to become English in looks, name, clothing, and religious
belief. Unfortunately, Bashaw's becoming English did not lead either to reliable work or to a home; with his wife by his side he continued to wander
from city to city, having and burying children as they went along so frequently that he had to sell his story in order to sustain himself, his wife, and
their single surviving child out of ten. Neither conversion nor anglicization
could effect his integration into the Christian society of England or Scotland.
Bashaw was an Other, defeated, impoverished, and alterized. He was in the
same situation as the straggling American Indians who entered New England
towns, sometimes to be beaten, sometimes pitied, and always to be viewed
as outsiders.[20]

* * *

It is an interesting coincidence that in the same decade Bashaw published his
account about the Muslim-as-Indian, another similar account was published
in the United States. American writers had generally shown little interest in
Islam or Muslims, except in the context of theological polemics or allusions
to captives among the North African corsairs.[21] If they were aware of
Muslims at all, they were aware of them as yet another nonwhite race from

whom whites should be segregated. In 1693, the House of Burgesses in Virginia declared "Negroes, Moores Molattoes, & Indians Slaues," and in 1705 the law stated that no "Negroes Mulattos, or Indians, although Christians, or Jews, Moors, Mahametans, or other Infidels shall, at any Time, purchase any Christian Servant, nor any other, except of their own Complexion."[22] By the end of the eighteenth century, however, United States merchants had begun trading in the Mediterranean, and many American sailors were captured by North African corsairs and kept for ransom. Indeed from 1775 on, hundreds of sailors and merchants were captured and enslaved in Algiers.[23]

Completely unfamiliar with the civilization of Islam, laymen and politicians immediately realized the need for information about the sociological and anthropological conditions of North African slavery; they feared that more Americans might be captured in the future. Congress felt a particular sense of responsibility, and therefore when one John Foss published a hasty account of his captivity around 1796 , Congress urged him to prepare a second edition in which he would elaborate on the religious and cultural environment of North Africa and correct inaccuracies that had appeared in his earlier account. Foss complied and in 1798 he published his *Journal of the captivity and sufferings of John Foss; several years a prisoner at Algiers; together with some account of the treatment of Christian slaves when sick: and observations on the manners and customs of the Algerines. 2nd ed. Pub. according to act of Congress.* This was the first detailed account of a captivity among the Muslims to be published in America.[24] As with the English captivity accounts, this account was intended to provide information about the Muslims and their strange new world—new at least to the Americans.

In line with the wishes of Congress, Foss emphasized that his text was for the "utility" of Americans: "should, at any future period, from causes not seen, more Americans be doomed to wear the galling chain . . . a knowledge of the habits, manners, and customs of the place, may not be unserviceable" (Preface). To make the text useful, Foss realized that he had to situate it within a society whose construction was already familiar to the American reader. And no better society presented itself to Foss than that of the American Indians, who had been amply described in scores of captivity accounts over the previous two centuries. The image of the savage Indian would define and legitimate the image of the Muslim. For Foss, the account would not be "serviceable" unless he used the criteria of the Indian captivity genre with which his audience was familiar. In the same manner that Defoe had superimposed models of colonization, Foss superimposed models of captivity. In both cases, one model explained two peoples.

Such superimposition was possible because it was being controlled by the White Man, who was not daunted by cultural complexity; he could simplify and translate everything that belonged to "natives." If Foss was aware of the early English and European writings about America, where the Moors had been superimposed on the Indians, he may have felt justified in his own superimposition. He was simply explaining the Muslims by situating them in the familiar context of the American Indians. [25] Inevitably, such clarification of the Muslims, based on the representation of the Indians in a literary genre that derived from half a globe away from Algiers, led Foss to confuse the differences between the Indian and the Muslim worlds. By confusing the differences between the two environments of captivity, Foss produced a *Journal* that represented the Muslims in the same hostile and disdainful manner as late eighteenth-century narratives of Indian captivity represented the Indians.

By the time Foss wrote his account, the Indian captivity narrative, which had passed through various phases in its development toward a genre, no longer served religious puritan goals as it had in the late seventeenth and early eighteenth centuries; rather, as Roy Harvey Pearce has shown, this narrative represented a "vehicle of Indian-hatred." [26] The narrative elaborated on Indian horrors and physical outrages to show the "savagery" of the captor, and to solicit pity for the authors, many of whom used for that purpose a sensationally excessive and rhetorical style. The narratives reflected the contemporary American ethos that was against accommodating the Indians and very much in favor of "cleaning up the wilderness." The accounts therefore proved instrumental in invigorating the emergent nationalism of late eighteenth-century America.

Foss followed this criterion faithfully, and like the Indian captivity accounts of the late eighteenth century, his *Journal* excluded theological allusions; there was not in the whole account a single reference to the New Testament or to Christ. For Foss, the three-year ordeal of captivity had no religious relevance. This indifference to religion did not, however, prevent Foss from advancing a strong anti-Muslim invective. Just as the Indian captivity account served to foment anti-Indian hatred, Foss used his own account to generate anti-Muslim sentiment. He made the analogy quite clear: the Moors of North Africa were similar to the Indians of North America in skin color and stature. The Americans, however, were similar to the Turks in being "well built robust people, their complexion not unlike Americans."[27] The reason for the latter superimposition was that the Turks were the rulers of North Africa—they were conquerors of the native Moors. But then Foss added that the dress of the Turks makes them "appear more like monsters than human beings." There were no humans among the Muslims. Either there were monster-like Turks, or Indian-like Moors.

To confirm this image of the "barbarians"—a term that would henceforth be used repeatedly in American accounts of captivity among the Muslims—[28] Foss described in great detail the cruelty of the Muslims to the slaves, and elaborated on the various kinds of punishment that were meted out in North Africa. As in the numerous accounts that described Indian cruelty and torture,[29] Foss was graphic in his description of "oriental" horror. He described the "bastinadoe," and spent pages distinguishing between the numerous methods of execution and reflecting on the brutality of pain the "Algerines" inflicted: "But for murder of a Mahometan he [the perpetrator] is cast off from the walls of the city, upon iron hooks, which are fastened into the wall about half way down. These catch by any part of the body that happens to strike them, and sometimes they hang in this manner in the most exquisite agonies for several days together before they expire."[30] Further evidence of Muslim cruelty and heartlessness was derived from episodes about slaves who were crushed under the rocks they were moving. Foss also recorded the story of a "blackman belonging to New-York," who died the same day he left the hospital because the man's master had taken him out before he had fully recovered.[31] The Muslims were ruthless.

Finally, Foss tried to show that Muslims had no historical legitimacy in North Africa—an argument similar to one used since the seventeenth century to legitimate a holy war against them. Similarly, other American writers in the late eighteenth and throughout the nineteenth century claimed that there was a manifest destiny that upheld their right to the American Zion, a right that necessitated the destruction of the Indian "usurpers." Foss used a similar argument, although he did not apply to Algiers the biblical model of the promised land; North Africa was and had been the land of the great civilizations of Carthage and of Rome. Under those civilizations the land had "abounded with many populous cities, and to have residence here was considered as the highest state of luxury."[32] Muslims had violently replaced the Carthaginians and the Romans—who had become the Christians of North Africa, according to Foss—and as usurpers, had devastated the land. What greatness in "science" and "wisdom" that once prevailed among the Arabs no longer remained. Foss lamented the loss of Carthage and Rome to those "merciless Barbarians, whose very breath seems to dry up every thing noble, great or good."[33] Just as the barbarity of the Indians had justified their conquest, the barbarity of the North Africans also justified their conquest and destruction. Only after they were expelled would the old glory be reinstituted. Only with their annihilation would the Euro-American civilization of the classical world reassume its rightful land.

This argument by Foss is similar to American arguments against the Indians. A contrast between a sordid present and a glorious past, whether of Zion or Rome, resulted in the illegitimization of the present, whether of Indians or of Muslims, and the aspiration toward a glorious future by the chosen and the American. In both cases, the present was without legitimacy because it was either a usurpation of the past or a hindrance to the future. Foss was emphasizing here that North Africa in the past was different from the world of cruel and strange "Mahometans" of his day, and very different from the world of the Americans. That is why he showed in his description not what the Muslims had, but what they lacked, since what they lacked was precisely what Americans had and what made Americans the measure of civilization. The world of the Muslims was different from the world of the Americans, and therefore, like the world of the Indians, alien, undesirable, and ultimately expendable.

A unique literary genre in American writing about the Indians defined the

Muslims. The *Journal*, which served future Americans in understanding North African Islam, confirmed a construction of Islam that drew on a literary narrative completely alien to the environment it purported to portray. It confirmed that just as the Indian—who had been a danger in the past—was Other because of his "violence" and primitiveness, the Muslim—who was a danger of the present and the future—was Other in his violence and "Mahometanism." The first document in American writing about a Muslim captivity described the Muslims through an Indian-hating American lens.

* * *

The triangle was then complete. As John Smith had viewed the Indians through the lens of his Muslim/Turkish antipathy, John Foss viewed the Muslims through the lens of Indian antipathy. And as the lands of the North American Indians had been "allotted" to the French, the English, and the Spanish, the lands of the Muslims were to be allotted, as Defoe hoped, to "new [European] Nations."

Exactly a century after the second edition of *A Plan of the English Commerce* was published, in 1830, France invaded, de-peopled, and dominated Algiers and turned it into a satellite in its empire of trade and power. Defoe's prophecy of empire was fulfilled; the conquest of the Middle East had begun.

APPENDIX A

ENGLISH CAPTIVITY ACCOUNTS, 1577–1704

Unless otherwise indicated, the place of publication is London.

1. 1563–1577: *The worthie enterprise of Iohn Fox an Englishman in deliuering 266. Christians out of the captiuitie of the Turkes at Alexandria, the 3. of Ianuarie 1577* (in Hakluyt, *Principal Navigations*, 1589, pp. 150–153).

2. 1583. Thomas Sanders, *The voyage made to Tripolis in Barbarie, in the yeere 1583. with a ship called the Iesus, wherein the aduentures and distresses of some Englishmen are truely reported, and other necessary circumstances obserued* (in Hakluyt, *Principal Navigations*, 1599, 2:184–191).

3. Edward Webbe, *The Rare and Most Wonderfvll Things which Edward Webbe an Englishman borne, hath seene and passed in his troublesome trauailes, in the cities of Ierusalem, Damasko, Bethlem and Galely: and in the lands of Jewrie, Egypt, Grecia, Russia, and Prester Iohn* (1590).

4. 1593. Richard Hasleton, *Strange and Wonderfvll Things. Happened to R. Hasleton, borne at Braintree in Essex, In his ten yeares trauailes in many forraine countries* (1595).

5. 1593. Richard Johnson et al., *The casting away of the Tobie neere Cape Espartel corruptly called Cape Sprat without the Straight of Gibralter on the coast of Barbarie. 1593* (in Hakluyt, *Principal Navigations*, 1599, 1: 201–203).

6. c. 1604. *The True Travels, Adventvres, and Observations of Captaine Iohn Smith, In Europe, Asia, Affrica, and America, from Anno Domini 1593. to 1629* (1630).

7. Anthony Munday, *The Admirable Deliverance of 266. Christians by Iohn Reynard Englishman from the captiuitie of the Turkes, who had beene Gally slaues*

many yeares in Alexandria (1608).

8. 1610—1612. Henry Middleton, *The sixth Voyage, set forth by the East-Indian Company in three Shippes; the Trades Increase, of one thousand Tunnes, and in her the Generall Sir HENRY MIDDLETON, Admirall; the Pepper-Corne of two hundred and fiftie, Vice-Admirall, the Captaine NICHOLAS DOVNTON: and the Darling of ninetie. The Barke Samuel Followed as a Victualler of burthen one hundred and eightie: written by Sir H. MIDDLETON* (in Purchas, *Purchas his Pilgrimes*, 1625, pp. 247—266).

9. 1622. John Rawlins, *The Famovs and Wonderfvll Recoverie of a Ship of Bristoll, called the Exchange, from the Turkish Pirates of ARGIER* (1622).

10. c. 1628. James Wadsworth, *The English Spanish Pilgrime. Or a New Discoverie of Spanish Popery, and Iesviticall Stratagems* (1629), chapter 5.

11. 1631—1638. Francis Knight, *A Relation of Seaven yeares Slaverie vnder the Turkes of Argeire, suffered by an English Captive Merchant* (1640).

12. Devereux Spratt, "The Capture of a Protestant Divine, by an Algerine Corsair, in the Seventeenth Century" (in T. A. B. Spratt, *Travels and Researches in Crete*. Amsterdam: Adolf M. Hakkert, 1984. First publ. in 1865. 1: 384—387).

13. 1642. *Newes from Sally: of a Strange Delivery of Foure English Captives from the slavery of the Turkes* (1642).

14. c. 1639—1644. William Okeley. *Eben-Ezer: or, A Small Monument of Great Mercy, Appearing in the Miraculous Deliverance of William Okeley . . . from the Miserable Slavery of Algiers* (1676).

15. c. 1648. T. S. *The Adventures of (Mr. T. S.) an English Merchant, Taken Prisoner by the Turks of Argiers, and carried into the Inland Countries of Africa* (1670).

16. c. 1655. Abraham Browne, "A Book of Remembrance of God's Provydences towards me, A. B., throughout the cours of my Life, written for my own medytacon in New Engl." The captivity account appears as a selection in T. Riley, "Abraham Browne's Captivity by the Barbary Pirates," *Seafaring in Colonial Massachusetts*. Boston: The Colonial Society of Massachusetts, 1980, pp. 31—42.

17. c. 1657—58. Edward Coxere, *Adventures by Sea of Edward Coxere*, ed. by E. H. W. Meyerstein. Oxford: Clarendon Press, 1946.

18. c. 1670. Adam Elliot, "A Narrative of my Travails, Captivity and Escape

from Salle, in the Kingdom of Fez," in A *Modest Vindication of Titus Oates the Salamanca-Doctor from Perjury* (1682).

19. 1680–87. Joshua Gee, *Narrative of Joshua Gee of Boston, Mass.* (Hartford, 1943).

20. Thomas Phelps, A *True Account of the Captivity of Thomas Phelps, at Machaness in Barbary* (1685).

21. c. 1681–92. Francis Brooks, *Barbarian Cruelty. Being A True History of the Distresed Condition of the Christian Captives under the Tyranny of Mully Ishamel Emperor of Morocco, and King of Fez and Macqueness in Barbary.* (1693).

22. cc. 1678–1690s. Joseph Pitts, *A True and Faithful Account of the Religion and Manners of the Mahommetans in which is a particular Relation of their Pilgrimage to Mecca* (1704).

The Journey of the First Levantine to America: Being the Wandering of the Priest Ilyas son of the Cleric Hanna al-Mawsuli from the Ammoon al-Kildani family: 1668–1683.[*]

Edited by Fr. Antoon Rabbat al-Yasooi'i
(Beirut: Catholic Press, 1906).

The journal of Hanna al-Mawsuli constitutes the first account of Spanish America to be written in Arabic. Although the account, *Rihla*, was not published until the beginning of the twentieth century, and therefore had no influence on Arabic thought, it provides an important perspective on the "Levantine" view of America and of the Spanish and American Indian populations in the early modern period.

The writer was a Syriac Catholic priest who belonged to an oriental church that was Uniate with the Papacy. His church retained its Syriac liturgy and language, but was ecclesiastically administered from Rome. This link with Rome is crucial as it helps explain not only the familiarity al-Mawsuli showed with Christian European writings about America, but his adoption of the European discourse in those writings. Despite the difference

[*] All translations from Arabic are mine. The numbers in brackets refer to the Arabic edition.

in liturgy, background, language, and history between himself and Rome, al-Mawsuli used the European discourse as the lens through which to view the New World.

From the very outset al-Mawsuli confirmed that the native populations of America were "savage" and not "different from animals."They worshipped "Satan" or trees or wild animals, and offered sacrifices to the "cursed devil"(p. 2). Not surprisingly, these observations repeated the views that appeared in the Spanish texts about America by Pedro di Candia and D'Acosta, which al-Mawsuli had read, and some of which he had translated into Arabic. Al-Mawsuli adopted without reflection the anti-Indian position of the conquerors. Furthermore, the term he used for America was again the Spanish term, *India of the West,(Hind al-gharb),* or simply *India (al-Hind)*; the term had been used at the end of the sixteenth century by the Moroccan historian al-Fishtali, while in the early seventeenth century, the term *al-Hunood al Maghribiyya* had been used by the Morisco writer Ahmad bin Qasim. [1] Such usage confirms that the Arabic was a direct translation from the Spanish and that the Arabs derived their nomenclature for America from the Europeans. Curiously, neither in al-Fishtali nor in al-Mawsuli does the name "America" appear. Also from the Spanish/European sources was the racial categorization al-Mawsuli used for the American Indians—"red"—which appears both as an adjective and as a noun: "The red came out and shouted" (p. 19). Not unlike other visitors to America, al-Mawsuli saw what he had read.

Al-Mawsuli was very conscious of himself as a Uniate Christian from the Ottoman Empire. After arriving in Paris he had to stay in the city for eight months because the messenger from Sultan Mohammad, who was visiting the French King in August of 1669, needed him to act as a translator from French into Arabic andTurkish. Later in Syracuse, he mentioned his servant, who was a "Roman Catholic" (ruumi) from Aleppo (p. 10). He was sensitive about the difference between the Catholic and the Syriac Church—a sensitivity that has continued into the twentieth century. Throughout his journey in America, al-Mawsuli celebrated mass in Syriac and distributed rosaries and crucifixes from Jerusalem, much to the devout joy of the Spanish congregation and clergy. Meanwhile, he was thrilled at the Spaniards' wonderment at his different clothes and long beard—the Syriac clergy do not trim

their beards. People often sought his benediction and were eager to participate in a Syriac mass (pp. 30, 34). Al-Mawsuli also practiced oriental medicine, and after successfully curing patients with frog powder he recalled how
the people had eagerly tried to keep him permanently among them (p. 50).
When he reconciled the governor of Provincial with the Dominican abbot,
he recalled how the latter praised God and said, "Here is a priest who came
from the city of Baghdad to reconcile us" (p. 62).

Al-Mawsuli recognized himself as a cultural stranger in the land of the
Indians and the Spaniards, but he was assured of his place there because of
his allegiance to the same church to which the Spaniards belonged. America,
for him, was a Christian land. The proof of this was that he met with many
miracles there that were performed chiefly but not exclusively by the Virgin
Mary (pp. 14, 25, 43, 46), whom he described on one occasion as "a-sitt al-
isbanyuliyya"—the Spanish lady (p. 65). That Mary, whose city of Nazareth
al-Mawsuli had visited early on in his *Rihla*, was a Spanish lady demonstrates
the power and awe with which he viewed Spanish/Catholic Christianity. For
him, the imperial hegemony of Spain in America could only have been
assisted by a Spanish, not a Jewish or a Levantine Mother of God. It is no
wonder that America was suffused with Catholic miracles, and no wonder
that, as a Uniate with the Catholics, he was eager to enjoy the legitimacy to
wander in Spanish America and to study its people and geography, just like
any other Catholic. Christianity was empowerment.

This Christianity was repeatedly confirmed as Catholic and therefore
anti-Protestant. In his introduction to the *Rihla*, al-Mawsuli explained that it
was apropos of the rebellion of some Christians against the Roman Church
that Jesus compensated for the loss of the heretics by inviting into His church
peoples of different races and traditions. During his journey he repeatedly
met and therefore mentioned those "heretics." From Iskandaroon to Europe,
he used an English ship to transport him (p. 4), and in Caracas, he learned,
the Indians sold nutmeg to the English and the Dutch, but not to the
Spaniards (p. 26). Having realized that the heretics were both in the
Mediterranean and in the Atlantic, al-Mawsuli started to share in the anxiety
that fellow Catholics felt at the growing presence of Protestants in "their"
part of the world.

In spite of his religious and polemical identification with the Catholics of the New World, al-Mawsuli never forgot that he was a Levantine and therefore frequently compared and contrasted what he saw among the Indians with his native society and land—in the same way Spanish and English writers did. The fish he saw in the river Colan resembled the fish in the Tigris (p. 29); when he saw the raging sea, he recalled a description he had read in the *Thousand and OneNights* (p. 20). Later he compared the desolate and waterless path he traveled to the "land of Egypt" (p. 30). In Buenos Aires there was a medicinal drink that was as popular as "coffee in our country" (p. 51). In Misque the Indians used horses and spears like "the Arabs" (p. 52). As he looked at the Indians al-Mawsuli relied on both his Western readings and his Levantine geography. He could not help but sometimes be reminded of the Mediterranean world of Islam. At one point he met a priest who had been captured by Algerian pirates while returning from the West Indies to Spain (p. 63). When he realized that in the southern hemisphere it rained between May and September, he observed that this was different from "the habits and weather of our country" (p. 66). Most interestingly, however, in this Mediterranean-American cross referencing is al-Mawsuli's use of the word *futuh* to describe the Spanish conquest of America—the word that in Arabic describes the early Muslim conquests of the Levant, North Africa, and central Asia (p. 52). Was al-Mawsuli favorably comparing the spread of Islam in the Middle East with the spread of Christianity in America?

With regard to the American Indians al-Mawsuli had very little to say at the beginning of his account, except to repeat the Spanish epithets about their heathenism and devil worship. He was confused and perhaps even afraid; after all, he had steeped himself in the anti-Indian discourse of European texts. That is why he repeatedly added the adjective *kafara* (infidels) when describing Indians, recalling the term *heathen,* which was always applied to them in European writings. For al-Mawsuli, however, the term must have had an especially negative connotation—it was the same term the Ottoman Turks often pejoratively and derisively applied to Christians. Perhaps in a kind of unconscious vindictiveness, al-Mawsuli used the same epithet for the Indians that the Ottomans used for the Christians: just as he and other Christians had been denigrated as *kafara,* he would denigrate the

Indians as *kafara* too. Perhaps he felt he could do unto others what others had done unto him.

As he progressed in his text, however, al-Mawsuli began to provide some accurate, albeit brief, descriptions of the Indians. At one point he mentioned how the Indians did not want the Spaniards to discover their use of "darseen" for fear that the Spaniards would attack them and "take their country" (p. 26). At another point he observed that some Indians were real Christians while others were Christians "out of fear" (p. 30). But al-Mawsuli was no Las Casas—actually he seemed not to have read him. Although he described Spanish violence against the Indians, he did not commiserate with them, but seemed to position himself firmly on the Spanish side. The Spaniards fought the Indians, killed hundreds of them, and the survivors were to be taught Christianity. That, to al-Mawsuli, seemed to be the Catholic God's design for the Indians. Whatever he wrote about the Indians, therefore, reflected their infidelity and their savagery. Before the Spaniards "took possession of the country," he noted, the Indians did not know the true God (p. 33). During "the time of their infidelity," the Indians buried their dead above ground (p. 40); "infidel" Indians worshipped the "red mountain" (p. 44). On one occasion he had an Indian tortured because the Indian would not speak to him in Spanish. After the Indian was brutally whipped he spoke Spanish, and when al-Mawsuli asked him why he had resisted using Spanish the man answered: "We Indians do not obey the Spaniards if they do not beat us" (p. 47). When later he arrived in Potosi, where silver had been extracted with devastating results to the Indians, al-Mawsuli had no comment to make except to describe in detail the intricate process of production (pp. 47–49).

But the more al-Mawsuli traveled in America, the more he softened toward the Indians, especially after an Indian boy saved his life by alerting him to a plot on his life by a "mestico" (p. 28). Later, when an Indian priest told him there were seven Indian men in jail who were innocent, he went down and released them (p. 45). When he asked an Indian why he had not divulged his knowledge about a silver mine, the Indian answered: "I have seen Indians before me who informed the Spaniards and then died under torture. That is the reason. I believed his words regarding the tyranny which I saw them inflict on the Indians" (p. 53). But al-Mawsuli never went beyond such a statement to condemn the Spanish treatment of the natives; much as he may have sympathized with individual cases of injustice and pain, he remained committed to the Christian ideology that had made possible the conquest of America and the journey he had undertaken.

* * *

It is unfortunate that although al-Mawsuli came from the Middle East, he did not have a distinct or truly individual view of America or the American Indians. It is also unfortunate that he was not a more compassionate priest or was not more original in his perspective; after all he did belong to a unique community within Christendom. His description reflects Spanish views and shows how ignorant the Arab and Ottoman East was about the India of the West. While al-Mawsuli cited Spanish writers, he did not cite a single work about the New World by Levantine Christians or Muslims. Obviously, none existed. [2] That is why al-Mawsuli translated material from Spanish into Arabic and wrote down the account of his journey, thereby providing the first material in Arabic about the New World.

Looked on in a wider context, however, this document sheds some light on the dissemination of anti-Indian sentiment in countries and among communities that had no interaction with America. The Spaniards and their Catholic institution developed racist views of the "reds" to justify their conquest. Racism was necessary for empire and therefore, in the world of realpolitik, serviceable and indispensable. But as the texts that had explained and justified conquest spread from among the Spaniards to other peoples—in this case the Arabs—these texts introduced a hostile and demeaning view of the Indians to groups who had nothing to do with Spain's imperial goals. Al-Mawsuli had no reason to develop a negative attitude toward the Indians simply because he was not part of the conquering race; yet he did. Had his text been published it would have disseminated a hostile view of the Indians to his seventeenth-century Arabic-speaking audience. This transferability of discourses is yet another bane of imperialism: not only do imperialists denigrate and alterize "natives," but they establish the definition that is adopted and propagated about the "natives." In this case, the Arabic-speaking al-Mawusli learned from Spaniards to denigrate Indians in the same way Indians learned to denigrate the African slaves, Africans the mulattos, and mulattos the mesticos. Each group learned from the imperialist the language of racial and ethnic polarization, or as Caliban put it, they learned how "to curse"— not the conqueror but the conquered.

APPENDIX C

AHMAD BIN QASIM ON SODOMY

Ahmad bin Qasim al-Hajari al-Andalusi, *Nasir al-Deen 'ala Qawm al-Kafireen*: pp. 50–52.

One day, I read in the front page of his [a man in Paris whom bin Qasim had met] copy of the Qur'an, written in Frankish, the following words: "Based on this, the Muslims condone sodomy." I asked him: "Who told you that it is condoned among us?" He answered that it was apparent in this verse: "Women are your fields: go, then, into your fields whence you please" (Cow : 223).*

I said: "For us, sodomy is a worse sin than adultery, for if a married man commits adultery, he is stoned unto death; and if he is unmarried, he is given a hundred lashes and is driven out of his country and is jailed for a year. But if a man commits the act of Lot's people, whether he is married or unmarried, by religious law, he is stoned to death. How do you presume to interpret the Qur'an while those who interpret it require knowledge in numerous disciplines, and you know neither the Arabic language nor its grammar, nor other things?"

So I said to him: "Erase what you have written." But he refused to erase what he had written on the book. He had mentioned that in a certain church there were Arabic books. So I told him: "I like to read them." So we walked and found a big cupola, and found chairs and books lined on the shelves.

*The translation is by N. J. Dawood, *The Koran* (Penguin Books, 1990).

Every book was tied by two iron rings and an iron chain passed through all the books. All this was done so that the books would neither be lost nor stolen. And the books were in every language.

We searched until we found an Arabic book and we opened to read it. We came across the place where there was a commentary on the verse that had been written on the front page of his book, "Women are your fields." I had not intended the verse, but God had guided me in His might to prove what I had said to the Christian. The information in the commentary about the verse included a few lines of poetry, so I took a pencil, and I wrote, the Christian being present, a few lines of verse, which were later improved for me by the learned sheikh al-Ajhouri:

Virtuous women are for breeding and for confirming religion.

God gives virtuous women to whomever He chooses,

But their wombs are our fields to plow;

We plant, and God nurtures.

The Christian said: "What have you written"? I answered: "Some commentary on the verse which you had written on the front page about condoning intercourse from the rear." I told him the meaning of the poem in his language. And then I said to him the words of God almighty, "Women are your fields." He said: "Yes." I said to him: "Have you seen or heard of anyone who plants his seed in stone"? He said: "No." I said: "Nobody plants his seed except in the place of planting and seeding, and women are the planting place for men, just like plants, whether she was facing the man or turning her back to him." Then he took his pencil and erased what he had written in . . . . [blank] the verse. The sheikh al-Ajhouri reported about our Seyyid Malek [bin Anas, a jurist] that some credited to him that he had condoned sexual intercourse from the rear, so he told them: "What uncouth bedouins you are! Can you plant seeds other than in a place of planting"?

As for this heinous deed [sodomy], it is widespread among Muslims so much so that the Christian imagined that it was condoned in our religion, because it is so widespread and because it is not punished. It has been said that some keep boys specifically for this purpose, and they do not remember that it is forbidden in the religion of Islam and that God almighty grew so angry because of this deed that he destroyed four cities with all the people in them.

NOTES

INTRODUCTION

1. I say this notwithstanding the work of James Shapiro, *Shakepeare and the Jews*, and the review, "An English Obsession," by Stephen Greenblatt, *The New York Times Book Review*, 11 August 1996, pp. 12–13.

2. For the number of Jews in Elizabethan and Jacobean England see E. R. Samuel, "Portuguese Jews in Jacobean London," *Jewish Historical Society of England—Transactions*, 18 (1953–1955): 171–187; Theodore K. Rabb, "The Stirrings of the 1590s and the Return of the Jews to England," ibid., 26 (1974–1978): 26–33; Lewis S. Feuer, "Francis Bacon and the Jews: Who was the Jew in the *New Atlantis?*" ibid., 29 (1982–1986): 1–25. See also chapter 1 in David S. Katz, *Philo-Semitism and the Readmission of the Jews to England, 1603–1655*.

3. See the account by James Rosier, *A Trve Relation of the most prosperous voyage made this present yeere 1605, by Captaine George Waymouth*, C4r-Dr.

4. For accounts of the Indians who came (or were brought) to England, see Carl Bridenbaugh *Jamestown 1544–1699*, chapter 3; Carolyn Thomas Foreman, *Indians Abroad 1493–1938*, chapter 1; Lee, "The American Indian in Elizabethan England," in *Elizabethan and Other Essays*, Boas, ed., pp. 263–302; Cawley, *The Voyagers*, pp. 357 ff. For Indians in English drama, *ibid*, pp. 359 ff. and Loren E. Pennington, "The Amerindian in English promotional literature 1575–1625," in *The Westward Enterprise*, K. R. Andrews et al., eds., pp. 175–194.

5. Ahmad Gunny has dealt with writers who traveled into central Asia and the subcontinent in *Images of Islam in Eighteenth-Century Writings*, esp. chapters 1 and 7. See also Sir Denis Wright, *The English amongst the Persians*, and my introduction in *Islam in Britain*, pp. 2–4.

6. Parker, *Books to Build an Empire*, p. 131. See also the dedication to Sir Robert Cecil in the second volume of *Navigations* (1599), where Hakluyt describes how the English have traveled "into the Leuant within the Streight of Gibraltar, & from thence ouer land to the South and Southeast Parts of the world."

7. Suraiya Faroqhi, *Pilgrims and Sultans: The Hajj under the Ottomans*, p. 16.

8. G. K. Hunter, "Elizabethans and Foreigners," p. 52. See Hall, *Things of Darkness*, p. 11 and Hall's description of the "blackmoors" (sub-Saharan Africans) in late Elizabethan England, "Guess Who's Coming to Dinner? Colonization and Miscegenation in *The Merchant of Venice*," *Renaissance Drama*, n. s. (1992): 87–111. In his discussion of race, Kwame Anthony Appiah stated that in Shakespeare's England, the Moors "were barely an empirical reality." "Race," in *Critical Terms for Literary Study*, p. 277.

9. Harris, "A Portrait of a Moor," pp. 89–97; Eldred Jones, *Othello's Countrymen*: pp. 12 ff.; Jack D'Amico, *The Moor in English Renaissance Drama*, chapter 1. Emily C. Bartels mentioned in her article, "Imperialist Beginnings: Richard Hakluyt and the Construction of Africa," that during "the Elizabethan period, too, Moors appeared prominently at court as ambassadors and diplomats," p. 528.

10. Hall, *Things of Darkness*. Only once did she allude to the encounter with Barbary, p. 17. Jack D. Forbes, in *Africans and Native Americans*, also drew little distinction between North Africans and sub-Saharans, pp. 54–56. The earlier studies by Jordan, *White over Black*, and Tokson *The Popular Image of the Black Man*, failed to distinguish between the two geographical communities.

11. *Purchas his Pilgrimage* (1617 ed.), p. 276; see also John Brereton: "if it were as farre and dangerous as the Moores trade is from Fess and Marocco (ouer the burning and moueable sands, in which they perish many times, and suffer commonly great distresses) unto the riuer called Niger in Africa, and from thence, up the said river manie hundred miles; afterwards ouer-land againe, unto the riuer Nilus," *A Briefe and true Relation of the Discouerie of the North part of Virginia*, p. 23.

12. For a discussion of these terms, see the introduction in Barthelemy, *Black Face, Maligned Race* and in D'Amico, *The Moor in English Renaissance Drama*.

13. Jonathan Haynes, *The Humanist as Traveler*, pp. 119–121; Emily C. Bartels, *Spectacles of Strangeness: Imperialism, Alienation and Marlowe*, p. 59 and "Making More of the Moor: Aaron, Othello, and Renaissance Refashionings of Race," *Shakespeare Quarterly*, 41 (1990): 433–454; Relihan, "Suppressing Islam: The Geography of Sidney's Arcadian Landscape," a paper read at the MLA Conference, Chicago, December 1995; Virginia Mason Vaughan, *Othello: A Contextual History*, p. 14; Jean E. Howard, "An English Lass amid the Moors: Gender, race, sexuality, and national identity in Heywood's 'The Fair Maid of the West'," in *Women, "Race," and Writing in the Early Modern Period*, Margo Hendricks and Patricia Parker, eds. pp. 101–117, especially the last page; Karen Newman, " 'And wash the Ethiop white': Femininity and the Monstrous in *Othello*," in *Shakespeare Reproduced*, Jean E. Howard and Marion O'Connor, eds. p. 150. Although Jack D'Amico focused in his study on the literary representation of the Moor, he also alluded to England's "budding colonialism" and "expanding colonial empire," *The Moor in English Renaissance Drama*, pp. 61–62.

14. E. S. Bates, *Touring in 1600*, p. 189. See also my *Islam in Britain*, pp. 11–14 and the

discussion against supposed English imperialism (with specific reference to *The Tempest*) in Meredith Anne Skura, "Discourse and the Individual: The Case of Colonialism in *The Tempest*," *Shakespeare Quarterly*, 40 (1989): 42–69; Leo Salingar, "The New World in *The Tempest*," in *Travel and Drama in Shakespeare's Time*, Jean-Pierre Maquerlot and Michèle Willems, eds., pp. 209–223. The works of Mary C. Fuller and Jeffrey Knapp are also important in this context.

15. *A Dialogue of Comfort* in *The Complete Works of St. Thomas More*, Martz and Manley, eds., "The third boke," pp. 188 ff.

16. R. Carr, *The Mahumetane or Turkish Historie*, p. 111 v.

17. See my *Islam in Britain*, pp. 40–45.

18. Dahiru Yahya, *Morocco in the Sixteenth Century*, p. 187. Chapter 8 is very informative about English-Moroccan relations.

19. De Castries, *Les Sources inédites de l'histoire du Maroc . . . d'Angleterre*, 2:208. See also Bovill, *The Battle of Alcazar*, chapter 17.

20. De Castries, *Les Sources inédites de l'histoire du Maroc . . . d'Angleterre*, 2:222 ff.

21. Ibid., 3:129.

22. Ibid., 3:165.

23. A. N. Porter, ed., *Atlas of British Overseas Expansion*, pp. 5–22. In this period, England also came into possession of Barbados (claimed in 1605, occupied in 1624), Bermuda (1609–1615), half of St. Kitts (1623–25); it made "some feeble pretence" at occupying Nova Scotia (Innes, *The Maritime and Colonial Expansion*, p. 123), and colonized New Providence but only for a short period.

24. Eburne, *A Plain Pathway to Plantations*, pp. 65–67.

25. *The Letters and the Life of Francis Bacon*, Spedding et al., eds., 13:176–181. For an excellent survey of the impact of the Barbary Corsairs on England, see Hebb, *Piracy and the English Government*. Some earlier studies include R. L. Playfair, *The Scourge of Christendom*; Samuel C. Chew, *The Crescent and the Rose*, units I and II; G. N. Clark, "Barbary Corsairs in the Seventeenth Century," *Cambridge Historical Journal*, 8 (1945- 1946): 22–35; Sir Godfrey Fisher, *Barbary Legend*; Peter Earle, *Corsairs of Malta and Barbary*, chapters 1–4; Stephen Clissold, *The Barbary Slaves*.

26. *By the Protector. A Proclamation Giving Encouragement to such as shall transplant themselves to Jamaica* (October 1655).

27. David B. Quinn, "New Geographical Horizons: Literature," in *Explorers and Colonies*, pp. 86–89 especially. See also the study of English (and other European) colonial "ceremonies of possesion" in Patricia Seed, *Ceremonies of Possession in Europe's Conquest of the New World*.

28. See David B. Quinn's analysis of the term *colonization* in "Renaissance Influences in English Colonization," *Explorers and Colonies*, pp. 97–118.

29. Richard Beacon, *Solon his Follie*, p. 140.

30. See the introduction in Felsenstein, *Anti-Semitic Stereotypes* for an analysis of the term *stereotype*.

31. See chapter 4 in Barthelemy, *Black Face, Maligned Race* for a discussion of the racism in these plays.

32. See the discussion of *Othello* by Daniel Vitkus: "Turning Turk in *Othello* : The Conversion and Damnation of the Moor," *Shakespeare Quarterly* , 48 (1997): 145–177.

33. Tokson, *The Popular Image of the Black Man*, p. x.

34. Ibid., p. 138.

35. See chapter 5 in my *Islam in Britain*.

36. Hodgen, *Early Anthropology in the Sixteenth and Seventeenth Centuries*, p. 28.

37. W. R. Jones, "The Image of the Barbarian in Medieval Europe," *Comparative Studies in Society and History*, 13 (1971): 376–407. See also chapter 2 in Pagden, *The fall of natural man*.

38. See the valuable discussion on the link between barbarity and domination in Lotfi Ben Rejeb, "Barbary's 'Character' in European Letters, 1514–1830: An Ideological Prelude to Colonization," *Dialectical Anthropology*, 6 (1982): 345–355.

39. See the discussion of this "superiority" in Jeffrey Knapp, *An Empire Nowhere: England, America, and Literature from Utopia to The Tempest*, and the critique in Fuller, *Voyages in Print*, chapter 3.

40. Chantal de la Véronne, *Tanger sous l'occupation anglaise d'après une description anonyme de 1674*, p. 27. It is significant that the English had viewed Tangier as a "colonial" outpost. It was the only place in the Muslim world to which they had sent men accompanied by their wives and children, and the only place whose geography they had tried to anglicize, imposing names such as Cambridge, Whitehall, York, and Charles Fort.

41. Al-Wufrani, *Nuzhat al-Hadi*, p. 309: Mulay Ismail "sent his armies and they surrounded [Tangier] and all the Christians who were there until they got in their ships and fled by sea, leaving it empty." The translation is my own.

1. TURKS AND MOORS IN ENGLAND

1. See Appendix VIII in M. Epstein, *The Early History of the Levant Company*, where English merchants explained to Queen Elizabeth the benefits of their trade with the Turks and therefore justified their dealings with them.

2. Hakluyt, *Navigations*, 5:170. This was confirmed a year later in "The charter of the privileges granted to the English, & the league of the great Turke with the Queenes majestie in respect of traffique, dated in June 2580," *Navigations*, 5:178–189.

3. Ibid., 5:177.

4. From the report sent to Rudolf II in March 1579, quoted in Susan Skilliter, *William Harborne* , p. 63.

5. *Calendar of Scottish Papers, 1589–1593*, 10:404. *Calendar of Scottish Papers, 1597–1603*, 13:532.

6. *The Portable Hakluyt's Voyages*, Blacker, ed., p. 516.

7. See *The Fugger News-Letter, Second Series*, Klarwill, ed., 11 September 1588: "A hundred Turks and Moors who had been at the oars in a Spanish galleass were here recently. Our King had caused them to be brought here with an archer from Calais at his own expense and sent them from here to Marseilles by water. From there they sail at the King's expense to Constantinople," p. 176.

8. *C. S. P, Domestic, Elizabeth, 1591*, 3:109.

9. In 1587, Sir Francis Drake's account included the following payment: "For a charge of the Turk, lighterage, and other charges paid by Alderman Martyn by the Commissioners' warrant," *Papers Relating to the Navy*, ed. Corbett, p. 95. In February 1589, "News that Gondy's Moor, who was [brought to] England by Drake, attacked d'[Omal] in Paris because he took away Gondy's horse, which the Moor had in his charge. 'D'Omal was armed, and so had no great harm. . . . The poor Moor is drawn with four horse.'" *C. S. P. , Foreign Series, Elizabeth, January–July 1589*, 23:90.

10. Matthews, ed., *News and Rumor in Renaissance Europe (The Fugger Newsletters)*, pp. 220–221.

11. See Meredith Hanmer, *The Baptizing of a Turke*. For a study of Chinano, see chapter 4 in my *Islam in Britain* and the article by Quinn, "Turks, Moors, Blacks," in *Explorers and Colonies*; Robert Burton, *The Anatomy of Melancholy*, part 3, section 4, p. 330.

12. *Acts of the Privy Council, 1597–1598*, 28:408: "forasmuch as there ar fewe of late yeres taken by the turke and that at this present divers poore marryners that ar come over hither out of Spaine, whereof som have bin in the gallies, others have bin cruelly and barbourously racked and most of them have indured great missery, wee have bin moved with compassion of their poore estates to recomend them to your Lordship [Mayor of London], that of the collection that shalbe gathered at the Spitle sermons there maie somethinge be reserved to be distributed emongst them to releive their necessityes and to send them home into their contries." De Castries, *Les Sources . . . d'Angleterre*, 2:220.

13. John Manningham, *The Diary of John Manningham of the Middle Temple, 1602–1603*, p. 150.

14. *Letters from George Lord Carew*, p. 125.

15. *Acts of the Privy Council, July 1621–May 1623*, pp. 329, 467.

16. Ibid, *June 1630–June 1631*, p. 257

17. *Mercurius Fumigosus*, June 28–July 5.

18. John Evelyn, *The Diary De Beer, ed.*, 3: 197. See also the following extract from John Cotgrave's, *Wits Interpreter* (1655, 2nd ed., 1662), pp. 322–325 for the whole poem: "A Wight there is come out of the East, / A mortal of great fame; / He looks like a man, for he is not a beast, / Yet he has never a Christian name: / Some say he's a Turk, some call him a Jew, / For ten that believe him, / scarce one tels true, / Let him be what he will, 'tis all one to you; / But yet he shall be a Turk."

19. Thomas Warmstry, *The Baptized Turk, or a Narrative of the Happy Conversion of Signior Rigep Dandulo*, pp. 18–19.

20. *C. S. P. Domestic Commonwealth, 1656–1657*, 10:289.

21. S. P. 18/182/ f. 193.

22. S. P. 18/182/f. 194.

23. *C. S. P. Domestic, Charles II, 1669*, 9:163.

24. "Hamett Clavecho and Braham MacKaden, imployed as Commissioners to his Majestie from Sally," in *The Acts of the Privy Council of England, 1628 July–1629 April*, p. 311.

25. *C. S. P. Domestic, Charles I, 1635*, 8:533.

26. De Castries, *Les Sources . . . d'Angleterre*, 3:176.

27. Ibid., 3:332.

28. *C. S. P. Domestic, Commonwealth, 1655*, 8:365.

29. *C. S. P. Domestic, Commonwealth, 1657–58*, 11:309. Such articles continued to appear in treaties well into the eighteenth century. See the treaty of 1721 cited by John Windus, article XII, which stipulated that the "Subjects of the King of Fez and Morocco shall be suffered to transport out of the Dominions of the King of Great Britain, any sort of Goods whatsoever, to the Dominions of the said King of Fez and Morocco," in John Windus, *A Journey to Mequinez*, p. 246.

30. Hakluyt, *Navigations*, 5:279.

31. *C. S. P. Domestic, William III, 1 January–31 December 1697*, pp. 2, 24.

32. Ibid., pp. 63, 98.

33. *C. S. P. and Manuscripts . . . Venice, 1619–1621*, 16:486; John Rawlins, *The Famous and Wonderful Recovery of a Ship of Bristol*, in Firth, ed., *An English Garner*, pp. 274, 272.

34. De Castries, *Les Sources . . . d'Angleterre*, 2:526.

35. S. P. 14/183/ff. 51 and 51 I. All subsequent quotations in the paragraph are from these two documents.

36. *Acts of the Privy Council of England, 1625–1626*, p. 31.

37. S. P. 16/30/f. 37. All subsequent quotations in the paragraph are from this document.

38. *The Negotiations of Sir Thomas Roe in his Embassy to the Ottoman Porte*, p. 346.

39. Ibid., p. 376.

40. De Castries, *Les Sources . . . d'Angleterre*, 3:7–8.

41. S. P. 16/31/f. 164.

42. *Acts of the Privy Council of England June–December 1626*, p. 120.

43. *C. S. P. Domestic, Charles I, 1626*, 1:418; De Castries, *Les Sources . . . d'Angleterre*, 3:8.

44. *C. S. P. Domestic, Charles I, 1625–1626*, 1:113.

45. De Castries, *Les Sources . . . d'Angleterre*, 3:94.

46. Fisher, *Barbary Legend*, p. 141. In *Things of Darkness*, Hall reproduced numerous paintings of "Moorish" and "Negro" slaves. For Muslim slaves on English ships, see the ref-

erence in *The Lives and Deaths of the Two English Pyrats Purser, and Clinton*, B3r.

47. Lawdon Vaidon, *Tangier: A Different Way*, p. 24.

48. Thomas Phelps, *A True Account of the Captivity of Thomas Phelps*, p. 2.

49. Comte Henry De Castries, *Moulay Ismail et Jacques II*, pp. 48–49; and the anonymous article on "Le Raiss Abdallah Ben Aicha Corsaire de Sale et Amiral de la Flotte Cherifienne," *La Revue Maritime*, New Series, no. 140 (August 1931): 194–200. See also the reference to Muslim slaves owned by Sir Dudley North, *The Lives*, 3:64–65.

50. *C. S. P. Domestic, Charles I, 1636*, 10:173.

51. S. P. 16/408/f. 119.

52. *C. S. P. Domestic, Charles I, 1636*, 10:532.

53. *Acts of the Privy Council of England, June–December 1626*, p. 297. All subsequent quotations in the paragraph are from this document.

54. Ibid., pp. 402–403.

55. De Castries, *Les Sources . . . d'Angleterre*, 3:12. See also Harrison's reference to this commission in September 1627, Ibid., 3:35.

56. *The Manuscripts of the Earl Cowper, K. G.*, 1:311.

57. For the accusation, see *C. S. P. Domestic, Charles I, 1625–1626*, 1:529; S. P. 71/12/f. 126.

58. *Acts of the Privy Council of England, January–August, 1627*, p. 48.

59. S. P. 71/1/ f. 74.

60. *Discovery of 29 Sects, here in London* (1641), p. 4.

61. Yungblut, *Strangers Settled Here*, chapter 4. See also C. W. Chitty, "Aliens in England in the Sixteenth Century," *Race* 8 (1966): 129–145.

62. S. P. 16/332/f. 30 vi.

63. S. P. 16/332/f. 30 i.

64. S. P. 16/322/f. 52.

65. S. P. 16/332/f. 30 vi.

66. *C. S. P. Domestic, Charles I, 1636–1637*, 10:146; ibid., 1637, 11:294. See also for other ships that were captured: *C. S. P. Domestic, Charles I, 1626*, 1:257 and the reference to the Algiers man-of-war that was brought into the Downs and "received by the people with no little satisfaction," *C. S. P. Domestic, Charles II, January–November 1671*, 11:170.

67. S. P. 16/332/f. 30 and 16/370/f. 12.

68. *Acts of the Privy Council of England, January–August 1627*, p. 191.

69. *C. S. P. Domestic, Charles I, 1636–37*, 10:177.

70. *C. S. P. Domestic, Charles I, 1637*, 11:742.

71. *C. S. P. Domestic, Charles II, 1669*, 9:234.

72. *Acts of the Privy Council of England, Colonial Series, 1670*, entry 1338.

73. Hakluyt, *Navigations*, 6:137.

74. *Calendar of Letters and State Papers, relating to English Affairs preserved principally in the*

Archives of Simancas, Elizabeth 1568–1579, 2:699.

75. Skilliter, *William Harborne*, pp. 50–51.

76. Ibid., p. 77.

77. Harris, "A Portrait of a Moor," p. 96.

78. De Castries, *Les Source . . . d'Angleterre*, 1:512.

79. *The Fugger News-Letters, Second Series*, Klarwill, ed., (17 February 1595): English vessels "are to meet the corsair Amurad and then the combined force is to join the English Armada sailing this spring to lie in wait for the Indian fleet," p. 263.

80. De Castries, *Les Sources . . . d'Angleterre*, 2:158; John Nichols, *The Progresses . . . of Elizabeth*, 2:9–10.

81. Quoted in Harris, "A Portrait of a Moor," p. 92. See also De Castries, *Les Sources . . . d'Angleterre*, 2:164–67.

82. De Castries, *Les Sources . . . d'Angleterre*, 2:203.

83. Ibid.

84. Nichols, *The Progresses . . . of Elizabeth*, 2:10. Years after the visit Londoners still recalled the stinginess of the ambassador. See *Calendar of the Manuscripts of . . . Salisbury*, Giuseppi and Lockie, eds., part 19: 287.

85. *The Chamberlain Letters*, McClure, ed., 1:108.

86. See H. B. Rosedale, *Queen Elizabeth and the Levant Company*, p. 16; S. A. Skilliter, "Three Letters from the Ottoman 'Sultana' Safiye to Queen Elizabeth I," in *Documents from Islamic Chanceries*, S. M. Stern, ed., p. 143, and my "Renaissance England and the Turban," pp. 41–43.

87. *The Progresses, Processions, and Magnificent Festivities, of King James the First*, Nichols, ed., 2:157 n.

88. Ibid., p. 158.

89. As Ben Jonson noted in *The Alchemist*, in *The Works of Ben Jonson*, Percy and Simpson, eds., 10:61. "Each was given 30 £ by the King," *Calendar of the Manuscripts of . . . Salisbury*, 21:315.

90. John Finet, *Finetti Philoxenis* (1656), p. 58. In a similar manner, Christians in the Ottoman Empire got "a holy man, though a Turk, to read over a sick child," North, *The Lives*, 3:56.

91. *C. S. P. Domestic, Charles I, 1625–1626*, 1:12 and 113.

92. *C. S. P., Colonial Series, East Indies, China and Persia, 1625–1629*, p. 84.

93. De Castries, *Les Sources . . . d'Angleterre*, 3:25 n.

94. John Finet, *Ceremonies of Charles I, The Note Books of John Finet 1628–1641*, Loomie, ed., p. 231.

95. *The Arrivall and Intertainemes of the Embassador, Alkaid Jaurar Ben Abdella*, p. 9. The name of the ambassador was spelled in different ways. See "Alcayde Taudar Ben Abdala" in

C. S. P. Domestic, Charles I, 1637–1638, 12:476.

96. John Finet, *Ceremonies*, Loomie, ed., p. 231; *Arrivall*, p. 12.

97. The description that follows derives from John Finet, *Ceremonies*, Loomie, ed., pp. 233–234.

98. *Arrivall*, p. 5.

99. See the letter from Mulay al-Mansur to Queen Elizabeth, where there is mention of the Dutch captives, De Castries, *Les Sources . . . d'Angleterre*, 2:149–151.

100. See chapter 2, below, the unit on "Pirates," for English piratical attacks on North Africa.

101. See De Castries, *Les Sources . . . d'Angleterre*, 3:524.

102. Finet, *Ceremonies*, Loomie, ed., pp. 293–295.

103. *C. S. P. and Manuscripts . . Venice, 1657–1659*, 3:534.

104. *The Writings and Speeches of Oliver Cromwell*, Abbot, ed., 4:515, 568.

105. See the account of Cigala in John Evelyn, *The History of the Three late famous Imposters*, pp. 33–34 especially.

106. For Evelyn's account of this visit see *Diary*, De Beer, ed., 4:265–266. See also E. M. G. Routh, *Tangier: England's Lost Atlantic Outpost, 1661–1684*, chapter 12; see, for a more detailed account, Wilfrid Blunt, *Black Sunrise: The Life and Times of Mulai Ismail, Emperor of Morocco 1646–1727*, chapters 16 ff.

107. Yungblut, *Strangers Settled Here*, p. 30.

108. During the occupation of Tangier by British forces between 1661–1684, Moors visited the outpost and were entertained by the soldiers there: "we daily entertain," wrote Sir Hugh Cholmeley to the Ambassador in Madrid in 1665, "Christians and Turks that come to see us." *Calendar of the Manuscripts of the Marquis of Bath*, 2:150.

109. *C. S. P., Colonial Series, East Indies, China and Japan, 1513–1616*, pp. 335 and 347.

110. S. P. 16/311/f. 9.

111. T. S., *The Adventures of (Mr. T. S.)*, pp. 205 ff.

112. Ibid., pp. 56, 57.

113. Fisher, *Barbary Legend*, p. 101. See for an account of this woman Francis Brooks, *Barbarian Cruelty*, pp. 27–34.

114. Routh, *Tangier: England's Lost Atlantic Outpost*, p. 22.

115. Thomas Rymer, *Shakespeare: The Critical Heritage*, Brian Vickers, ed., 2:29. This desire on the part of English women to seduce or marry Muslim royalty continued into the modern period. From November 1809 until June 1810 the Iranian ambassador to London, Abul Hassan Khan, resided in London. As he complained in his journal, he was pestered by "a shameless woman who writes to me declaring her love and begging to come with me to Iran," p. 245. And throughout his stay the Prince of Wales queried him about alleged affairs he was having with English women. In *A Persian at the Court of King George, 1809–1810*, Margaret Morris Cloake, ed. and trans.

116. See my paper "Britons, Muslims, and American Indians: Gender and Power," presented at the South Central Renaissance Conference, Waco, Texas, 2–4 April, 1998.

117. For anti-alien riots see Yungblut, *Strangers Settled Here*, pp. 40–41.

118. See my "Eurocentrism or Islamocentrism? The Anglo-Spanish Conflict in Islamic Documents," forthcoming in *A Festschrift for Hussam Al Khateeb*, Mohammad Shaheen, ed.

2. SOLDIERS, PIRATES, TRADERS, AND CAPTIVES: BRITONS AMONG THE MUSLIMS

1. Henry Robinson, *Libertas, or Reliefe to the English Captives in Algier*, p. 5. This figure was engrained in Christian memory. Over a century and a half later Royall Tyler still recalled it in *The Algerine Captive*, p. 95.

2. Sha'ban, "The Mohammedan World in English Literature, c. 1580–1642: Illustrated by a text of the Travailes of the Three English Brothers," p. 226.

3. Ferguson, *The Indian Summer of English Chivalry*, p. 225.

4. Ide, *Possessed with Greatness*, p. 4.

5. Quoted in Paul A. Jorgensen, "Theoretical Views of War in Elizabethan England," *J. H. I.*, 12 (1952): 476.

6. Barret, *The Theorike and Practike of Moderne Warres*, p. 7.

7. Quoted in Shepherd, *Marlowe and the Politics of Elizabethan Theatre*, p. 143.

8. Writers against the new technology included the following: Sir John Smythe, *Discourses Concerning Weapons* (1590); and Sir Henry Knyvett, *Briefe Discourse of Warre* (1596). Writers in support included Sir Roger Williams, *Briefe Discourse* (1590) and Robert Barret. For a survey of this controversy, see Draper, *The Othello of Shakespeare's Audience*, chapter VIII.

9. *C. S. P. Domestic, Edward, Mary, Elizabeth I*, 1:506.

10. Vella, *An Elizabethan-Ottoman Conspiracy*, p. 8.

11. *C. S. P. Foreign Series, Elizabeth, 1578–79*, 13:476; *C. S. P. Foreign Series, Elizabeth, 1583–84*, 18:309.

12. All references are to the edition by John Yoklavich in *The Dramatic Works of George Peele*. Stukley's name has been spelled in various ways—I shall use Peele's. For a study of the development of the play's background see Thorleif Larsen, "The Historical and Legendary Background of Peele's *Battle of Alcazar*," *Transactions of the Royal Society of Canada*, 2 (1939): 185–197. See also Joseph Candido, "Captain Thomas Stukeley: The Man, the Theatrical Record, and the Origins of Tudor 'Biographical' Drama, *Anglia*, 105 (1987): 50–68.

13. De Castries, *Les Sources . . . d'Angleterre*, 1:282.

14. *The Fugger News-Letter, Second Series*, Klarwill, ed., p. 188.

15. Ibid., pp. 290–291.

16. Hakluyt, *Navigations*, 12:102.

17. Petruccio Ubaldini, S. P. 9/102: "To Lord Burleigh from Petruccio Ubaldini, citizen of Florence, a veracious account of the Enterprise which Pope Gregory XIII made in Ireland against the Queen of England" (1580).

18. See the account in Z. N. Brooke, "The Expedition of Thomas Stukeley in 1578," *English Historical Review*, 28 (1913): 330–337.

19. As confirmed by one of the ballads about Stukley, quoted in *The Famous History of the Life and Death of Captain Thomas Stukeley*, in Simpson, *The School of Shakespeare*, 1:147.

20. Quoted in Izon, *Sir Thomas Stucley*, p. 222.

21. The play, *The Famous History*, is reproduced in Simpson, *The School of Shakespeare*, vol. 1.

22. Hakluyt, *Navigations*, 6:294.

23. Fuller, however, concluded his description by confirming that Stukley had been "a bubble of emptiness, and meteor of ostentation," *The History of the Worthies of England*, 1:415.

24. *Purchas his Pilgrimes*: 6:70.

25. Ibid., 6:91.

26. Quoted in a letter by R. Cocks to Thomas Wilson in Penz, *Les Captifs Francais*, p. 5. See also De Castries, *Les Sources . . . d'Angleterre*, 2: 308, where there is reference to English and French men who were taken in March 1607 to "serve . . . the warres [in Morocco], promising them good recompence."

27. R. C., *A True Historicall discourse of Muley Hamets rising to the three Kingdomes of Moruecos, Fes and Sus*, G1r.

28. Ibid., G1v.

29. Penz, *Les Captifs Francais*, p. 5.

30. Hasleton, *The Miserable Captivity*, 2:174. English gunners were also prized by the Spaniards, see Coxere, *Adventures by Sea*, p. 64.

31. Hasleton, *The Miserable Captivity*, 2:174.

32. *Purchas his Pilgrimes*, 8:312.

33. *Letters from the great Turke lately sent vnto the holy Father the Pope and to Rodulphus naming himselfe King of Hungarie, and to all the Kinges and Princes of Christendome*, Bv. Renegades were in high numbers in the North African armies. See the references in de la Véronne, ed., *Les Sources Inédites de L'histoire du Maroc, Archives et Bibliothèques d'Espagne*, 3: 259. The army of Abdel-Malek consisted of twelve thousand soldiers, two thousand of whom were "renégats"; by 1577, his army was "au moins 30000 cavaliers, tous de la région ou renégats," ibid., p. 352. Unfortunately, it is not known how many of those were Britons.

34. Shirley, *Discours of the Turkes*, p. 4; De Castries, *Les Sources . . . d'Angleterre*, 2:290.

35. Coryat, *Master Coryats in Purchas His Pilgrimes*, 10:422–423; Roe, *The Negotiations of Sir Thomas Roe*, p. 205.

36. Rawlins, *The Famous and Wonderful Recovery* in *An English Garner*, Firth, ed., p. 258;

The Chamberlain Letters, McClure, ed., 2:507.

37. Blount, *A Voyage*, p. 112.

38. As late as 1691, "the Number of Deserters that come over to the Turks is almost incredible," wrote the traveler the Sieur du Mont. There were "several compleat French Regiments in the Ottoman Army" who joined because of "the favourable Treatment they receive[d] at their Arrival." *A New Voyage*, pp. 180–181.

39. Coxere, *Adventures by Sea*, p. 82.

40. The quotation continues with a condemnation of "the greater number of French and other nations, renegades and volunteers, who in the act of serving the Turks make themselves more barbarians than the barbarians themselves." *C. S. P. and Manuscripts . . . Venice*, 33:276

41. Brooks, *Barbarian Cruelty*, p. 81.

42. Baker, *Piracy and Diplomacy*, Pennell, ed., p. 126.

43. Pellow, *The Adventures of Thomas Pellow*.

44. Pitts, *A True and Faithful Account*, p. 143.

45. Harris, "A Portrait of a Moor," p. 90.

46. De Castries, *Les Sources . . . d'Angleterre*, 3:56.

47. Blount, *A Voyage*, p. 15.

48. Carteret, *The Barbary Voyage of 1638*, p. 10. For a detailed study of the English attack on Salee see Kenneth R. Andrews, *Ships, Money and Politics: Seafaring and Naval Enterprise in the Reign of Charles I*, chapter 7.

49. *The Arrivall and Intertainements of the Embassador, Alkaid Jaurar Ben Abdella*, pp. 23, 31.

50. Jorgensen, *Shakespeare's Military World*, chapter 4.

51. See Ralston, *Importing the European Army*, pp. 43 ff.

52. Braudel, *The Mediterranean and the Mediterranean World*, Reynolds, trans., vol. 2; Tenenti, *Piracy and the Decline of Venice*, chapter 4; Senior, *A Nation of Pirates*.

53. H. Timberlake, *A True and strange discourse of the trauailes of two English Pilgrimes* (1603), p. 7.

54. Davis, *A True Relation*, B4v.

55. Middleton, *An Account of the Captivity*, p. 263.

56. In 1577 Father Luis de Sandoval warned the Moroccan ruler against sending ships to ransom his captives in Spain for fear of English, along with other Protestant "Lutheran" pirates. De Castries, *Les Sources . . . d'Espagne*, 3:286.

57. De Castries, *Les Sources . . . d'Angleterre*, 1:482.

58. *Acts of the Privy Council, 1599–1600*, 30:744.

59. De Castries, *Les Sources . . . de France*, 3:321, 363.

60. Roe, *Negotiations*, p. 605.

61. Tenenti, *Piracy and the Decline of Venice*, p. 61.

62. See Henry and Renée Kahane and Andreas Tietze, *The Lingua Franca in the Levant*,

entry 251.

63. Roe, *Negotiations*, p. 140. Actually, when the expedition against Algiers was being discussed in 1617, Sir William Monson suggested that all captured "Turks and Moors" be sold as slaves, Morgan, *History of Algiers*, p. 633.

64. *C. S. P. D., James I, 1623–25 with Addenda*, 11:430.

65. De Castries, *Les Sources . . . d'Angleterre*, 3:160; *C. S. P. D., Charles I, 1639*, 14:315.

66. Thurloe, *A Collection of State Papers*, Birch, ed., 7:567.

67. *The Journals of Thomas Allin*, 1:178, 2:240–242. See also the agreement between the government of Algiers and Allin: "De plus les vaisseaux anglais où il se recontra des turcs ou turques et mores escalves pour le transport [à] vendre en autre lieu, nous le[s] ferons aussi de bonne prise," 2:227.

68. See the chapter entitled "Pirates" in Christopher Hill, *Liberty Against the Law*, pp. 114–122. For other studies on British pirates see Williams, *Captains Outrageous: Seven Centuries of Piracy*, chapter 4; Kenneth R. Andrews, *Elizabethan Privateering*; Lloyd, *English Corsairs on the Barbary Coast*.

69. *Ferdinando Gorges and His Province of Maine*, Baxter, ed., p. 174. The same information in Gorges appear in De Castries, *Les Sources . . . d'Angleterre*, 2:463.

70. Smith, *The Description of New England* (1616), in *Travels and Works*, Arber, ed., 1:217.

71. Morgan, *History of Algiers*, p. 634.

72. Senior, *A Nation of Pirates*, p. 37.

73. Drake, *The World Encompassed* (1628), pp. 4–5.

74. Quoted by Vella, *An Elizabethan-Ottoman Conspiracy*, p. 45

75. De Castries, *Les Sources . . . d'Angleterre*, 2:309.

76. Tenenti, *Piracy and the Decline of Venice*, p. 75.

77. Penz, *Les Captifs Francais*, p. 6.

78. Tenenti, *Piracy and the Decline of Venice*, p. 81.

79. Manwaring, ed., *The Life and Works of Sir Henry Mainwaring*, 2:11.

80. Ibid., 2:25.

81. Ibid., 2:25 n.

82. Ibid., 2:26; Coindreau, *Les Corsairs de Salé*, p. 48.

83. *The Chamberlain Letters*, McClure, ed., 2:433.

84. *Nevves from Sea, Of two notorious Pyrats Ward the Englishman and Danseker the Dutchman*, B3v.

85. Daborne, *A Christian turn'd Turke*, Swaen, ed., line 1916.

86. Quoted by Senior, *A Nation of Pirates*, p. 90.

87. Ibid., p. 96.

88. Ibid., pp. 90–91.

89. Ibid., p. 93.

90. Hebb, *Piracy and the English Government*, p. 14, n. 1.

91. Ibn Abi Dinar, *Kitab al-Munis*, p. 192. The translation is my own.

92. Williams, *Captains Outrageous*, p. 100.

93. Ibid., p. 92.

94. Pringle, *Jolly Roger*, p. 49.

95. Senior, *A Nation of Pirates*, p. 98.

96. Morgan, *History of Algiers*, p. 634.

97. Rawlins, *The Famous and Wonderful Recovery of a Ship of Bristol*, Firth, ed., p. 274.

98. *A Fight at Sea*, B2v.

99. De Castries, *Les Sources . . . d'Angleterre*, 2:569, 588.

100. Byam, *A Retvrne from Argier*, pp. 33–35.

101. De Castries, *Les Sources . . . d'Angleterre*, 3:114.

102. *The Manuscripts of the Earl Cowper*, 2:117.

103. De Castries, *Les Sources . . . d'Angleterre*, 1:438.

104. Hakluyt, *Navigations*, 6:433.

105. See also the introduction to "La Barbary Company" in De Castries, *Les Sources . . . d'Angleterre*, 1:445 ff.

106. Ibid., 1:101, 1:107.

107. *Tudor Economic Documents*, 2:48–49.

108. Ibid., 2:65. See also pp. 58–61.

109. De Castries, *Les Sources . . . d'Angleterre*, 1:431.

110. Ibid., 1:511, 2:56–57, 2:237.

111. Hakluyt, *Navigations*, 5:289.

112. De Castries, *Les Sources . . . d'Angleterre*, 1:362.

113. *The Travells and Adventures* in *Travels and Works*, Arber, ed., 2:871.

114. C. S. P. and Manuscripts . . . *Venice, 1617–1619*, 15:196.

115. Hebb, *Piracy and the English Government*, p. 92, n. 2.

116. C. S. P. Domestic, James I, *1623–1625, with Addenda*, 11:27.

117. *Acts of the Privy Council of England, 1630 June–1631 June*, p. 264.

118. Cartaret, *The Barbary Voyage*, p. 24.

119. Coindreau, *Les Corsairs de Salé*, p. 49.

120. Skilliter, *William Harborne*, p. 10.

121. Ibid., p. 33.

122. Hakluyt, *Navigations*, 5: 187. Cf. Skilliter's translation of Murad's incorporation: "Those people from England and the lands which are dependent upon it who have settled down in our well-protected dominions, whether they be married or bachelors, shall pursue their professions," *William Harborne*, p. 88.

123. C. S. P. Domestic, Elizabeth I, *1598–1601*, 5:249.

124. Robinson, *Liberty of Conscience: or the sole means to obtaine Peace and Truth*, "Epistle to the Reader"; C. S. P. Domestic, *1652–53*, p. 238.

125. See the detailed study in Daniel Goffman, *Britons in the Ottoman Empire 1642–1660.*

126. Milton, *The Life Records of John Milton, 1655–1669,* French, ed., 4:173–174.

127. De Castries, *Les Sources . . . d'Angleterre,* 1:112. The translation is my own.

128. Willan, *Studies in Elizabethan Foreign Trade,* pp. 108 ff. and the unit on "Sugar and the Elizabethans."

129. See for instance her request in De Castries, *Les Sources . . . d'Angleterre,* 2:120.

130. Ibid., 3:108.

131. Ibid., p. 112.

132. Shirley, *Discours of the Turkes,* p. 11.

133. De Castries, *Les Sources . . . d'Angleterre,* 3:175.

134. Industrial spying had been going on between Europe and Islam since the early Renaissance. See Jardine, *Worldly Goods,* chapter 1, "Conditions for Change: Goods in Profusion."

135. See the complaint about dishonesty in *Tudor Economic Documents,* 2:218.

136. *Tudor Economic Documents,* 2:50.

137. Ibid., 2:51–53.

138. Hakluyt, *Navigations,* 5:230.

139. Ibid., p. 234 Less than half a century later, circa. 1621, English merchants were still unable to compete in international markets because their "cloths" were not "well made as in former times or not well dyed," *Seventeenth-Century Economic Documents,* p. 12; see also pp. 29 ff.

140. Hakluyt, *Navigations,* 5:234–237. The transfer of crafts and knowledge was therefore not just from Christians to Muslims, as Braudel maintains. *The Mediterranean,* Reynolds, trans., 2:799–800.

141. *New American World,* Quinn, ed., 3:122.

142. Skilliter, *William Harborne,* p. 78.

143. Charles H. Talbot, "America and the European Drug Trade," in *First Images of America,* Chaippelli, ed., 2:833: "Since the key texts studied and commented on in the medieval universities were those of Rhazes, Avicenna and Averroes, it followed that all physicians trained in the schools were impregnated with Arabic ideas on materia medica. As a result, European dependence on the Levant for its spices and drugs lasted for at least 400 years."

144. De Castries, *Les Sources . . . d'Angleterre,* 2:169.

145. Al-Wufrani, *Nuzhet al-Hadi,* p. 51.

146. *Purchas His Pilgrimes,* 6:57.

147. *Acts of the Privy Council, 1600–1601,* 31:365. The appointment of these two English doctors came immediately after the departure of Mulay's French physician, Etienne Hubert, who had been in Morocco since 1598. Elizabeth was eager to replace the French

in such a sensitive position.

148. S. P., 16/373/f. 135.

149. De Castries, *Les Sources . . . d'Angleterre*, 2:559.

150. Heywood, *The Dramatic Works of Thomas Heywood*, 5:23–24.

151. Gascoigne, *The Posies*, Cunliffe, ed., pp. 75–85; *The Plays and Poems of Philip Massinger*, 4:277, 5.3, 17–36; *A Brave and Memorable and Dangerovs Sea-Fight,* (1636), p. 10.

152. Jones, *Designs by Inigo Jones for Masques & Plays at Court*, p. 102.

153. See the description and analysis of this theme in Donald P. McCrory, ed. and trans., *The Captive's Tale*, especially appendix 1.

154. *The Works of Beaumont and Fletcher*, 5:135. British Library MS. Add 5489 shows how 29 Algiers captives (including three women) in 1645 owed 2107 pounds and 18 shillings for their ransom.

155. There is still no study of the genre of English captivity writings among the Muslims. Daniel Vitkus and I are currently preparing a select edition of writings from 1577 to 1704.

156. Cited in Hebb, *Piracy and the English Government*, p. 117, n. 2.

157. See for instance S. P. 16/5, f. 24; S. P. 16/329, f. 29; S. P. 16/332, fols. 30 and 30 V.

158. S. P. 16/316, f. 52

159. S. P. 16/316, f. 52 I.

160. Hakluyt, *Navigations*, 5: 153–165. See the expanded version in *The Admirable Deliverance of 266. Christians by Iohn Reynard Englishman from the captiuitie of the Turkes* (1608).

161. Webbe, *His Trauailes, 1590*, p. 25.

162. Ibid., p. 21.

163. Hasleton, *The Miserable Captivity*, 2:151–185.

164. T. S., *The Adventures of (Mr. T. S.)*, p. 67.

165. Ibid., pp. 43, 93..

166. Ibid., pp. 31–33.

167. Ibid., pp. 161–162.

168. Elliott, *A Modest Vindication of Titus Oates*, pp. 11–12.

169. Pitts, *A True and Faithful Account*, p. 162.

170. *Coryats Crudities*, pp. 64–66; Henry Marsh, *A New Survey of the Turkish Empire*, pp. 69–72; John Covel, *Extracts from the Diaries*, Bent, ed., pp. 270–271.

171. *The Works of Thomas Kyd*, Boas, ed.

172. *The Travailes of The Three English Brothers*, Sha'ban, ed., p. 240. See further on this English religious latitude my forthcoming article, "The Toleration of Muslims in Renaissance England."

173. Spratt, *Travels and Researches in Crete*, 1:386.

3. The Renaissance Triangle: Britons, Muslims, and American Indians

1. Geoffrey W. Symcox, "The Battle of the Atlantic, 1500–1700," *First Image of America*, Chiapelli, ed., 1:269.

2. *The Mediterranean and the Mediterranean World in the Age of Philip II*, Reynolds, trans., vol. 2; David Beers Quinn, *England and the Discovery of America, 1481–1620*, prologue and chapter 2. Marvin Arthur Breslow also ignored the Muslim world completely although "Barbaria" is prominent on the map that is printed on the cover jacket of his *English Puritan Views of Foreign Nations, 1618–1640*. Similarly, K. R. Andrews et al. described *The Westward Enterprise*, but ignored the eastward one. A. D. Innes described the Far Eastern enterprise but ignored the venture into the Mediterranean: *The Maritime and Colonial Expansion of England*.

3. See Helen Wallis, "The Cartography of Drake's Voyage," in *Sir Francis Drake and the Famous Voyage, 1577–1580*, Norman J. W. Thrower, ed., pp. 121–164. For White, see *The New World*, Stefan Lorant, ed., p. 169. See also the reference by C. M. Senior, *A Nation of Pirates*, p. 65, to the English pirate Tibald Saxbridge, who stopped at Mogador, in Morocco, before sailing to the West Indies. In the eighteenth century Defoe's Robinson Crusoe was captured by Moors off the western coast of Morocco, then sailed down to sub-Saharan Africa before launching out toward the West Indies.

4. Fuller, *Voyages in Print: English Travel to America, 1576–1624*, p. 12.

5. When Purchas published his *Pilgrimes in Five Bookes* in 1625, the description of America occupied only a part of the second book, while the third, fourth, and fifth books described English navigation in Africa and the "Arabian, Persian, Indian Shoares," "beyond the East Indies to the Ilands of Iapan, China, Cauchinchina, the Philippinae," and in "the Easterne parts of the World" (title page).

6. William Harrison, *The Description of England*, Georges Edelen, ed., p. 182. It is important to note that Barbary was England's admission to the Mediterranean. As K. R. Andrews has observed, "the Barbary connection . . . provided the incentive and opportunity" for the English incursion into the Mediterranean"—an incursion that developed into a permanent presence. "Sir Robert Cecil and Mediterranean plunder," *The English Historical Review*, 87 (1972), p. 519.

7. Robert Johnson, *Nova Britannia*, E3r.

8. Ibid., B2v-B3r. For studies on the motives of the early transatlantic adventurers see David Cressy, *Coming Over*, chapter 3; David B. Quinn, "Why They Came," in *Explorers and Colonies*, pp. 151–179; Carl Bridenbaugh, *Vexed and Troubled Englishmen, 1590–1642*. For the Roanoke project see Kenneth R. Andrews, "Elizabethan Privateering," in *Raleigh in Exeter*, Joyce Youings, ed., pp. 1–20, especially p. 10: "It has been established beyond reasonable doubt that one of the main purposes of founding a colony there was to provide a base for

privateering action against the Spanish treasure fleets bound from Havana to Seville and against the ports and shipping of Spain's Caribbean in general."

9. Cressy, *Coming Over*, pp. 6–7. A similar situation was taking place in the Caribbean too: see Francis Jennings, *The Invasion of America*, p. 32; "Certainly no question arose of permanent colonization with the Caribbean" in the Elizabethan period, K. R. Andrews, "The English in the Caribbean, 1560- 1620," in *The Westward Enterprise*, K. R. Andrews et al., eds., p. 115.

10. "The Discourse of the Old Company, 1625," in Lyon Gardiner Tyler, ed., *Narratives of Early Virginia*, p. 434. That is why the population had consisted chiefly of males. See Karen Ordahl Kupperman, *Settling with the Indians*, p. 10. See also Cressy, *Coming Over*, pp. 37–38.

11. *Stuart Royal Proclamations*, 1:108–109.

12. Ibid., p. 571.

13. Ibid., pp. 98, 206. Johnson, The New Life, Force, ed., 1:21.

14. Ibid., pp. 52, 378.

15. As estimated by Thomas Mun, the seventeenth-century economic historian, and cited in Wood, *A History of the Levant Company*, p. 42.

16. *Stuart Royal Proclamations*, 1:146 n.

17. See Peter N. Carroll, *Puritanism and the Wilderness*, chapter 2, for a detailed survey of the impact of the ocean on New England emigrants. See also Cressy, *Coming over*, chapter 6, "The vast and furious ocean."

18. Edward Johnson, *Johnson's Wonder Working Providence*, J. Franklin Jameson, ed., chapter XVI and *passim*; Thomas Tillam, "Upon the first sight of New England June 29, 1638" in Messerole, ed., *Seventeenth-Century American Poetry*, p. 397.

19. Sir Thomas Gates, " A true reportory of the wracke" (1609), in *Purchas his Pilgrimes*, 19:8.

20. *An Account of the Captivity of Sir Henry Middleton* in Jean de Laroque, *A Voyage to Arabia Foelix through the Eastern Ocean and the streights of the Red-Sea*, p. 268.

21. Eburne, *A Plain Pathway to Plantations*, p. 44.

22. See for instance Jennings, *The Invasion of America*, chapters 3 ff.; David Stannard, *American Holocaust*, chapter 1.

23. *The Letters of John Chamberlain*, McClure, ed., 1:367.

24. Bridenbaugh, *Jamestown*, p. 45; David Ransom, "Wives for Virginia, 1621," *The William and Mary Quarterly*, 3rd series, 48 (1991): 3–18; Kuperman, *Settling with the Indians*, p. 19.

25. For a brief account of the negative propaganda see Cressy, *Coming Over*, pp. 13–16. For White's refutation see his account in *The New World*, Stefan Lorant, ed., pp. 169 ff. For Smith and Levett see *Sailors' Narratives of Voyages along the New England Coast, 1524–1624*, George Parker Winship, ed., pp. 242–247, 290–291. See also Howard Mumford Jones,

"The colonial impulse: an analysis of the 'promotion' literature of colonization," *Proceedings of the American Philosophical Society*, 90 (1946): 131–161. For the earthly paradise motif see Bernard W. Sheehan, *Savagism and Civility*, chapter 1; Robert Ralston Cawley, *The Voyagers and Elizabethan Drama*, pp. 290 ff.

26. Sir Sidney Lee, *Elizabethans and Other Essays*, Boas, ed., p. 322.

27. William L. Sachse, "The Migration of New Englanders to England, 1640–1660," *American Historical Review*, 53 (1948): 251–278. See also the introduction to the facsimile reproduction of Johnson's *Wonder-Working Providence*, p. v; Andrew Delbanco, "Looking Homeward, Going Home: The Lure of England for the Founders of New England," *New England Quarterly*, 59 (1986): 358–386; Cressy, *Coming Over*, chapter 8.

28. Okeley, *Eben-Ezer*, pp. 46–47. It is possible that this hesitation to return home was in response to the propaganda for the settlement of America. See for instance Eburne's "Epistle to Readers," in which he denounced the poor and the indigent for staying in England and increasing the country's "misery and decay" instead of relocating to the plantations, *A Plain Pathway*, pp. 11–12 especially.

29. George Alsop, *A Character of the Province of Maryland* (1666), Newton D. Mereness, ed., p. 106.

30. All the information is from Hebb, *Piracy and the English Government*, pp. 18, 89, 139, 138, 139–140.

31. Knight, *A Relation*, A3v; *The Statutes of the Realm*, 5:134.

32. *List and Analysis of State Papers*, Wernham, ed., 1:450.

33. Hebb, *Piracy and the English Government*, p. 163.

34. Christopher Hill, "Impressment and Empire," in *Liberty Against the Law*, p. 165; see also James D. Butler, "British Convicts shipped to American Colonies," *American Historical Review*, 2 (1896): 12–34, and the extensive survey by Abbot Emerson Smith, *Colonists in Bondage: White Servitude and Convict Labor in America, 1607–1776*, and chapter 1 in Ballagh, *White Servitude*.

35. "Of Plantations," in *Essays in Selected Writings of Francis Bacon*, Hugh G. Dick, ed., p. 90.

36. Hill, "Impressment and Empire" in *Liberty against the Law*, p. 169.

37. *C. S. P., Colonial, 1574–1660*, p. 268.

38. Edmund S. Morgan, "The First American Boom: Virginia 1618 to 1630," *The William and Mary Quarterly*, 3rd series, 28 (1971): 197.

39. *The Records of the Virginia Company of London*, Kingsbury, ed., 1:334–335.

40. Richard S. Dunn, "Experiments holy and unholy, 1630–1631," K. R. Andrews et al., eds., *The Westward Enterprise*, p. 272. In 1616 Bermuda had 600 inhabitants while Virginia had 350. See David D. Smits, " 'Abominable Mixture': Toward the Repudiation of Anglo-Indian Intermarriage in Seventeenth-Century Virginia," *The Virginia Magazine of History and Biography*, 95 (1987): 157–193. A detailed study of the colonists in Virginia appears in

Morgan, "The First American Boom," p. 170 and the references in note 4. Morgan asserts that in 1624 the number of colonists in Virginia was 1292 ; a year later, the number had fallen to 1210.

41. For the figures of captives see *C. S. P. Domestic, Charles I, 1625–1626*, 1:343; for the American figures see Alden T. Vaughan and Daniel K. Richter, "Crossing the Cultural Divide: Indians and New Englanders, 1605–1763," *Proceedings of the American Antiquarian Society*, 90 (1980), pp. 27, 46. See also Nicholas Canny, "The permissive frontier: social control in English Settlements in Ireland and Virginia, 1550–1650," in K. R. Andrews et al., eds., *The Westward Enterprise*, pp. 30- 32.

42. For Wales see David B. Quinn, "Wales and the West," in *Explorers and Colonies,* pp. 397–415.

43. Richard Slotkin, *Regeneration through Violence*, p. 37.

44. See the analysis of White's list in Quinn, *Set Fair for Roanoke*, pp. 55 ff. The data about the social status of the emigrants before the Great Migration are less detailed than those after the Migration. See John Camden Hotten, ed., *The Original Lists of Persons of Quality . . .Who went from Great Britain to the American Plantations, 1600–1700*, pp. 169–196, 201–265, 266–274; the lists in W. S., *The Proceedings of the English Colonie in Virginia since their first beginning from England in the yeare of our Lord 1606, till this present 1612*, in Barbour, ed., *The Jamestown Voyages*, 2:382–383, 397–400, 418–422; chapter 2 in Cressy, *Coming Over*. For an analysis of 273 migrants in 1637, see T. H. Breen and Stephen Foster, "Moving to the New World," *William and Mary Quarterly*, 3rd. series, 30 (1973): 189–222.

45. Waterhouse, *A Declaration of the State of the Colony in Virginia*, pp. 35–43.

46. Josiah Child, *A New Discourse of Trade* (1694), p. 183. See the study by David Souden, " 'Rogues, Whores and Vagabonds'?: Indentured Servant Emigrants to North America and the Case of Mid-Seventeenth Century Bristol," *Social History*, 3 (1978): 23–41.

47. Alexander Young, ed., *Chronicles of the Pilgrim Fathers of the Colony of Plymouth, 1602–1625*, 2:257.

48. Paul Baepler, "The Barbary Captivity Narrative in Early America," *Early American Literature*, 30 (1995), p. 96.

49. Smith, *Travels and Works*, Arber, ed., 1:240; *Bradford's History of Plymouth Plantation, Davis, ed.*, p. 206.

50. *Voyage to Maryland*, Lawtasch-Boomgaarden, trans. and ed., p. 27; *C. S. P., Colonial Series, 1574–1660*, p. 309; *C. S. P. and Manuscripts . . .Venice, 1640–1642*, 25:18.

51. *Winthrop's Journal*, "History of New England, 1630–1649," Hosmer, ed., 2:126–27.

52. See the edition of Joshua Gee's journal, *Narrative of Joshua Gee of Boston, Mass.; Diary of Cotton Mather, 1681–1709*, 1:260. Before Gee, Abraham Browne had written an account of his captivity. See Stephen T. Riley, "Abraham Browne's Captivity by the Barbary Pirates, 1655," in *Seafaring in Colonial Massachusetts,* (Boston: Colonial Society of Massachusetts,

1980), pp. 31–42.

53. Mather, *The Goodness of God Celebrated* (1700), preface. There were many other references in the third quarter of the seventeenth century to American captives in North Africa. In 1676, a memorandum to King Charles II called for the protection of the Virginia fleet from the attacks of the "Algerines." *C. S. P., Colonial Series, America and West Indies, 1675–1676, also Addenda, 1574–1674*, p. 516. Three years later the future governor of the province of Albemarle was captured by the "Turks and carried into Algiers"; in April 1680, a petitioner in Jamaica complained about "the Algiers men-of-war infesting the seas," and in the following month, a similar complaint about the "Algerine pirates" came from Barbados: the dread of pirates, wrote the governor, Sir Jonathan Atkins, had forced the ships to "go round by Ireland and Scotland, which will make their voyages longer than ever." *C. S. P., Colonial Series, America and West Indies, 1677- 1680*, pp. 326, 530, 532. In 1681, *The Impartial Protestant* reported in London that "Mr. Seth Southel Sailing to the Colony of Carolina, in October 1678. with a Commission to be Governour thereof, and to Collect His Majesties Duty there, in his Passage was taken Captive by the Turks, and carried into Argier, where for about two years he under went a most intollerable and Barbarous Slavery." *The Impartial Protestant*, no. 41, September 9–13, 1681.

54. Edmund S. Morgan, "The First American Boom," p. 196. See also Sheehan, *Savagism & Civility*, pp. 112–114; J. Norman Heard, *White into Red*, where the author maintains that when individuals of either race, white or Indian, experienced both civilizations— English and Native American—they "so frequently preferred the Indian life style," p. 13; John Canup, *Out of the Wilderness*, p. 125.

55. For a study of converts to Islam, see chapter 1 in my *Islam in Britain*.

56. Stephen Greenblatt, *Renaissance Self-Fashioning*, p. 9.

57. Strachey, *Historie*, p. 45; Rawlins, *The Famous and Wonderful Recovery of a Ship of Bristol*, Firth, ed., p. 274.

58. The term *renegade* or *runnugate* had also applied to an Englishman who went native among the Irish. For the use of the term among the Indians see, for instance, Captain Edward Maria Wingfield's use in 1608 of "our men runnugates," in Barbour, ed., *Jamestown Voyages*, p. 216, and the reference to Joshua Tift as a "Renegadoe" in N. S., *A Continuation of the State of New-England* (1676) in *Narratives of the Indian Wars, 1675–1699*, Lincoln, ed., p. 67.

59. *Puritans among the Indians*, Alden T. Vaughan and Edward W. Clark, eds., p. 15. For the change in attitude toward the Indians after 1622 see Vaughan, " 'Expulsion of the Salvages': English Policy and the Virginia Massacre of 1622," *The William and Mary Quarterly*, 3rd. Series 35 (1978): 57–84; Vaughan and Richter, "Crossing the Cultural Divide," p. 48.

60. Vaughan and Richter, "Crossing the Cultural Divide," p. 63, figure 5; Vaughan and Clark, *Puritans among the Indians*, pp. 15–16. See the detailed study of the daughter of John Williams in John Demos, *The Unredeemed Captive: A Family Story from Early America*. On the

other hand, Britons of mature age who were captured and forcibly Indianized often yearned to return home. See for instance John Tanner's eighteenth-century account, *The Falcon: A Narrative of the Captivity & Adventures of John Tanner During Thirty Years Residence among the Indians in the Interior of North America.* James Axtell concluded that at the end of the colonial period, "large numbers of French and English settlers had chosen to become Indians." *The Invasion Within,* chapter 13, pp. 302–305 especially.

61. Penrose, *Travel and Discovery in the Renaissance,* pp. 237–238.

62. See the biography of Pory by William S. Powell, *John Pory, 1572–1636;* Brenner, *Merchants and Revolution,* p. 150.

63. D'Amico, *The Moor,* p. 220. For a reproduction of the coat of arms see Kim F. Hall, *Things of Darkness,* p. 20.

64. Morison, *Builders of the Bay Colony,* p. 10; Smith, *A Description of New England* (1616), in *Sailors' Narratives,* p. 243.

65. *A Brief Narration . . . New-England,* in *Sir Ferdinando Gorges and his Province of Maine,* Baxter, ed., p. 163 n.

66. *The Roanoke Voyages,* Quinn, ed., 1:464; *Records of the Virginia Company of London,* Kingsbury, ed., 4:43; Marvell, *The Complete Poems,* Donno, ed., p. 116.

67. Patricia Seed has shown how the Portuguese and the Spaniards used the same methods for colonizing the Indians as they had for subduing the Muslims. *Ceremonies of Possesion in Europe's Conquest of the New World,* chapter 3.

68. Quoted in Sheehan, *Savagism & Civility,* p. 52; David B. Quinn, ed., *New American World,* 1:362 ff. See especially p. 416 where Coronado speaks of the "Indian Turk." In the encounter with the American Indians, wrote Kevin Terraciano, the Spaniards "especially use[d] the Moors as model," in "Discourses of Tolerance and Intolerance of Native Culture and History in Early Spanish American Writings," paper given at the "Seminar on Toleration," U. C. L. A., 24–25 April 1997. But the Spaniards later realized that the actual methods used in Christianizing the Moors "were inappropriate in America." John Parry, "A Secular Sense of Responsibility," in *First Images of America,* Chiappelli, ed., 1:303.

69. Hakluyt, *Navigations,* 5:62–63.

70. Parker, *Books to Build an Empire,* pp. 39–40.

71. Richard Eden, *The first Three English books on America [circa 1511]–1555 A. D.,* Edward Arber, ed., pp. xxviii, 23, 25, 27, 374. See also Eden's *The History of Trauayle in the West and East Indies, and other countreys lying eyther way . . . Persia, Arabia, Syria, AEgypte, Ethiopia . . . Newly set in order, augmented, and finished by Richarde Willes* (1577).

72. For a general comparison between the first two editions of *Navigations,* see chapters 2 and 3 in E. G. R. Taylor, *Late Tudor and Early Stuart Geography.* See also Parker, *Books to Build an Empire,* p. 174. For a study of Hakluyt's ideological position in regard to Africa see Emily Bartels, "Imperialist Beginnings: Richard Hakluyt and the Construction of Africa," *Criticism,* 34 (1992): 517–538. See also C. F. Beckingham, "The Near East: North

and North-east Africa," in D. B. Quinn, ed., *The Hakluyt Handbook* pp. 176–196. For Hakluyt's view of the Indians see Alfred A. Cave, "Richard Hakluyt's Savages: The Influence of 16th Century Travel Narratives on English Indian Policy in North America," *International Social Science Review*, 60 (1985): 3–24.

73. In the 1613 edition of *Purchas his Pilgrimage*, the "Third Book" was about the Muslims (along with parts of the fifth too, which includes descriptions of Egypt and Barbary), and the eighth book was about America. The 1614 edition of *Purchas* further expanded the material. The 1617 edition expanded the "Third Booke," which is about the "Arabians, Saracens, Turkes," from the 110 pages in the 1614 edition (pp. 227–337) to 130 pages (pp. 255–385).

74. Mather, *The Life of the Renowned John Eliot*, p. 84.

75. *Further English Voyages to Spanish America, 1583–1594*, Irene A. Wright, ed. and trans., pp. 54, 212, 173. It is important to recall that Spain had instituted very strict laws against the travel or emigration of Moors and/or Moriscos to America. Peter Boyd-Bowman, "Spanish Emigrants to the Indies, 1595–98: A Profile," in *First Images of America*, Chiappelli, ed., 2:738, 756.

76. *Purchas His Pilgrimage* (1617 ed.), p. 276. For Moors settled in America, see Father Escobedo, *Pirates, Indians, and Spaniards*, Covington, ed., pp. 76 ff. See also the fascinating study by Louis Cardillac, "Qadiyyat al-Moriskiyyeen bi America" (The Case of the Moriscos in America) in *Al-Muriskiyyoon al-Andalusiyyoon wal Maseehiyyoon*, al-Tamimi, trans., pp. 145–166. See further the interesting thesis by N. Brent Kennedy, *The Melungeons*, especially pp. 108–126.

77. D'Avenant, *The Dramatic Works*, 4:54–55. For a discussion of D'Avenant, see Barthelemy, *Black Face, Maligned Race*, pp. 171 ff.

78. *Puritans, Indians, and Manifest Destiny*, Segal and Stineback, eds., p. 143; John White, *The Planters Plea* (1630): "[S]ome conceive the Inhabitants of New-England to be Chams posterity," p. 54; and earlier, Strachey, *Historie*, pp. 54 ff. See also William Mckee Evans, "From the Land of Canaan to the Land of Guinea: The Strange Odyssey of the 'Sons of Ham,'" *American Historical Review*, 85 (1980): 15–43.

79. Strachey, *Historie*, pp. 81, 84, 60, 61, 87, 116.

80. *Travels and Works*, Arber, ed., 2:811–813.

81. John Smith, *A Map of Virginia, 1612*, reproduced in *Travels and Works*, Arber, ed., 1:182.

82. Ibid., p. 280.

83. Arber, ed., *Travels and Works*, 2:817–18.

84. Arber, ed., *Travels and Works*, 2:972. For other Muslim-Indian allusions, see William Wood, *New Englands Prospect* (1634), where the Indians are described as "lolling on the Turkish fashion," p. 68. "The Mahometans have 1000 monks in a monastery; the like saith Acost of Americans," Burton, *Anatomy of Melancholy*, part 3, section 4, p. 359.

85. Hulme, *Colonial Encounters*, pp. 35, 97.

86. Ibid., p. 108.

87. See the numerous references to "wild Arab" in Cawley, *The Voyagers and Elizabethan Drama*, pp. 178–181.

88. Waterhouse, *A Declaration*, p. 13. See the study of the interpreters in J. Frederick Fausz, "Middlemen in Peace and War: Virginia's Earliest Indian Interpreters, 1608–1632," *The Virginia Magazine of History and Biography*, 95 (1987): 41–64.

89. Wood, *New Englands Prospect*, p. 111. See Greenblatt, "Learning to Curse: Aspects of Linguistic Colonialism in the Sixteenth Century," in *Learning to Curse*, pp. 16–39.

90. De Castries, *Les Sources . . . d'Angleterre*, 1:353.

91. See the definitive work on the subject in Toomer, *Eastern Wisedome and Learning: The Study of Arabic in Seventeenth-Century England*.

92. Thurloe, *A Collection of the State Papers*, Birch, ed., 1:745.

93. *Calendar of the Clarendon State Papers*, Routledge, ed., 5:235.

94. *C. S. P. and Manuscripts . . . Venice, 1655–1656*, 30:311, "Relation of England by Giovanni Sagredo."

95. Gainsford, *The Glory of England*, pp. 191–92, and all of the seventh chapter.

96. Lord Carew, *Letters from George Lord Carew to Sir Thomas Roe, Ambassador to the Court of the Great Mogul, 1615–1617*, p. 83. See also p. 78. In 1653, Sir Thomas Bendish reported that in Aleppo "about two yeares since, our consul was dragged about the streets, our merchants houses broke open." Thurloe, *A Collection of the State Papers*, Birch, ed., 2:138–39. Britons could be humiliated, robbed, and disgraced and little could be done about it. In 1655, William Clarke, secretary to the Council of the Army, reported that the Grand Signior was "causing the throats of the English Ambassadour and all the English merchants to be cut, and their estates to be confiscated, amounting to 18 millions of crownes" in revenge for the attack of the British fleet on Tunis. *The Clarke Papers. Selections from the Papers of William Clarke*, Firth, ed., 3:45. For every British action Britons knew they had to reckon with a Muslim retaliation. Although no violence is reported to have been committed on the ambassador, a year later, in September 1656, it was reported to Secretary Thurloe, the intelligence gatherer of the Cromwellian administration, that the "Turke" had "cutt of the heads of two Venetian embassadors at Constantinople," and just over a week later, "seized all the French, Flemish ships in his dominions.'" Thurloe, *A Collection of the State Papers*, Birch, ed., 5:403, 438.

97. Anthony Pagden, *European Encounters with the New World*, chapter 2.

98. As I shall show in a paper under preparation, one of many reasons for the Civil War in England was the anger and dissatisfaction felt by thousands of men, women, and children at the continued captivity of their kin in North Africa, and at the king's inability or unwillingness to redeem them.

99. Anonymous, *New Englands First Fruits*, p. 2.

100. Kingsbury, *Records*, 1:220."Charter of Harvard College, May 31, 1650," in *American Colonial Documents to 1776*, Merrill Jensen, ed., p. 558.

101. Breitwieser, *American Puritanism and the Defense of Mourning*, p. 94.

102. Alfred A. Cave, *The Pequot War*, p. 17.

103. Quoted in Henderson and McManus, *Half Humankind*, p. 269. The Indian and the Irish were often superimposed on each other. See James Muldoon, "The Indian as Irishman," *Essex Institute Historical Collections*, 3 (1975): 267–289; Nicholas P. Canny, "The Ideology of English Colonization from Ireland to America," *William and Mary Quarterly*, 30 (1973): 575–598. It is interesting that the Muslims also reminded the English of the Irish. See Gainsford, *The Glory of England*, p. 23; Adam Elliott, *A Modest Vindication of Titus Oates the Salamanca-Doctor*: the Moors who came out to see the captives "wellcomed us with horrid barbarous Shouts somewhat like the Irish hubbub," p. 6.

4. SODOMY AND CONQUEST

1. Trexler, *Sex and Conquest*, p. 60.

2. *Islamic Homosexualities*, Murray and Roscoe, eds., p. 24. For the "berdache" in America, see Charles Callendar and Lee M. Kochems, "The North America Berdache," *Current Anthropology*, 24 (1983): 443–470.

3. *Historia*, in *New Iberian World*, Parry and Keith, eds., 1:13.

4. Ibid.

5. Todorov, *The Conquest of America*, p. 177. Las Casas denied the sodomy accusation in *History of the Indies*, Andrée Collard, ed. and trans., xiv and 48.

6. Canup, *Out of the Wilderness*, chapter 2, "The Disafforestation of the Mind." See also R. F. Oaks, "Things Fearful to Name: Sodomy and Buggery in Seventeenth-Century New England," in *Journal of Social History* 12 (1978–1979): 268–281.

7. *Bradford's History of Plymouth Plantation*, Morison, ed., pp. 404–413.

8. Quoted in Segal and Stineback, eds., *Puritans, Indians, and Manifest Destiny*, p. 90.

9. Ibid., p. 154.

10. Quoted in Bruce R. Smith, *Homosexual Desire in Shakespeare's England*, p. 45.

11. *Winthrop Papers*, 2:91, quoted in Segal and Stineback, eds., *Puritans, Indians, and Manifest Destiny*, p. 50.

12. See Nowell, *Abraham in Arms*, pp. 1–9.

13. *The History and Description of Africa*, Pory, trans. 2: 2, 294.

14. Jordan, *White over Black*, p. 40.

15. Tokson, *The Popular Image of the Black Man*, p. 17.

16. Davis, *Trve Relation of the Trauailes and most miserable Captiuitie*, B2v.

17. There is still no comprehensive study of homosexuality in Islamic history. See the brief discussion with useful notes in Boswell, *Christianity, Social Tolerance, and Homosexuality*,

pp. 194–98; Bullough, *Sexual Variance in Society and History*, pp. 229 ff.; *Homoeroticism in Classical Arabic Literature*, Wright and Rowson, eds. These sources, however, rely on literary texts only and not on historical or sociological surveys. *Islamic Homosexualities*, Murray and Roscoe, eds., conflates literary models from medieval Islam with twentieth-century practices.

18. Burg, *Sodomy and the Pirate Tradition*, p. xvi; Craigie, ed., *The Basilicon Doron of King James VI*, 1:65.

19. See the detailed study of the literary "myths" in Smith, *Homosexual Desire*.

20. Bray, *Homosexuality in Renaissance England*; Hill, "Male Homosexuality in 17th-Century England," in *The Collected Essays of Christopher Hill*, 3:226–235; Bullough, "The Sin Against Nature and Homosexuality," in *Sexual Practices and the Medieval Church*, Bullough and Brundage, eds., pp. 55–72; Burg, *Sodomy and the Pirate Tradition*.

21. For an interesting case study of a seventeenth-century trial see Caroline Binham, "Seventeenth-Century Attitudes toward Deviant Sex," *Journal of Interdisciplinary History*, 1 (1971): 447–468.

22. Nicolay, *The Nauigations, peregrinations and voyages*, T. Washington, trans., p. 8r.

23. Hanmer, *The Baptizing of a Turke*, 4v.

24. Lithgow, *The Rare Adventures*, Phelps, ed., p. 99.

25. Knolles, *General Historie of the Turkes,* 2nd ed. (1610), p. 962.

26. "Relations of the Christianitie of Africa" in *Purchas His Pilgrimes*, 9:282. See also Cameron McFarlane, *The Sodomite in Fiction and Satire, 1660–1750*, pp. 38–40.

27. Hanmer, *The Baptizing of a Turke*, 4v.

28. Grimeston, *The History of the Serrail*, pp. 163–64.

29. Calvert, *The blessed Jew of Morocco*, p. 219.

30. Purchas *Pilgrimage*, (1613 edition), p. 246.

31. Al-Wufrani, *Nuzhat al-Hadi*, pp. 77, 179; Ahmad bin Qasim, *Nasir al-Deen,* pp. 50–52. See appendix C for a translation.

32. Quoted in Hebb, *Piracy and the English Government*, p. 150.

33. *The Case of many Hundreds of Poor English Captives, in Algier*, p. 1.; Fox, *To The Great Turk and the King at Argiers*, p. 4. See my article "Some Notes on George Fox and Islam," *The Journal of the Friends' Historical Society*, 55 (1989): 271–276.

34. Quoted in Carroll, "Quaker Slaves in Algiers, 1679–1688," in *The Journal of the Friends' Historical Society*, 54 (1982), p. 308.

35. Berckman, *Victims of Piracy*, pp. 51–52; Burg, *Sodomy and the Pirate Tradition*, chapters 2 and 3 especially.

36. Rowse, *Homosexuals in History*, chapter 4.

37. Trexler, *Sex and Conquest*, p. 91.

38. Grimeston, *The History of the Serrail*, p. 62.

39. *Purchas His Pilgrimes*, 9:281. In 1614, during a debate in the House of Commons, it

was noted that because certain English merchants were poor and traded in unprotected ships, their goods were seized by the "Algerines" and "their Children buggered and made slaves." *Commons Debate*, Notestein et al., eds., 7:637.

40. Rycaut, *The Present State*, p. 33.

41. St. Serfe, *Tarugo's Wiles: or the Coffee-House (1668)*, Park, ed., p. 233.

42. Grimeston, *The History of the Serrail*, p. 163.

43. Rycaut, *The Present State*, p. 33.

44. Sanderson, *A Discourse of the most notable things of the famous Citie Constantinople*, in *Purchas His Pilgrimes*, 9:483.

45. For a discussion of the satirical attitude to sodomy in the Shakespearean period, see chapters 3 and 4 in Smith, *Homosexual Desire*.

46. Lithgow, *The Rare Adventures*, Phelps, ed., pp. 209–210.

47. Baker, *Piracy and Diplomacy in Seventeenth-Century North Africa*, Pennell, ed., p. 161.

48. Elliott, *A Modest Vindication of Titus Oates*, p. 13.

49. Hammond, "Titus Oates and 'Sodomy,'" in *Culture and Society in Britain 1660–1800*, Black, ed., p. 98.

50. Bray, *Homosexuality*, p. 28.

51. Boswell, *Christianity*, p. 279, n. 32.

52. Osborne, *Politicall Reflections upon the Government of the Turks*, p. 81.

53. T. S., *The Adventures of (Mr. T. S.)*, p. 28.

54. Gainsford, *The Glory of England*, 25r.

55. Bray, *Homosexuality*, p. 62.

56. Boswell, *Christianity*, p. 159.

57. Rowse, *Homosexuals in History*, p. 17.

58. Rycaut, *The Present State*, p. 31.

59. For Bruce R. Smith, however, there was a sexual element behind the literary use of Neoplatonic concepts and models: *Homosexual Desire*, chapter 2.

60. Rycaut, *The Present State*, p. 31.

61. Bray, *Homosexuality*, p. 17.

62. Rycaut, *The Present State*, p. 34.

63. Grimeston, *The History of the Serrail*, p. 166.

64. Rycaut, *The History of the Turkish Empire*, p. 69.

65. Purchas, *Pilgrimage* (1613 ed.), p. 246.

66. Quoted in Patricia Parker, "Fantasies of 'Race' and 'Gender': Africa, Othello and bringing to light," in *Women, "Race," and Writing in the Early Modern Period*, Hendricks and Parker, eds., p. 84

67. Sandys, *A Relation of a Journey begun An. Dom. 1610*, p. 69.

68. Nicolay, *The Nauigations, peregrinations and voyages*, T. Washington, trans., p. 60r.

69. Shirley, *Discours of the Turkes*, p. 2.

70. Goodich, *The Unmentionable Vice*, p. 20.

71. Jonathan Goldberg, "Colin to Hobbinol: Spenser's Familiar Letters," *South Atlantic Quarterly*, 88 (1989), p. 115.

72. Jordan, *White over Black*, p. 25. Why such prurience should be a mark of the "civilized" is unclear.

73. *Sir Anthony Sherley and His Persian Adventure*, Ross, ed., p. 187.

74. Ibid., p. 107.

75. Ibid., p. 217.

76. See for instance Grimeston's translation of an account of the Persians by Pierre d'Avity: "although they marrie many wiues, yet they loue boies, and pursue them as eagerly or rather more than women: wherein they imitate the Turkes and moreouer they haue detestable places appointed for those pleasures, whereas they keepe young boies to that end." Edward Grimeston, *The Estates, Empires, & Principallities*, p. 793. See also *The Second Volume of the Post-boy*, p. 81.

77. Coryat, *Master Coryats Constantinopolitan Observations abridged* in *Purchas His Pilgrimes*, 10:425.

78. Kadir, *Columbus and the Ends of the Earth*, p. 70

5. Holy Land, Holy War

1. See Kadir, *Columbus and the Ends of the Earth*, pp. 30–31 esp.; Eden, *The Decades* (1555), pp. aiiiir–v. See also the survey by Roger B. Merriman, *The Rise of the Spanish Empire in the Old World and the New*, vol. 3: chapter 25; Charles Verlinden, Yvonne Freccero, trans., *The Beginnings of Modern Colonization*, chapter 1; and "The Muslim Frontier," in *New Iberian World*, Parry and Keith, eds., 1:189–234.

2. In his *American Holocaust*, David Stannard showed how Spaniards applied their anti-Muslim holy war ideology on the American Indians—with devastating results. (Unit III).

3. Segal and Stineback, eds., *Puritans, Indians, and Manifest Destiny*, p. 49, quoting Cotton Mather. See also Gary B. Nash, "The Image of the Indian in the Southern Colonial Mind," *The William and Mary Quarterly*, 3rd series, 29 (1972): 197–230; Canup, *Out of the Wilderness*, p. 142; Roy Harvey Pearce, "The 'Ruines of Mankind': The Indian and the Puritan Mind," *J. H. I.*, 13 (1952): 200–217.

4. Mead's views were not confined to England but extended to New England too: see William Hubbard, *A General History of New England*, p. 26.

5. *The Jamestown Voyages*, Barbour, ed., 1:114.

6. *The State Papers of John Thurloe*, Birch, ed., 5:82–83.

7. *Eighth Report of the Royal Commission on Historical Manuscripts*, part 1, p. 239.

8. Samuel Lee, *Israel Redux* (1677), chapter 13; Ross, *A view of all Religions*, p. 37.

9. See the map by the first Turkish printer, Ibraheem Mutteferrika, "Iqleem Misr,"

(undated but engraved and printed in 1729), which refers to "ard Filisteen." I am grateful to Professor E. Birnbaum for permission to reproduce the map.

10. *The Jamestown Voyages*, Barbour, ed., 1:234.

11. Ibid., 1:79.

12. *Purchas his Pilgrimes*, 19:219.

13. Ibid., p. 243.

14. Cave, "Richard Hakluyt's Savages: The Influence of 16th Century Travel Narratives on English Indian Policy in North America," *International Social Science Review*, 60 (1985), p. 9. See the earlier discussion of this theme in Wright, *Religion and Empire*, chapter 4, and Miller, *Errand Into the Wilderness*, chapter 4. By 1637 the theme was so common that Thomas Morton wrote a treatise on *New English Canaan or New Canaan* in which he described America (sometimes tongue-in-cheek) as the Promised Land to which the Christian colonists from England had divine right.

15. Robert Johnson, *Nova Britannia,* B3v; Robert Gray, *A Good Speed to Virginia*, D2r; Cushman, "Reasons and Considerations touching the lawfulness of removing out of England," in Young, ed., *Chronicles*, pp. 243–244.

16. Segal and Stineback, eds., *Puritans*, p. 91.

17. Ibid., p. 31. See Vaughan, *New England Frontier, Puritans and Indians 1620–1675*, who believes that this argument was used by far fewer of the Puritans than other English settlers, p. lxiii. See also Chester E. Eisinger, "The Puritans' Justification for Taking the Land," *Essex Institute Historical Collections*, 84 (1948): 131–143.

18. Mason, *A Brief History of the Pequot War*, reprinted in *History of the Pequot War*, Orr, ed., p. 44.

19. *The Worlde, or An historicall description of the most famous kingdomes and common-weales therein . . . Translated into English, and inlarged* (1601), pp. 54–55; Gainsford, *The Glory of England*, p. 37v.

20. T. S., *The Adventures of (Mr. T. S.)*, p. 114.

21. Gainsford, *The Glory of England*, p. 30v.

22. *Purchas his Pilgrimage* (1617), p. 361.

23. George Sandys, *A Relation*, "To the Prince." See also the comment by Haynes about Sandys' map with which the text opens: Sandys "nowhere recognizes Turkish or Arab jurisdiction . . One might conclude (with justice) that the Muslim presence was thought of as a shadow over the land rather than as an historical actuality to be assimilated." *The Humanist as Traveller*, p. 16.

24. *Purchas his Pilgrimes*, 19:235.

25. William S. Simmons, "Cultural Bias in New England Puritans' Perception of the Indians," *William and Mary Quarterly*, 38 (1981): p. 71.

26. Suriano, *Treatise on the Holy Land*, p. 29.

27. Thomas Brightman too emphasized this theme. See in particular, *A Revelation of the*

Reuelation that is the Revelation of St. John, p. 292.

28. Ashton, *A shorte treatise upon the Turkes Chronicles,* the introductory poem; John Ross, *Tangers Rescue; or a Relation of the late Memorable Passages at Tanger* "A Poem," (1680), p. 35; Defoe, see conclusion below; and Foss, *A Journal of the Captivity and Sufferings of John Foss,* pp. 47, 69.

29. De Castries, *Les Sources . . . d'Angleterre,* 2: 578.

30. See Mather, *Decennium,* in *Narratives of the Indian Wars,* Lincoln, ed.: "we Translated the Bible into Indian. That they might gather from hence, that the French [Catholics] had put Poison into the Good Drink," p. 257. See also Mather, *The Life of the Renowned John Eliot,* p. 124.

31. See Kellaway, *The New England Company 1649–1776,* chapters 2 and 5.

32. Erdmann, *The Origin of the Idea of Crusade*; John Kelsay and James Turner Johnson, *Just War and Jihad*; Stannard, *American Holocaust*; Bainton, *Christian Attitudes toward War and Peace*; Michael Walzer, *The Revolution of the Saints.* See also J. H. Parry, *The Age of Reconnaissance,* p. 390.

33. Turner, *Ideology, Reason and the Limitation of War,* chapter 2.

34. Bainton, *Christian Attitudes,* pp. 44–45.

35. Erdmann, *The Origin,* pp. 41–56.

36. David Little, " 'Holy War' Appeals and Western Christianity: A Reconsideration of Bainton's Approach," in *Just War,* Kelsay and Johnson, eds., p. 127.

37. Ibid., p. 129.

38. Craigie, *The Problem of War in the Old Testament,* pp. 49–50. Such a view was advanced in 1629 by the rector Richard Bernard, for whom holy war was exclusively the war of Yahweh. In his *The Bible-Battells or The Sacred Art Military* (1629), he presented "an History of Holy Warres"—the wars in the Old Testament between the Israelites and God's enemies.

39. Tenenti, *Piracy and the Decline of Venice, 1580–1615,* chapters 2 and 4.

40. Tyerman, *England and the Crusades 1095–1588,* pp. 369–370. For a brief discussion of "holy war" in medieval England see Schwoebel, *The Shadow of the Crescent,* pp. 135 ff.

41. Johnson, *Ideology,* p. 82. Braudel stated that after 1600 the idea of an anti-Muslim crusade gained ground, but went into decline as soon as the Thirty Years War started, *The Mediterranean,* 2:844.

42. *A Trve Declaration,* Force, ed. 3:7. See Alfred A. Cave, "Canaanites in a Promised Land: the American Indian and the Providential Theory of Empire," *American Indian Quarterly,* 12 (1988): 277–297.

43. Waterhouse, *A Declaration of the State of the Colony in Virginia* (1622), pp. 17, 23. See also *A Relation or Iournall of the beginning and proceedings of the English Plantation setled at Plimoth in NEW ENGLAND* (1622), pp. 65–72.

44. Mason, *A Brief History of the Pequot War,* in Orr, ed., *History of the Pequot War,* pp. 19, 23, 30.

45. Cited in Segal and Stineback, eds., *Puritans*, p. 111.

46. Underhill, in Orr, ed., *History of the Pequot War*, pp. 80–81.

47. Wigglesworth, *The Poems of Michael Wigglesworth*, Bosco, ed., p. 91. See also Canup, *Out of the Wilderness*, p. 80, for the Indian-Amalekite comparison.

48. Increase Mather, *A Brief History of the Warr with the Indians in Newe-England,* Slotkin and Folson, eds., p. 86. See the discussion of King Philip's War as a "just" and "holy" war in Jill Lepore, *The Name of War*, pp. 107–113.

49. Cotton Mather, *Decennium Luctuosum* (1699), in *Narratives of the Indian Wars, 1675–1699*, Lincoln, ed., pp. 201, 203, 208, 210, 227, 230, 231.

50. *The Works of the Right Reverend Joseph Hall, D. D.*, 7:349–354.

51. Newton, *A Notable History of the Saracens*, B4r–C1v. The author was Cornelius Augustinus Curio.

52. What may have motivated Heywood to write his play was the success, temporary as it was, of the Croatians in defending themselves against the Ottoman advance in Central Europe. In 1593, *A true discourse wherein is set down the Wonderfull mercy of God shewed towardes the Christians, on the two and twenty of Iune, 1592 against the Turke, before Sysck in Croatia* had appeared in London; in 1595, *The Warres betweene the Christians and the Turke* and *The Estate of Christians, liuing vnder the subiection of the Turke* also appeared.

53. *The Foure Prentises of London. With the Conquest of Ierusalem* in *The Dramatic Works of Thomas Heywood*, 2:221.

54. Ibid., p. 243.

55. Carew, *Godfrey of Bvlloigne or The Recouerie of Hierusalem An Heroicall Poeme written in Italian by Seig. Torquato Tasso, and translated into English by R. C. Esquire* (1594).

56. Lee, "Tasso and Shakespeare's England," 169–184 in *Elizabethans and Other Essays*. Boas, ed.

57. James I, *The Poems of James VI of Scotland*, Craigie, ed., 1:197–257.

58. De Castries, *Les Sources . . . d'Angleterre*, 2:223.

59. Ibid., pp. 225, 227.

60. Cited in Watson and Thomson, *History of Philip III*, 2: appendix.

61. *The Fugger News-Letters, Second Series*, Klarwill, ed., p. 346.

62. In 1596 a biography of Scanderberg was translated from French into English (with a prefatory poem by Edmund Spenser) in which the heroic achievements of this "scourge of the Turks" were presented. Iaqves de Lavardin, *The Historie of George Castriot*.

63. "London's Love to the Royall Prince Henrie, meeting him on the River of Thames (at his returne from Richmonde) with a worthie Fleete of her Citizens, on Thursday the last of May 1610," in *The Progresses, Processions, and Magnificent Festivities, of King James the First,* Nichols, ed., 2:315 ff.

64. Nichols, ed., *Progresses . . . James the First*, p. 323.

65. Nichols, ibid, p. 528.

66. Ibid., p. 529.

67. Ibid.

68. Ibid., p. 528.

69. Ibid.

70. *The Letters of John Chamberlain*, McClure, ed., 1:416.

71. Ibid., p. 418. He repeated the same words to Sir Dudley Carleton, p. 421.

72. Bergeron, *English Civic Pageantry 1558–1642*, p. 96.

73. Nichols, ed., *Progresses . . . of King James*, 2:541.

74. Akrigg, *Jacobean Pageant, The Court of King James I*, p. 146.

75. Nichols, eds., *Progresses . . . of King James*, 2:659–660.

76. Ibid., p. 662.

77. Ibid., p. 664.

78. Cited in Nichols, *Progresses . . . of King James*, 2:647. See also Bergeron, *English Civic Pageantry*, pp. 98–99.

79. *The Letters and the Life of Francis Bacon*, Spedding et al. eds., 13:175–181.

80. *The Negotiations of Sir Thomas Roe*, p. 4.

81. Fisher, *Barbary Legend*, p. 186.

82. Anderson, *An Historical and Chronological Deduction of the Origin of Commerce*, 2:291.

83. *Algiers Voyage in a Iournall or Briefe Reportary of all occurents hapning*, A3v.

84. See chapters 5 and 6 in Hebb, *Piracy and the English Government* for a detailed analysis of this expedition.

85. Bacon, *Letters and the Life,* Spedding et al., eds., 7:17–36. The text, however, only appeared in print in 1629.

86. J. Max Patrick, "Hawk versus Dove: Francis Bacon's Advocacy of a Holy War by James I against the Turks," *Studies in the Literary Imagination*, 4 (1971), p. 161.

87. Bacon, *Letters and the Life*, Spedding et al., eds., 7:28.

88. Ibid., p. 32.

89. Ibid.

90. Ibid., p. 19.

91. It is interesting that when William Monson looked back at this unsuccessful expedition during the reign of King Charles I, he too viewed it as having been motivated by James's religious zeal. Although Monson did not use the phrase "holy war," he emphasized at the outset of his treatise how the king had been concerned for his subjects and "all other Christian people in Europe" who were being captured by the Turks: "The ill-managed Enterprise upon Algiers," in *Sir William Monson's Naval Tracts*, 3:94.

92. *Commons Debate 1621*, Notestein et al., eds., 4:14.

93. *Godfrey of Bulloigne: A critical edition of Edward Farifax's translation of Tasso's Gerusalemme Liberata, together with Farifax's Original Poems*, Lea and Gang, eds., pp. 590–91.

94. Ibid., pp. 88–93.

95. *C. S. P. and Manuscripts . . .Venice, 1621–1623*, 27:483–484. A decade earlier the cru-

sade was aimed against France. See George Marcelliue, *The French Herald Summoning all True Christian Princes to a generall Croisade, for a holy warr against the great Enemy of Christendome, and all his slaves. Upon the Occasion of the most execrable murther of Henry the great* (1611).

96. De Castries, *Les Sources . . . d'Angleterre*, 3:49.

97. Ibid., pp. 125–127.

98. Kellet, *A Retvrne from Argier*, p. 66.

99. Marsh, *A New Survey of the Turkish Empire*, pp. 59 ff.

100. Ibid., pp. 64–65.

101. Ibid., pp. 65–66.

102. Ibid., p. 75.

103. Ibid., p. 76.

104. Ibid., p. 85.

105. Ibid., p. 84.

106. S. P. 16/279 fols. 61r–v.

107. *A Letter from the King of Morocco, To his Majesty the King of England Charles I* (London, 1680, and republished in 1682). I am using the latter version.

108. Ibid. See another version of this letter in De Castries, *Les Sources . . . d'Angleterre*, 3:357.

109. Ibid., 3:431. My translation.

110. Waller, *Poems* (1645), "Of Salley."

111. See Hebb, *Piracy and the English Government*, chapter 11.

112. Trevor-Roper, *Archbishop Laud, 1573–1645*, p. 369.

113. Walzer, *The Revolution*, p. 290. Walzer erroneously stated that Mead was the influential eschatologist, but the Fast Sermons reveal the preeminence of Brightman's influence.

114. Zinck, "Of Arms and the Heroic Reader: The Concept of Psychomachy in Spenser, Milton and Bunyan," pp. 59–60.

115. Fuller, *The Historie of the Holy Warre*, p. 283.

116. Ibid., p. 15.

117. Ibid., p. 278.

118. Ibid., p. 16.

119. So it is not accurate to state, as Johnson has, that English seventeenth-century writers did not reject "holy war *per se*" (*Ideology*, p. 97 n).

120. *Poems of Edmund Waller*, Thorn Drury, ed., pp. 35 and 156.

121. *Newes from the Great Turke*, title page.

122. Ross, *The Alcoran of Mahomet*, Ff r-v.

123. Camoes, *The Lusiads, or Portugals Historicall Poem*, VII, 5.

124. *Rome for the Great TURKE, Or Else, The Great Turke for little Rome . . . With an humble*

perswasion to all Christian Princes to joyne couragiously [against] *Rabshakeh* (1664), frontispiece.

125. See my discussion of "Christendom" in "The Individual and the Unity of Man in the Writings of Thomas Traherne," pp. 240–249.

126. *The Letters of Robert Blake*, Powell, ed., and *The Journals of Sir Thomas Allin*, Anderson, ed.

127. I am grateful to Professor Robert G. Collmer for discussing Bunyan's work with me and for sending me a copy of the first Arabic translation of *The Pilgrim's Progress*.

128. *C. S. P. Domestic, Charles I, 1636–37*, 10:87.

129. *John Josselyn, Colonial Traveler*, Lindholdt, ed., p. 190.

130. *Johnson's Wonder-Working Providence, 1628–1651*, Jameson, ed., pp. 272–273.

131. *The Diary of Samuel Sewall, 1674–1729*, 1:165.

132. *Diary of Cotton Mather*, 1:242–243.

CONCLUSION

1. Joseph Pitts, *A True and Faithful Account of the Religion and Manners of the Mohammetans*, p. 3. About a century later the American novelist Royall Tyler also mentioned that the "Arabs" ate their prisoners. *The Algerine Captive*, p. 201.

2. Phelps, *A True Account of the Captivity of Thomas Phelps*, pp. 8–9.

3. *A Plan of the English Commerce Being a Compleat Prospect of the Trade of this Nation, as well the Home Trade as the Foreign*, pp. xiii–xiv.

4. Ibid., pp. 234 and 238.

5. Ibid., p. 239.

6. Ibid., p. 241.

7. Ibid., p. 243–45. For the imperialism of Defoe see J. A. Downie, "Defoe, Imperialism, and the Travel Books Reconsidered," in *Critical Essays on Daniel Defoe*, Roger D. Lund, ed, pp. 78–96.

8. *A Plan of the English Commerce*, p. 243.

9. Ronald Takaki, "*The Tempest* in the Wilderness: The Racialization of Savagery," *The Journal of American History*, 79 (1992), p. 912.

10. *The Turkish Refugee: Being a Narrative of the Life, Sufferings, Deliverances, and Conversion, of Ishmael Bashaw, a Mahometan Merchant, from Constantinople, who was taken Prisoner by the Spaniards, and Made a Wonderful Escape to England. Where, having become a Convert to the Christian Faith, He was Publicly Baptized, with the Approbation of the Right Reverend the Lord Bishop of Lincoln* (1797).

11. Ibid., p. 16.

12. Ibid., p. 17.

13. Ibid., p. 20.

14. Ibid., p. 21.

15. Ibid., p. 27.

16. Ibid., p. 28.

17. Ibid.

18. Ibid., p. 29.

19. Ibid., p. 30.

20. It is important to distinguish between Bashaw's account, which seems quite realistic, and the Muslim "pose" that was adopted by a writer calling himself "Gaifer." In *The Conversion of a Mahometan to the Christian Religion Described in a Letter from Gaifer, in England, to Aly-Ben-Hayton, His Friend in Turkey*, the author sought to show the superiority of non-conformist Christianity to the Anglican Church.

21. See Sha'ban, *Islam and Arabs in Early American Thought*: chapter 3, although the discussion chiefly covers the nineteenth century and later.

22. *Journals of the House of Burgesses of Virginia*, McIlwaine, ed., p. 476; quoted by Alden T. Vaughan, "From White Man to Redskin: Changing Anglo-American Perceptions of the American Indian," *The American Historical Review*, 87 (1982), p. 935.

23. See chapter 5 in Allison, *The Crescent Obscured*.

24. For references to earlier short texts see Sha'ban, *Islam and Arabs*, p. 76.

25. In Tyler's novel, *The Algerine Captive*, a similar superimposition was made. p. 36 n.

26. Roy Harvey Pearce, "The Significances of the Captivity Narrative," *American Literature*, 19 (1947): 1–20. For other studies on the captivity narratives among the Indians, see Marius Barbeau, "Indian Captivities," *Proceedings of the American Philosophical Society* 94 (1950): 522–548; Richard VanDerBeets, " 'A Thirst for Empire': The Indian Captivity Narrative as Propaganda," *Research Studies*, 40 (1972): 207–215; Slotkin, *Regeneration through Violence*, chapter 5; Vaughan and Clark, *Puritans among the Indians*, introduction.

27. Foss, *A Journal*, p. 74.

28. See Maria Martin's account and Thomas Nicholson's *An Affecting Narrative of the Captivity & Sufferings of Thomas Nicholson, [A Native of New. Jersey.]*.

29. Nathaniel Knowles, "The Torture of Captives by the Indians of Eastern North America," *Proceedings of the American Philosophical Society*, 82 (1940): 151–225.

30. Foss, *A Journal*, pp. 32–33.

31. Ibid., pp. 52–53. Foss missed the irony: a black slave would not have been better treated in "Christian" America. In 1800, James Wilson Stephens denounced slavery in Algeria in the same breath as he denounced it in America. *An Historical and Geographical Account of Algiers*, p. 243.

32. Foss, *A Journal*, p. 47.

33. Ibid., p. 69.

Appendix B

1. Al-Fishtali, *Manahil as-safa*, p. 196.

2. Turkish cartography, however, shows Islamic familiarity with America. See Kemal Ozdemir, *Ottoman Nautical Charts and the Atlas of Ali Macar Reis*. (Marmara Bank Publication, 1992).

Bibliography

Primary Sources

Unless otherwise indicated, the place of publication of books before 1900 is London.

British Government Documents

Acts of the Privy Council.

Calendar of State Papers, Domestic Series.

Calendar of State Papers, Foreign Series.

Calendar of Letters and State Papers, relating to English Affairs preserved principally in the Archives of Simancas, Elizabeth 1568–1579.

Calendar of State Papers and Manuscripts, Relating to English Affairs existing in the archives and collections of Venice and in other libraries of Northern Italy.

Calendar of State Papers, Colonial Series, East Indies, China and Japan, 1513–1616. Edited by W. Noel Sainsbury. London, 1862.

Calendar of State Papers, Colonial Series, 1574–1660.

Calendar of State Papers, Colonial Series, America and West Indies.

Calendar of Scottish Papers.

List and Analysis of State Papers, Foreign Series, Elizabeth, August 1589–June 1590. Edited by Richard Bruce Wernham. London: HMSO, 1964.

State Papers, Public Record Office.

Other Primary Sources

The Admirable Deliverance of 266. Christians by Iohn Reynard Englishman from the captiuitie of the Turkes, (1608.)

Africanus, Leo. *The History and Description of Africa.* Translated by John Pory (1600).

Al-Fishtali, Abu Faris. *Manahil as-safa fi ma'athir mawaleena ash- shurafa'*. Edited by K. Kuriem. Rabat, 1974.

Algiers Voyage in a Iournall or Briefe Reportary of all occurents hapning (1621).

Al-Mawsuli, Hanna. *Rihla*. Edited by Antoon Rabbat al-Yasooi'i. Beirut: Catholic Press, 1906.

Alsop, George. *A Character of the Province of Maryland* (1666). Edited by Newton D. Mereness. Freeport, New York: Books for Libraries Press, 1902, reprinted in 1972.

Al-Wufrani, Mohammad bin Abdallah. *Nozhet al-Hadi bi-Akhbar Mulook al-Qarn al-Hadi*. Edited by O. Houdas. Paris: Ernest Leroux, 1888.

Allin, Thomas. *The Journals of Thomas Allin. 1660–1678* 2 vols. Edited by R. C. Anderson. London: Navy Records Society, 1939–1940.

The Arrivall and Intertainements of the Embassador, Alkaid Jaurar Ben Abdella, with his Associate, Mr. Robert Blake (1637).

Ashton, Peter. *A shorte treatise upon the Turkes Chronicles* (1546).

Bacon, Francis. *Essays*. In *Selected Writings of Francis Bacon*. Edited by Hugh G. Dick. New York: Random House, 1955.

———. *The Letters and the Life of Francis Bacon*. 14 vols. Edited by James Spedding et al. London: Longmans, 1889.

Baker, Thomas. *Piracy and Diplomacy in Seventeenth-Century North Africa*. Edited by C. R. Pennell. London and Toronto: Associated University Presses, 1989.

Barbour, Philip L., ed. *The Jamestown Voyages under the First Charter*. 2 vols. Cambridge: Cambridge University Press, 1969.

Barret, Robert. *Theoricke and Practike of Modern Warres* (1598).

Bashaw, Ishmael. *The Turkish Refugee: Being a Narrative of the Life, Sufferings, Deliverances, and Conversion, of Ishmael Bashaw, a Mahometan Merchant, from Constantinople, who was taken Prisoner by the Spaniards, and Made a Wonderful Escape to England. Where, having become a Convert to the Christian Faith, He was Publicly Baptized, with the Approbation of the Right Reverend the Lord Bishop of Lincoln* (1797).

Bath, Marquis of. *Calendar of the Manuscripts of the Marquis of Bath*. Dublin: HMSO, 1907.

Beacon, Richard. *Solon his Follie, or A Politique Discourse touching the Reformation of common-weales conquered, declined or corrupted*. Edited by Clare Carroll and Vincent Carey. Binghamton, N.Y.: Medieval & Renaissance Texts & Studies, 1996.

Beaumont, Francis and Fletcher, John. *The Works of Beaumont and Fletcher*. 11 vols. Edited by Alexander Dyce. Freeport, New York: Books for Libraries Press, 1970. First published between 1843–1846.

Bernard, Richard. *The Bible-Battells or The Sacred Art Military* (1629).

Beverley, Robert. *The History and Present State of Virginia* (1705). Edited by Louis B. Wright. Chapel Hill: University of North Carolina Press, 1947.

Bin Qasim, Ahmad. *Nasir al-Deen 'ala Qawm al-Kafireen*. Edited by Mohammad Razzuk.

Addar al-Bayda': Publications of the School of Literature and Social Sciences, 1987.

Blake, Robert. *The Letters of Robert Blake Together with Supplementary Documents.* 2 vols. Edited by J. R. Powell. London: Navy Records Society, 1937.

Blount, Henry. *A Voyage into the Levant. A Briefe Relation of a Journey, lately performed by Master Herny Blunt, Gentleman, from England by the way of Venice, into Dalmatia, Sclavonica, Bosnah, Hungary, Macedonia, Thessaly, Thrace, Rhodes and Egypt, unto Gran Cario:With particular observations concerning the moderne condition of the Turkes.* 3rd ed., 1638. First published in 1636.

Bradford, William. *Bradford's History of Plymouth Plantation, 1606–1646.* Edited by William T. Davis. New York: Barnes & Noble, Inc., 1908.

———. *Of Plymouth Plantation, 1620–1647.* Edited by Samuel Eliot Morison. New York: Alfred A. Knopf, 1966.

A Brave Memorable and Dangerovs Sea-Fight, foughten neere the Road of Tittawan in Barbary (1636).

Brereton, John. *A Briefe and true Relation of the Discouerie of the North part of Virginia; being a most pleasant, fruitfull and commodious soile* (1602).

Brightman, Thomas. *A Revelation of the Reuelation that is the Revelation of St. John opened clearly with a logicall Resolution and Exposition.* Amsterdam, 1615.

Brooks, Francis. *Barbarian Cruelty Being a True History of the Distressed Condition of the Christian Captives under the Tyranny of Mully Ishmael Emperor of Marocco* (1693).

Bunyan, John. *The Holy War, made by Shaddai upon Diabolus, for the regaining of the metropolis of the World* (1682).

Burton, Robert. *The Anatomy of Melancholy.* Edited by Holbrook Jackson. London: J. M. Dent, 1977.

Byam, Henry. *A Retvrne from Argier. A Sermon Preached at Minhead in the County of Somerset the 16. of March, 1627* (1628).

Calvert, Thomas. *The blessed Jew of Morocco: or, A Blackmoor made White* (1648).

Camoes, Luiz Vas de. *The Lusiads, or Portugals Historicall Poem . . . Now newly put into English by Richard Fanshaw Esq., 1655.* Edited by Geoffrey Bullough. Carbondale, Illinois: Southern Illinois University Press, 1963.

Carew, Lord George. *Letters from George Lord Carew to Sir Thomas Roe, Ambassador to the Court of the Great Mogul, 1615–1617.* Edited by John Maclean. London: Camden Society, 1860. Reprinted in 1968.

Carew, Richard. *Godfrey of Bvlloigne or The Recouerie of Hierusalem An Heroicall Poeme written in Italian by Seig. Torquato Tasso, and translated into English by R. C. Esquire* (1594).

Carr, R. *The Mahumetane or Turkish Historie, containing three Bookes* (1600).

Carteret, Sir George. *The Barbary Voyage of 1638.* Edited by Boies Penrose. Philadelphia, 1929.

The Case of many Hundreds of Poor English Captives, in Algier (1680).

Casas, Bartholomé de las. *History of the Indies.* Translated and edited by André Collard. New York: Harper & Row, 1971.

Chamberlain, John. *The Letters of John Chamberlain.* 2 vols. Edited by Norman Egbert McClure. Philadelphia: The American Philosophical Society, 1939.

Child, Josiah. *A New Discourse of Trade* (1694).

Clarendon, Earl of. *Calendar of the Clarendon State Papers.* 5 vols. Edited by F. J. Routledge. Oxford: Clarendon Press, 1970.

The Clarke Papers. 3 vols. Edited by C. H. Firth. London: Longmans, Green, and Co., 1899.

Commons Debate 1621. 7 vols. Edited by Wallace Notestein et al. New Haven: Yale University Press, 1935.

The Conversion of a Mahometan to the Christian Religion Described in a Letter from Gaifer, in England, to Aly-Ben-Hayton, His Friend in Turkey. 10th ed. Concord, 1797.

Corbett, Julian S., ed. *Papers Relating to the Navy during the Spanish War, 1585–1587.* London: Navy Records Society, 1987.

Coryat, Thomas. *Master Coryats Constantinopolitan Observations abridged.* In *Purchas His Pilgrimes,* vol. 8.

———. *Coryats Crudities hastily gobled up in five moneths travells* (1611).

Cotgrave, John. *Wits Interpreter* (1655, 2nd ed., 1662).

Covel, John. *Extracts from the Diaries of Dr. John Covel, 1670–1679.* In *Early Voyages and Travels in the Levant.* Edited by J. Theodore Bent. New York: Burt Franklin, 1964. First published in 1893.

Cowper, Earl. *The Manuscripts of the Earl Cowper, K. G., preserved at Melbourne Hall, Derbyshire.* 3 vols. London: HMSO, 1888.

Coxere, Edward. *Adventures by Sea of Edward Coxere.* Edited by E. H. W. Meyerstein. New York and London: Oxford University Press, 1946.

C. R.; *A True Historicall discourse of Muley Hamets rising to the three Kingdomes of Moruecos, Fes and Sus* (1609).

Cromwell, Oliver. *The Writings and Speeches of Oliver Cromwell.* 4 vols. Edited by W. C. Abbott. Cambridge: Harvard University Press, 1937–1947.

———. *By the Protector. A Proclamation Giving Encouragement to such as shall transplant themselves to Jamaica* (October 1655).

Daborne, Robert. *A Christian turn'd Turke.* Edited by A. E. H. Swaen. In Anglia: Zeitschrift für Englische Philologie. Band XX. Halle: Max Niemeyer, 1898.

D'Aranda, Emanuel. *The History of Algiers and it's Slavery* (1666).

D'Avenant, Sir William. *The Dramatic Works of Sir William D'Avenant.* 4 vols. New York: Russell & Russell Inc., 1964.

Davis, William. *A True Relation of the Travels and most miserable Captivity of William Davis, Barber-Surgeon of London* (1614).

De Castries, Le Comte Henry, editor. *Les Sources Inédites de L'Histoire du Maroc: Archives et*

Bibliothèques D'Angleterre. Vol. 1. Paris: Editions Ernest Leroux, 1918; vol. 2. Paris: Paul Geuthner, 1925.

―――. *Les Sources Inédites de L'Histoire du Maroc: Archives et Bibliothèques de France*. 3 vols. Paris: Ernest Leroux, 1909.

―――. *Une Description du Maroc sous le Règne de Moulay Ahmed el-Mansour (1596) D'Apres un Manuscrit Portugais de la Bibliothèque Nationale*. Edited and translated by De Castries. Paris: Ernest Leroux, 1909.

De Cenival, Pierre, and Philippe de Cossé Brissac, eds. *Les Sources Inédites de l'Histoire du Maroc: Archives et Bibliothèques Nationale*. Vol. 3. Paris: Paul Geuthner, 1936.

Defoe, Daniel. *A Plan of the English Commerce Being a Compleat Prospect of the Trade of this Nation, as well the Home Trade as the Foreign*. 1st ed., 1728; 2nd ed., 1730.

De Lavardin, Iaqves. *The Historie of George Castriot, Svrnamed Scanderbeg, King of Albanie* (1596).

"The Discourse of the Old Company, 1625." In Lyon Gardiner Tyler, ed., *Narratives of Early Virginia*. New York: Barnes and Noble, 1907. Reprinted in 1959.

Discovery of 29 Sects, here in London (1641).

Drake, Sir Francis. *The World Encompassed* (1628).

Eburne, Richard. *A Plain Pathway to Plantations (1624)*. Edited by Louis B. Wright. Ithaca, New York: Cornell University Press, 1962.

Eden, Richard. *The Decades of the newe worlde or west India* (1555).

―――. *The first Three English books on America [? 1511]–1555 A. D.* Edited by Edward Arber. New York: Kraus Reprint Co., 1971. First published in 1885.

―――. *The History of Trauayle in the West and East Indies . . . Newly set in order, augmented, and finished by Richarde Willes* (1577).

Eighth Report of the Royal Commission on Historical Manuscripts. London, 1881.

Eliot, Sir John. *An Apology for Socrates and Negotium Posterorum*. 2 vols. Edited by Alexander B. Grosart. London, 1881.

Elliot, Adam. *A Modest Vindication of Titus Oates the Salamanca-Doctor from Perjury or an Essay to Demonstrate him only forsworn in several Instances* (1682).

Escobedo, Father. *Pirates, Indians and Spaniards: Father Escobedo's "La Florida."* Edited by James W. Covington. Translated by A. F. Falcones. St. Petersburg, Florida: Great Outdoors Publishing, 1963.

The Estate of Christians, liuing vnder the subiection of the Turke (1595).

Evelyn, John. *The Diary of John Evelyn*. 6 vols. Edited by E. S. De Beer. Oxford: Clarendon Press, 1955.

―――. *The History of the Three late famous Imposters* (1669).

Fairfax, Edward. *Godfrey of Bulloigne: A critical edition of Edward Farifax's translation of Tasso's "Gerusalemme Liberata," together with Fairfax's Original Poems*. Edited by Kathleen M. Lea and T. M. Gang. Oxford: Clarendon Press, 1981.

The Famous History of the Life and Death of Captain Thomas Stukeley. In Richard Simpson, *The School of Shakespeare*. vol. 1. London: Chatto and Windus, 1878.

A Fight at Sea, Famously fought by the Dolphin of London against fiue of the Turkes Men of Warre (1617).

Finet, John. *Finetti Philoxenis* (1656).

————. *Ceremonies of Charles I The Note Books of John Finet 1628–1641*. Edited by Albert J. Loomie, S. J. New York, Fordham University Press, 1987.

Foss, John. *A Journal of the Captivity and Sufferings of John Foss*. Newburyport, 1798.

Fox, George. *To The Great Turk and the King at Argiers* (1680).

The Fugger News-Letters, First Series. Edited by Victor von Klarwill. Translated by Pauline de Chary. New York: Books for Libraries Press, 1970. First published in 1924.

The Fugger News-Letters, Second Series. Edited by Victor von Klarwill. Translated by L. S. R. Byrne. London: John Lane the Bodley Head Ltd., 1926.

Fuller, Thomas. *The Historie of the Holy Warre* (1639).

————. *The History of the Worthies of England*. 3 vols. Edited by P. Austin Nuttall (1840).

G[ainsford], T[homas], *The Glory of England, or A Trve Description of many excellent prerogatiues and remarkeable blessings, whereby She Triumpheth ouer all the Nations of the World* (1618).

Gascogine, George. *The Posies*. Edited by John W. Cunliffe. New York: Greenwood Press, 1969. Originally publ. 1907.

Gee, Joshua. *Narrative of Joshua Gee of Boston, Mass*. Hartford, 1943.

Gorges, Ferdinando. *Sir Ferdinando Gorges and His Province of Maine*. 3 vols. Edited by James Phinney Baxter. Boston, 1890.

Gray, Robert. *A Good Speed to Virginia* (1609).

Grimeston, Edward. *The History of the Imperiall Estate of the Grand Seigneurs* (1635).

————. *The Estates, Empires & Principallities of the World* (1615).

Hakluyt, Richard. *The Principall Navigations, Voiages and Discoveries of the English nation* (1589).

————. *The Principal Navigations, Voyages, Traffiques & Discoveries of the English Nation*. 8 vols. Glasgow: James MacLehose and Sons, 1904.

————. *The Portable Hakluyt's Voyages*. Edited by Irwin R. Blaker. New York: Viking Press, 1965.

Hall, Joseph. *The Works of the Right Reverend Joseph Hall, D. D.* 10 vols. Edited by Philip Wynter. Reprinted, New York: AMS Press, 1969. First published in 1869.

Hanmer, Meredith. *The Baptizing of a Turke: A Sermon preached at the Hospitall of Saint Katherin, adioyning unto her Maiesties Towne the 2 October 1586* (1586).

Harrison, William. *The Description of England*. Edited by Georges Edelen. Washington and New York: The Folger Shakespeare Library and Dover Publications, Inc., 1994.

Hasleton, Richard. *The Miserable Captivity of Richard Hasleton, born at Braintree in Essex*. In *An English Garner*. 2 vols. Edited by C. Raymond Beazley. New York: Cooper Square

Publishers, Inc. Reprinted in 1964.

Heywood, Thomas. *The Dramatic Works of Thomas Heywood Now First Collected with Illustrative Notes and a Memoir of the Author in Six Volumes.* New York: Russell & Russell Inc., 1964.

Hotten, John Camden, ed., *The Original Lists of Persons of Quality . . . Who went from Great Britain to the American Plantations, 1600–1700.* Baltimore, 1974. First published in 1874.

Hubbard, William. *A General History of New England from the Discovery to MDCLXXX.* New York: Arno Press. Reprinted in 1972. First published in 1815.

Ibn Abi Dinar, Abu Abdallah. *Kitab al-Munis fi akhbar Ifriqiyah wa Tunis.* Edited by Muhammad Shammam. Tunis: al-Maktabah al-Atiqah, 1967.

James I. *The Poems of James VI. of Scotland.* 2 vols. Edited by James Craigie. Edinburgh and London: William Blackwood & Sons, 1955.

———. *The Basilicon Doron of King James VI,* 2 vols. Edited by James Craigie. London and Edinburgh: W. Blackwood & Sons, Ltd., 1944–1950.

Johnson, Edward. *Johnson's Wonder Working Providence.* Edited by J. Franklin Jameson. New York: Barnes and Noble, 1910. Reprinted in 1959.

Johnson, Edward. *Wonder-Working Providence.* Delmar, New York: Scholars' Facsimiles & Reprints, 1974.

Johnson, Robert. *Nova Britannia. Offring most Excellent fruites by Planting in Virginia* (1609).

———. *The New Life of Virginea* (1612). In *Tracts and Other Papers, Relating Principally to the Origin, Settlement, and Progress of the Colonies in North America.* Vol. 3. Edited by Peter Force. Gloucester, Mass.: Peter Smith, 1963. First published in 1844.

Jones, Inigo. *Designs by Inigo Jones for Masques & Plays at Court.* Introduction by Percy Simpson and C. F. Bell. New York: Russell & Russell, 1924. Reprinted in 1966.

Jonson, Ben. *The Alchemist* in *Ben Jonson.* 11 vols. Edited by C. H. Herford and Percy and Evelyn Simpson. Oxford: Clarendon Press, 1925–1963.

Josselyn, John. *John Josselyn, Colonial Traveler: A Critical Edition of "Two Voyages to New England."* Edited by John Lindholdt. Hanover, N. H. and London: University Press of New England, 1988.

Journals of the House of Burgesses of Virginia, 1659/60–1693. Edited by H. R. McIlwaine. Richmond, Virginia, 1914.

Kellet, Edward. *A Retvrne from Argier* (1628).

Khan, Abul Hasan. *A Persian at the Court of King George, 1809–10.* Translated and edited by Margaret Morris Cloake. London: Barrie & Jenkins, 1988.

Kingsbury, Susan Myra, ed., *The Records of the Virginia Company of London.* 4 vols. Washington: Government Printing Office, 1906.

Knavery in all Trades: or, The Coffee-House. A Comedy. As it was Acted in the Christmas Holidays by several Apprentices With great Applause (1664).

Knolles, Richard. *General Historie of the Turkes.* 2nd ed., 1610.

Knott, Nathaniel. "Advise of a Sea-man touchinge the expidition intended agaisnt the

Turkish Pirates." S. P. 16/281.

Knyvett, Sir Henry. *Briefe Discourse of Warre* (1596).

Kyd, Thomas. *The Works of Thomas Kyd*. Edited by Frederick S. Boas. Oxford: Clarendon Press, 1967. First published in 1901.

Lee, Samuel. *Israel Redux: or The Restauration of ISRAEL Exhibited in Two Short Treatises* (1677).

A Letter from the King of Morocco, To his Majesty the King of England Charles I (1680, republished in 1682).

Letters from the great Turke lately sent vnto the holy Father the Pope and to Rodulphus naming himselfe King of Hungarie, and to all the Kinges and Princes of Christendome (1606).

Lincoln, Charles H., ed. *Narratives of the Indian Wars, 1675–1699*. New York: Barnes & Noble, 1913. Reprinted in 1959.

Lithgow, William. *The Rare Adventures and Painful Peregrinations of William Lithgow*. Edited by Gilbert Phelps and B. I. Lawrence. London: Folio Society, 1974.

The Lives and Deaths of the Two English Pyrats Purser, and Clinton (1639).

The Lives of the Right Hon. Francis North, Baron Guilford, . . . The Hon. Sir Dudley North . . . and The Hon. And Rev. Dr. John North (1826). 3 vols. Edited by Roger North.

Lorant, Stefan, ed. *The New World: The First Pictures of America*. New York: Duell, Sloan & Pearce, 1946.

Mainwaring, Henry. *The Life and Works of Sir Henry Mainwaring*. 2 vols. Edited by G. E. Manwaring. London: The Navy Records Society, 1920.

Manningham, John. *The Diary of John Manningham of the Middle Temple, 1602–1603*. Edited by Robert Parker Sorlien. Hanover, New Hampshire: University Press of New England, 1976.

Marcelline, George. *The French Herald Summoning all True Christian Princes to a generall Croisade, for a holy warr against the great Enemy of Christendome, and all his slaves. Upon the Occasion of the most execrable murther of Henry the great* (1611).

Marlowe, Christopher. *Tamberlaine. Part One and part Two: Text and Major Criticism*. Edited by Irving Ribner. Indianapolis, New York: Odyssey Press, 1974.

Marsh, Henry. *A New Survey of the Turkish Empire History and Government Compleated* (1633 and 1664).

Marvell, Andrew. *The Complete Poems*. Edited by Elizabeth Story Donno. Harmondsworth: Penguin Books, 1972.

Martin, Maria. *History of the Captivity and Sufferings of Mrs. Maria Martin, who was six years a slave in Algiers*. Boston, 1807.

Mason, John. *A Brief History of the Pequot War*. Reprinted in *History of the Pequot War*. Edited by Charles Orr. Cleveland: Helman-Taylor Company, 1897.

Massinger, Philip. *The Plays and Poems of Philip Massinger*. 5 vols. Edited by Philip Edwards and Colin Gibson. Oxford: Clarendon Press, 1976.

Mather, Increase. *A Brief History of the Warr with the Indians in New-England* (1676). In *So*

Dreadful a Judgment: Puritan Responses to King Philip's War, 1676–1677. Edited by Richard Slotkin and James K. Folson. Middletown, Connecticut: Wesleyan University Press, 1978.

Mather, Cotton. *Decennium Luctuosum* (1699). In *Narratives of the Indian Wars, 1675–1699*. Edited by Charles H. Lincoln. New York: Barnes & Noble, Inc. 1913.

———. *Diary of Cotton Mather*. 2 vols. New York: Frederick Ungar Publishing Co., 1957.

———. *The Life of the Renowned John Eliot; A Person justly Famous in the CHURCH OF GOD* (1691).

Matthews, George T., ed. *News and Rumour in Renaissance Europe (The Fugger Newsletters)*. New York: Capricorn Books, 1950.

Mercurius Fumigosus, June 28–July 5.

Messerole, Harrison T., ed. *Seventeenth-Century American Poetry*. New York: Anchor Books, 1968.

Middleton, Henry. *An Account of the Captivity of Sir Henry Middleton* in *Jean de Laroque, A Voyage to Arabia Foelix through the Eastern Ocean and the streights of the Red-Sea* (1732).

Milton, John. *The Life Records of John Milton, 1655–1669*. Edited by J. Milton French. New York: Gordian Press, Inc., 1966.

Monson, Sir William. *Sir William Monson's Naval Tracts*. 5 vols. Edited by M. Oppenheim. London: Navy Records Society, 1913.

More, Thomas. *Dialogue of Comfort* in *The Complete Works of St. Thomas More*. Edited by Louis L. Martz and Frank Manley. New Haven and London: Yale University Press, 1976.

Morgan, J. *A Complete History of Algiers* (1731, reprinted in 1739).

Morton, Thomas. *New English Canaan or New Canaan. Containing an Abstract of New England, Composed in three Bookes*. Amsterdam, 1637.

New Englands First Fruits (1643).

Nevves from Sea, Of two notorious Pyrats Ward the Englishman and Danseker the Dutchman (1609).

Newes from the Great Turke (1645).

Newton, Thomas. *A Notable History of the Saracens* (1575).

Nicolay, Nicholas. *The Nauigations, peregrinations and voyages, made into Turkie by Nicholas Nicholay. Translated by T. Washington* (1585).

Nichols, John, ed. *The Progresses and public Processions of Queen Elizabeth*. 3 vols., 1823.

———. *The Progresses, Processions, and Magnificent Festivities, of King James the First*. 4 vols., 1828.

Nicholson, Thomas. *An Affecting Narrative of the Captivity & Sufferings of Thomas Nicholson, [A Native of New. Jersey.]* Boston, 1816.

Nowell, Samuel. *Abraham in Arms: or The first Religious General with his Army engaging in a War*. Boston, 1678.

Okeley, William. *Eben-Ezer: or, A Small Monument of Great Mercy, Appearing in the Miraculous Deliverance of William Okeley, William Adam, John Anthony, John Jephs, John Carpenter* (1676).

Orr, Charles, ed. *History of the Pequot War.* Cleveland: Helman-Taylor Company, 1897.

Osborne, Francis. *Politicall Reflections upon the Government of the Turks* (1650 and 1656).

Oviedo, Gabriel de. *Historia general y natural de las Indias.* Translated by J. H. Parry and R. G. Keith. In *New Iberian World*, vol. 3. New York: Times Books, 1984.

Peele, George. *The Dramatic Works of George Peele.* Edited by John Yoklavich. New Haven and London: Yale University Press, 1961.

Pellow, Thomas. *The Adventures of Thomas Pellow, of Penryn, Mariner.* Edited by Robert Brown. London, 1890. First published in 1740.

Phelps, Thomas. *A True Account of the Captivity of Thomas Phelps, at Machaness in Barbary* (1685).

Pitts, Joseph. *A True and Faithful Account of the Religion and Manners of the Mohammetans.* Exeter, 1704.

Purchas, Samuel. *Purchas his Pilgrimage* (1613).

———. *Purchas his Pilgrimage* (1617).

———. *Hakluytus Posthumus or Purchas His Pilgrimes.* 20 vols. Reprinted in New York: AMS Press, 1965. First published in 1905.

Quinn, David B. et al., eds. *New American World, A Documentary History of North America to 1612.* 5 vols. New York: Arno Press, 1979.

Quinn, David Beers, ed. *The Roanoke Voyages 1584–1590.* New York: Dover, 1991. Originally published 1955.

Raleigh, Walter. *A relation of the second voyage to Guiana* (1596).

Rawlins, John. *The Famous and Wonderful Recovery of a Ship of Bristol, called the Exchange, from the Turkish Pirates of Argier* (1622). In *An English Garner: Stuart Tracts (1603-1693).* Introduction by C. H. Firth. New York: Cooper Square Publishers, Inc., 1964.

A Relation or Iournall of the beginning and proceedings of the English Plantation setled at Plimoth in NEW ENGLAND (1622).

Ricard, Robert and Chantal de la Véronne. *Les Sources Inédites de L'Histoire du Maroc . . . Archives et Biliothèques D'Espagne.* 3 vols. Paris: Paul Geuthner, 1956.

Robinson, Henry. *Libertas, or Reliefe to the English Captives in Algier* (1642).

———. *Liberty of Conscience: or the sole means to obtaine Peace and Truth* (1643).

Roe, Thomas. *The Negotiations of Sir Thomas Roe in His Embassy to the Ottoman Porte, from the Year 1621 to 1628 Inclusive* (1740).

Rome for the Great TURKE, Or Else, The Great Turke for little Rome . . .With an humble perswasion to all Christian Princes to joyne couragiously [against] *. . . Robshakeh* (1664).

Rosier, James. *A Trve Relation of the most prosperous voyage made this present yeere 1605, by Captaine George Waymouth* (1605).

Ross, Alexander. *The Alcoran of Mahomet, Translated out of Arabique into French; By the Sieur Du Ryer, Lord of Malezair, and Resident for the King of France, at Alexandria* (1649).

———. *A View of all Religions in the World.* Second Edition. *(1655).*

Ross, John. *Tangers Rescue; or a Relation of the late Memorable Passages at Tanger* (1681).

Rycaut, Paul. *The Present State of the Ottoman Empire* (1668).

————. *The History of the Turkish Empire, From the Year 1623, to the Year 1677* (1687).

Salisbury, The Marquess of. *Calendar of the Manuscripts of the Most Honourable The Marquess of Salisbury, Part XXI* (1609–1612). Edited by G. Dyfnallt Owen. London: HMSO, 1970.

Sanderson, John. *A Discourse of the most notable things of the famous Citie Constantinople: both in ancient and late time*. In *Purchas His Pilgrimes*, vol. 9.

Sandys, George. *A Relation of a Journey begun An.Dom.1610* (1615).

Segal, Charles M. and David C. Stineback, eds. *Puritans, Indians, and Manifest Destiny*. New York: G. P. Putnam's Sons, 1977.

Seventeenth-Century Economic Documents. Edited by Joan Thirsk and J. P. Cooper. Oxford: Clarendon Press, 1972.

Sewall, Samuel. *The Diary of Samuel Sewall, 1674–1729*. 3 vols. New York: Arno Press, 1972.

Sha'ban, Fuad. "The Mohammedan World in English Literature, c. 1580–1642: Illustrated by a text of the *Travailes of the Three English Brothers*." Ph. D. dissertation: Duke University, 1965.

Shirley , Anthony. *Sir Anthony Sherley and His Persian Adventure*. Edited by Sir. E. Denison Ross. London: George Routledge & Sons, Ltd., 1933.

Shirley, Thomas. *Discours of the Turkes by Sr. Thomas Sherley*. Edited by Sir E. Denison Ross. London: Camden Miscellany, 1936.

Smith, John. *Travels and Works of Captain John Smith*. 2 vols. Edited by Edward Arber and re-edited by A. G. Bradley. New York: Burt Franklin, 1966. First published in 1910.

————. *The Complete Works of Captain John Smith (1580- 1631)*. 3 vols. Edited by Philip L. Barbour. Chapel Hill and London: University of North Carolina Press, 1986.

Smythe, Sir John. *Certain Discourses Concerning Weapons* (1590).

Spratt, T. A. B. *Travels and Researches in Crete*. 2 vols. Amsterdam: Adolf M. Hakkert, 1984. First published in 1865.

The Statutes of the Realm (1819).

Stephens, James Wilson, *An Historical and Geographical Account of Algiers*. 2nd ed. Brooklyn, 1800.

Strachey, William. *A True Reportory of the Wracke* (1610). In *Purchas his Pilgrimes*, vol. 19.

————. *The Historie of Travell into Virginia Britania (1612)*. Edited by Louis B. Wright and Virginia Freund. London: Hakluyt Society, 1953.

Stuart Royal Proclamations. 2 vols. Edited by James F. Larkin and Paul L. Hughes. Oxford: Clarendon Press, 1983.

St. Serfe, Thomas. *Tarugo's Wiles: or the Coffee-House*. Edited by Philip A. Park. Ph.D. dissertation: University of Pennsylvania, 1968.

Suriano. Fra Francesco. *Treatise on the Holy Land*. Translated by Theophilus Bellorini and Euegene Hoade. Jerusalem: Franciscan Press, 1949.

Tanner, John. *The Falcon: A Narrative of the Captivity & Adventures of John Tanner During Thirty Years Residence among the Indians in the Interior of North America*. Introduction by Louise Erdrich. New York: Penguin, 1994.

Thevet, Andrewe. *The New Found Worlde of Antarctike* (1568).

Thurloe, John. *A Collection of the State Papers of John Thurloe Esq.* 7 vols. Edited by John Birch (1742).

Timberlake, H. *A True and strange discourse of the trauailes of two English Pilgrimes* (1603).

A Trve Declaration of the estate of the Colonie of Virginia (1610). In *Tracts and Other Papers, Relating Principally to the Origin, Settlement, and Progress of the Colonies in North America.* Vol. 3. Edited by Peter Force. Gloucester, Mass.: Peter Smith, 1963. First published in 1844.

A true discourse wherein is set down the Wonderfull mercy of God shewed towards the Christians, on the two and twenty of Iune, 1592 against the Turke, before Syssek in Croatia (1593).

T. S. [Thomas Smith] *The Adventures of (Mr. T. S.), An English Merchant, Taken Prisoner by the Turks of Argiers* (1670).

Tudor Economic Documents. 3 vols. Edited by R. H. Tawney and Eileen Power. London: Longmans, 1924.

Tyler, Royall. *The Algerine Captive*. Introduction by Jack B. Moore. Gainesville, Fl.: Scholars' Facsimiles & Reprints, 1967.

Véronne, Chantal de la. *Tanger sous l'occupation anglaise d'après une description anonyme de 1674*. Paris: Librarie Orientaliste Paul Geuthner, 1972.

Vickers, Brian, ed. *Shakespeare The Critical Heritage*. London and Boston: Routledge & Kegan Paul, 1976.

Viereck, Phillip. *The New Land: Discovery, Exploration and Early Settlement of Northeastern United States*. New York: John Day Co., 1967.

Voyage to Maryland (1633) Relatio Itineris in Marilandiam. Edited and Translated by Barbara Lawatsch-Boomgaarden with Josef IJsewijn. Wauconda, Illinois: Bolchazy-Carducci, 1995.

Waller, Edmund. *Poems* (1645).

———. *Poems of Edmund Waller*. Edited by G. Thorn Drury. New York: Greenwood Press, 1968. First published in 1893.

Warmstry, Thomas. *The Baptized Turk, or a Narrative of the happy Conversion of Signior Rigep Dandulo* (1658).

The Warres betweene the Christians and the Turke (1595).

Waterhouse, Edward. *A Declaration of the State of the Colony in Virginia* (1622).

Watson R. and W. Thomson, *History of Philip III* (1786). 2 vols.

Webbe, Edward. *Edward Webbe, Chief Master Gunner, His Trauailes, 1590*. Edited by Edward

Arber (1869).

Whitaker, Alexander. *Good Newes from Virginia* (1613).

White, John. *The Planters Plea or the Grovnds of Plantations Examined, And vsuall Objections answered* (1630).

Wigglesworth, Michael. *The Poems of Michael Wigglesworth*. Edited by Ronald A. Bosco. Lanham: University Press of America, 1989.

Williams, Sir Roger. *A Briefe Discourse of warre. Written by Sir Roger Williams, Knight; with his opinion concerning some parts of the martial discipline* (1590).

Windus, John. *A Journey to Mequinez; The Residence of the Present Emperor of Fez and Morocco* (1725).

Winship, George Parker, ed., *Sailors Narratives of Voyages along the New England Coast, 1524–1624*. Boston: Houghton, Mifflin & Co., 1905.

Winthrop, John. *Winthrop's Journal "History of New England, 1630–1649."* 2 vols. Edited by James Kendall Hosmer. New York: Barnes & Noble, Inc., 1908.

Wood, William. *New England's Prospect* (1634).

The Worlde, or An historicall description of the most famous kingdomes and common-weales therein . . . Translated into English, and inlarged (1601).

Wright, Irene, ed. and trans. *Further English Voyages to Spanish America, 1583–1594*. London: Hakluyt Society 1951.

Young, Alexander, ed. *Chronicles of the Pilgrim Fathers of the Colony of Plymouth, 1602–1625*. Boston, 1841.

Secondary Sources

Akrigg, G. P. V. *Jacobean Pageant, The Court of King James I*. New York: Athenauem, 1967.

Allison, Robert J. *The Crescent Obscured: The United States and the Muslim World, 1776–1815*. Oxford: Oxford University Press, 1995.

Anderson, Adam. *An Historical and Chronological Deduction of the Origin of Commerce*. 4 vols. (1801).

Anderson, R. C. *Naval Wars in the Levant, 1559–1853*. Princeton: Princeton University Press, 1952.

Andrews, K. R., N. P. Canny and P. E. Hair. *The Westward Enterprise: English Activities in Ireland, the Atlantic, and America, 1480–1650*. Detroit, Wayne State University Press, 1979.

Andrews, Kenneth R. *Elizabethan Privateering: English Privateering During the Spanish War, 1585–1603*. Cambridge: Cambridge University Press, 1964.

————. "Sir Robert Cecil and Mediterranean plunder." *The English Historical Review* 87 (1972): 513–532.

————. "Elizabethan Privateering." In *Raleigh in Exeter 1985 Privateering and Colonisation in the reign of Elizabeth I*. Edited by Joyce Youings. Exeter: University of Exeter, 1985.

———. *Ships, Money and Politics: Seafaring and Naval Enterprise in the Reign of Charles I*. Cambridge: Cambridge University Press, 1991.

Appiah, Kwame Anthony. "Race." In *Critical Terms for Literary Study*. Edited by Frank Lentricchia and Thomas McLaughlin. Chicago: University of Chicago, 1990.

Axtell, James. *The Invasion Within, The Conquest of Cultures in Colonial North America*. New York and Oxford: Oxford University Press, 1985.

Baepler, Paul. "The Barbary Captivity Narrative in Early America." *Early American Literature* 30 (1995): 95–120.

Bainton, Roland. *Christian Attitudes toward War and Peace: A Historical Survey and Critical Re-evaluation*. Nashville, Tenn.: Abingdon Press, 1960.

Ballagh, James Curtis. *White Servitude in the Colony of Virginia*. Baltimore: The John Hopkins Press, 1973. First published in 1895.

Barbeau, Marius. "Indian Captivities." *Proceedings of the American Philosophical Society* 94 (1950): 522–548.

Bartels, Emily C. *Spectacles of Strangeness: Imperialism, Alienation and Marlowe*. Philadelphia: University of Pennsylvania Press, 1993.

———. "Making More of the Moor: Aaron, Othello, and Renaissance Refashionings of Race." *Shakespeare Quarterly* 41 (1990): 433–54.

———. "Imperialist Beginnings: Richard Hakluyt and the Construction of Africa." *Criticism* 34 (1992): 517–538.

Barthelemy, Anthony Gerard. *Black Face, Maligned Race. The Representation of Blacks in English Drama from Shakespeare to Southerne*. Baton Rouge and London: Louisiana State University, 1987.

Bates, E. S. *Touring in 1600*. London: Century, 1987. Introduction by George Bull. First published in 1911.

Beckingham, C. F. "The Near East: North and North-east Africa." In D. B. Quinn, ed., *The Hakluyt Handbook*, 176–196.

Ben Rejeb, Lotfi. "Barbary's 'Character' in European Letters, 1514–1830: An Ideological Prelude to Colonization." *Dialectical Anthropology* 6 (1982): 345–355.

Berckman, Evelyn. *Victims of Piracy: The Admiralty Court, 1575–1678*. London: Hamish Hamilton, 1979.

Bergeron, David M. *English Civic Pageantry, 1558–1642*. Columbia: University of South Carolina Press, 1971.

Binham, Caroline. "Seventeenth-Century Attitudes toward Deviant Sex." *Journal of Interdisciplinary History* 1 (1971): 447–468.

Boswell, John. *Christianity, Social Tolerance, and Homosexuality*. Chicago and London: University of Chicago Press, 1980.

Bovill, E. W. *The Battle of Alcazar*. London: The Batchworth Press, 1952.

Braudel, Fernand. *The Mediterranean and the Mediterranean World in the Age of Philip II.* 2 vols. Translated by Siân Reynolds. New York: Harper & Row, Publishers, 1973. First published in 1949.

Bray, Alan. *Homosexuality in Renaissance England.* Boston: GMP Publishers, 1988. First published in 1982.

Breen, T. H. and Stephen Foster. "Moving to the New World: The Character of Early Massachusetts Immigration." *The William and Mary Quarterly*, 3rd series. 30 (1973): 189–222.

Breitwieser, Mitchell Robert. *American Puritanism and the Defense of Mourning: Religion, Grief, and Ethnology in Mary White Rowlandson's Captivity Narrative.* Madison: University of Wisconsin Press, 1990.

Brenner, Robert. *Merchants and Revolution: Commercial Change, Political Conflict, and London's Overseas Traders, 1550–1653.* Princeton: Princeton University Press, 1993.

Breslow, Marvin Arthur. *English Puritan Views of Foreign Nations, 1618–1640.* Cambridge, Mass.: Harvard University Press, 1970.

Bridenbaugh, Carl. *Vexed and Troubled Englishmen, 1590–1642.* New York: Oxford University Press, 1968.

————. *Jamestown 1544–1699.* New York and Oxford: Oxford University Press, 1980.

Brooke, Z. N. "The Expedition of Thomas Stukeley in 1578." *English Historical Review* 28 (1913): 330–337.

Bullough, Vern L. *Sexual Variance in Society and History.* Chicago and London: University of Chicago Press, 1976.

————. "The Sin Against Nature and Homosexuality." In *Sexual Practices and the Medieval Church.* Edited by Vern L. Bullough and James Brundage. New York: Prometheus Books, 1982.

Burg, B. R. *Sodomy and the Pirate Tradition: English Sea Rovers in the Seventeenth-Century Caribbean.* New York and London: New York University Press, 1983.

Butler, James D. "British Convicts shipped to American Colonies." *American Historical Review* 2 (1896): 12–34.

Callendar, Charles and Lee M. Kochems. "The North American Berdache." *Current Anthropology* 24 (1983): 443–470.

Candido, Joseph. "Captain Thomas Stukeley: The Man, the Theatrical Record, and the Origins of Tudor 'Biographical' Drama." *Anglia* 105 (1987): 50–68.

Canny, Nicholas P. "The Ideology of English Colonization from Ireland to America." *The William and Mary Quarterly* 30 (1973): 575–598.

Canup, John. *Out of the Wilderness: The Emergence of an American Identity in Colonial New England.* Middletown, Connecticut: Wesleyan University Press, 1990.

Cardillac, Louis. *Al-Muriskiyyoon al-Andalusiyyoon wal Maseehiyyoon.* Translated by Abdul Jalil al-Tamimi. Tunis, 1983.

Carroll, Kenneth L. "Quaker Slaves in Algiers, 1679–1688." *The Journal of the Friends' Historical Society* 54 (1982): 301–312.

Carroll, Peter N. *Puritanism and the Wilderness*. New York and London: Columbia University Press, 1969.

Cave, Alfred. "Richard Hakluyt's Savages: The Influence of 16th Century Travel Narratives on English Indian Policy in North America." *International Social Science Review* 60 (1985): 3–24.

———. "Canaanites in a Promised Land: the American Indian and the Providential Theory of Empire." *American Indian Quarterly* 12 (1988): 277–297.

———. *The Pequot War*. Amherst: University of Massachusetts Press, 1996.

Cawley, Robert Ralston. *The Voyagers and Elizabethan Drama*. New York: Kraus Reprint Corporation, 1966. First published in 1938.

Chew, Samuel C. *The Crescent and the Rose: Islam and England During the Renaissance*. New York: Octagon Press, 1974. First published in 1937.

Chiappelli, Fredi, ed. *First Images of America*. 2 vols. Berkeley: University of California Press, 1976.

Chitty, C. W. "Aliens in England in the Sixteenth Century." *Race* 8 (1966): 129–145.

Clark, G. N. "Barbary Corsairs in the Seventeenth Century." *Cambridge Historical Journal* 8 (1945–46): 22–35.

Clissold, Stephen. *The Barbary Slaves*. New York: Barnes and Noble, 1992. First published in 1977.

Coindreau, Roger. *Les Corsairs de Salé*. Paris, 1948.

Craigie, Peter C. *The Problem of War in the Old Testament*. Grand Rapids, Mich.: Eerdmans, 1978.

Cressy, David. *Coming over: Migration and communication between England and New England in the seventeenth century*. Cambridge: Cambridge University Press, 1987.

D'Amico, Jack. *The Moor in English Renaissance Drama*. Tampa, Fl.: University of South Florida Press, 1991.

Davies, D. W. *Elizabethans Errant*. Ithaca, New York: Cornell University Press, 1967.

De Castries, Comte Henry. *Moulay Ismail et Jacques II*. Paris: Ernest Leroux, 1903.

Delbanco, Andrew. "Looking Homeward, Going Home: The Lure of England for the Founders of New England." *New England Quarterly* 59 (1986): 358–386.

Demos, John. *The Unredeemed Captive: A Family Story from Early America*. New York: Alfred Knopf, 1994.

Downie, J. A. "Defoe, Imperialism, and the Travel Books Reconisdered." In *Critical Essays on Daniel Defoe.*. Edited by Roger D. Lund. New York: G. K. Hall & Co., 1997.

Draper, John W. *The Othello of Shakespeare's Audience*. New York: Octagon Books. Reprinted in 1966.

Earle, Peter. *Corsairs of Malta and Barbary*. London: Sidgwick & Jackson, 1970.

Eisinger, Chester E. "The Puritans' Justification for Taking the Land." *Essex Institute Historical Collections* 84 (1948): 131–143.

Epstein, M. *The Early History of the Levant Company*. London: George Routledge & Sons, 1908.

Erdmann, Carl. *The Origin of the Idea of Crusade*. Translated by Marshall W. Baldwin and Walter Goffart. Princeton: Princeton University Press, 1977.

Evans, William Mckee. "From the Land of Canaan to the Land of Guinea: The Strange Odyssey of the 'Sons of Ham.'" *American Historical Review* 85 (1980): 15–43.

Faroqhi, Suraiya. *Pilgrims and Sultans: The Hajj under the Ottomans*. London: I. B. Tauris & Co Ltd, 1994.

Felsenstein, Frank. *Anti-Semitic Stereotypes: A Paradigm of Otherness in English Popular Culture, 1660–1830*. Baltimore and London: The Johns Hopkins University Press, 1995.

Ferguson, Arthur B. *The Indian Summer of English Chivalry*. Durham: Duke University Press, 1960.

Feuer, Lewis S. "Francis Bacon and the Jews: Who was the Jew in the *New Atlantis?*" *Jewish Historical Society of England–Transactions* 29 (1982–86): 1–25.

Fisher, Sir Godfrey. *Barbary Legend: War, Trade and Piracy in North Africa, 1415–1830*. Oxford: Oxford University Press, 1957.

Forbes, Jack D. *Africans and Native Americans: The Language of Race and the Evolution of Red-Black Peoples*. Urbana and Chicago: University of Illinois Press, 1993.

Foreman, Carolyn Thomas. *Indians Abroad 1493–1938*. Norman: University of Oklahoma Press, 1943.

Fausz, J. Frederick. "Middlemen in Peace and War: Virginia's Earliest Indian Interpreters, 1608–1632." *The Virginia Magazine of History and Biography* 95 (1987): 41–64.

Fuller, Mary C. *Voyages in Print: English Travel to America, 1576–1624*. Cambridge: Cambridge University Press, 1995.

Goffman, Daniel. *Britons in the Ottoman Empire 1642–1660*. Seattle and London: University of Washington Press, 1998.

Goldberg, Jonathan. "Colin to Hobbinol: Spenser's Familiar Letters." *South Atlantic Quarterly* 88 (1989): 107–126.

Goodich, Michael. *The Unmentionable Vice: Homosexuality in the Later Medieval Period*. Santa Barbara, California: ABC-Clio, Inc., 1979.

Greenblatt, Stephen. *Renaissance Self-Fashioning: From More to Shakespeare*. Chicago and London: University of Chicago, 1980.

———. *Shakespearean Negotiations: The Circulation of Social Energy in Renaissance England*. Oxford: Clarendon Press, 1988.

———. "Learning to Curse: Aspects of Linguistic Colonialism in the Sixteenth Century." In *Learning to Curse*. New York and London: Routledge, 1990, 16–39.

———. "An English Obsession." *The New York Times Book Review*. 11 August 1996, 12–13.

Gunny, Ahmad. *Images of Islam in Eighteenth-Century Writings*. London: Grey Seal, 1996.

Hall, Kim F. "Guess Who's Coming to Dinner? Colonization and Miscegenation in *The Merchant of Venice*." *Renaissance Drama* n. s. (1992): 87–111.

———. *Things of Darkness: Economics of Race and Gender in Early Modern England*. Ithaca and London: Cornell University Press, 1995.

Hammond, Paul. "Titus Oates and 'Sodomy.' " In *Culture and Society in Britain 1660–1800*. Edited by Jeremy Black. Manchester and New York: Manchester University Press, 1997.

Harris, Bernard. "A Portrait of a Moor." *Shakespeare Survey* 11 (1958): 89–97.

Haynes, Jonathan. *The Humanist as Traveler: George Sandys' Relation of a Journey begun An. Dom. 1610*. London: Associated University Press, 1986.

Heard, J. Norman. *White into Red: A Study of the Assimilation of White Persons Captured by Indians*. Metuchen, N. J.: The Scarecrow Press, Inc., 1973.

Hebb, David Delison. *Piracy and the English Government, 1616–1642*. Aldershot, England: Scolar Press, 1994.

Henderson, Katherin Usher and Barbara F. McManus. *Half Humankind: Contexts and Texts of the Controversy about Women in England, 1540–1640*. Urbana and Chicago: University of Illinois Press, 1985.

Hill, Christopher, *Liberty Against the Law*. New York: Penguin Press, 1996.

———. "Male Homosexuality in 17th-Century England." In *The Collected Essays of Christopher Hill*. Amherst: University of Massachusetts Press, 1986, 3: 226–235.

Hodgen, Margaret Trabue. *Early Anthropology in the Sixteenth and Seventeenth Centuries*. Philadelphia: University of Pennsylvania Press, 1964.

Hoenselaars, A. J. "The Elizabethans and the Turk at Constantinople." *Cahiers Elisabethians* 47 (1995): 29–42.

Howard, Jean E. "An English Lass amid the Moors: Gender, race, sexuality, and national identity in Heywood's 'The Fair Maid of the West.' " In *Women, "Race," and Writing in the Early Modern Period*. Edited by Margo Hendricks and Patricia Parker. London and New York: Routledge, 1994.

Hulme, Peter. *Colonial Encounters: Europe and the native Caribbean, 1492–1797*. London and New York: Methuen, 1986.

Hunter, G. K. "Elizabethans and Foreigners." In *Shakespeare in his own Age*. Edited by Allardyce Nicoll. Cambridge: Cambridge University Press, 1965.

Ide, Richard S. *Possessed with Greatness: The Heroic Tragedies of Chapman and Shakespeare*. Chapel Hill: University of North Carolina Press, 1980.

Innes, A. D. *The Maritime and Colonial Expansion of England Under the Stuarts (1603–1714)*. London: Samspon Low, Marston and Co., Ltd., 1932.

Izon, John. *Sir Thomas Stucley, c. 1525–1578: Traitor Extraordinary*. London: Andrew Melrose, 1956.

Jardine, Lisa. *Worldly Goods: A New History of the Renaissance*. New York and London: Doubleday, 1996.

Jennings, Francis. *The Invasion of America: Indians, Colonialism, and the Cant of Conquest*. New York: W. W. Norton & Company, 1975.

Johnson, James Turner. *Ideology, Reason and the Limitation of War: Religious and Secular Concepts 1200–1740*. Princeton: Princeton University Press, 1975.

———. *The Holy War Idea in Western and Islamic Traditions*. University Park, Pennsylvania: Pennsylvania State University Press, 1997.

Jones, Eldred. *Othello's Countrymen: Africans in English Renaissance Drama*. Oxford: Oxford University Press, 1965.

Jones, Howard Mumford. "The colonial impulse: an analysis of the 'promotion' literature of colonization." *Proceedings of the American Philosophical Society* 90 (1946): 131–161.

Jones, W. R. "The Image of the Barbarian in Medieval Europe." *Comparative Studies in Society and History* 13 (1971): 376–407.

Jordan, Winthrop D. *White over Black: American Attitudes Toward the Negro, 1550–1812*. Chapel Hill: University of North Carolina Press, 1968.

Jorgensen, Paul A. "Theoretical Views of War in Elizabethan England." *J. H. I.* 12 (1952): 469–481.

———. *Shakespeare's Military World*. Berkeley, Los Angeles: University of California Press, 1956.

Kadir, Djelal. *Columbus and the Ends of the Earth*. Berkeley: University of California Press, 1992.

Kahane, Henry and Renée and Andreas Tietze. *The Lingua Franca in the Levant*. Urbana: University of Illinois, 1958.

Katz, David S. *Philo-Semitism and the Readmission of the Jews to England, 1603–1655*. Oxford: Clarendon Press, 1982.

Kellaway, William. *The New England Company 1649–1776: Missionary Society to the American Indians*. London: Longmans, 1961.

Kelsay, John and James Turner Johnson. *Just War and Jihad: Historical and Theoretical Perspectives on War and Peace in Western and Islamic Tradition*. New York: Greenwood Press, 1991.

Kennedy, N. Brent with Robyn Vaughan. *The Melungeons*. Macon, Georgia: Mercer University Press, 1997. First published in 1994.

Knapp, Jeffrey. *An Empire Nowhere: England, America, and Literature from "Utopia" to "The Tempest."* Berkeley: University of California Press, 1992.

Knowles, Nathaniel. "The Torture of Captives by the Indians of Eastern North America." *Proceedings of the American Philosophical Society* 82 (1940): 151–225.

Kupperman, Karen Ordahl. *Settling with the Indians: The Meeting of English and Indian Cultures in America, 1580–1640*. Totowa, New Jersey: Rowman and Littlefield, 1980.

Larsen, Thorleif. "The Historical and Legendary Background of Peele's 'Battle of Alcazar.' " *Transactions of the Royal Society of Canada* 2 (1939): 185–197.

Lee, Sir Sidney. *Elizabethans and Other Essays*. Edited by Frederick S. Boas. Freeport: New York, 1968. Originally published 1929.

Lepore, Jill. *The Name of War: King Philip's War and the Origins of American Identity*. New York: Alfred A. Knopf, 1998.

Little, David. " 'Holy War' Appeals and Western Christianity: A Reconsideration of Bainton's Approach." In *Just War*. Edited by Kelsay and Johnson, 121–139.

Lloyd, Christopher. *English Corsairs on the Barbary Coast*. London: Collins, 1981.

Matar, Nabil. "The Individual and the Unity of Man in the Writings of Thomas Traherne." Ph.D. dissertation: Cambridge University, 1976.

———. "Some Notes on George Fox and Islam." *The Journal of the Friends' Historical Society* 55 (1989): 271–76.

———. "Renaissance England and the Turban." In *Images of the Other: Europe and the Muslim World before 1700*. Edited by David R. Banks. Cairo: American University in Cairo Press, 1996.

———. "Britons, Muslims, and American Indians: Gender and Power." Paper presented at South Central Renaissance Conference. Waco, Texas, 2–4 April 1998.

Islam in Brtitain, 1558–1685. Cambridge: Cambridge University Press, 1998.

———. "Eurocentrism or Islamocentrism? The Anglo-Spanish Conflict in Islamic Documents." Forthcoming in *A Festschrift for Hussam Al Khateeb*. Edited by Mohammad Shaheen.

"The Toleration of Muslims in Renaissance England: Practice and Theory." In *Religious Toleration from Cyrus to Defoe: The Variety of Rites*. Edited by John C. Laursen. Forthcoming, St. Martin's Press, 1999.

McCrory, Donald P., ed. and trans. *The Captive's Tale (La historia del cautivo) Don Quixote, Part One, Chapters 39–41*. Warminster: Aris & Philips, 1993.

McFarlane, Cameron. *The Sodomite in Fiction and Satire, 1660–1750*. New York: Columbia University Press, 1997.

Merriman, Roger B. *The Rise of the Spanish Empire in the Old World and the New*. 4 vols. New York: Cooper Square Publishers, Inc., 1962. First published 1918–1934.

Miller, Perry. *Errand Into the Wilderness*. Cambridge: Harvard University Press, 1956.

Morgan, Edmund S. *American Slavery, American Freedom: The Ordeal of Colonial Virginia*. New York: W. W. Norton, 1975.

———. "The First American Boom: Virginia 1618 to 1630." *William and Mary Quarterly* 3rd series. 28 (1971): 169–198.

Morison, Samuel Eliot. *Builders of the Bay Colony*. Boston: Houghton Mifflin Company. 2nd edition, 1958.

Muldoon, James. "The Indian as Irishman." *Essex Institute Historical Collections* 3 (1975):

267–289.

Murray, Stephen O. and Will Roscoe, eds. *Islamic Homosexualities: Culture, History, and Literature*. New York and London: New York University Press, 1997.

Nash, Gary B. "The Image of the Indian in the Southern Colonial Mind." *The William and Mary Quarterly* 3rd series, 29 (1972): 197–230.

Oaks, R. F. " 'Things Fearful to Name": Sodomy and Buggery in Seventeenth-Century New England." *Journal of Social History* 12 (1978–79): 268–282.

Pagden, Anthony. *European Encounters with the New World: From Renaissance to Romanticism*. New Haven and London: Yale University Press, 1993.

———. *The fall of natural man: the American Indian and the origins of comparative ethnology*. Cambridge: Cambridge University Press, 1982.

Parker, John. *Books to Build an Empire*. Amsterdam: N. Israel, 1965.

Parker, Patricia. "Fantasies of 'Race' and 'Gender': Africa, Othello and bringing to Light." In *Women, 'Race' and Writing in the Early Modern Period*. Edited by Margo Hendricks and Patricia Parker. London and New York: Routledge, 1994.

Parry, John H. and Robert G. Keith, eds. *New Iberian World*. 5 vols. New York: Times Books, 1984.

Parry, J. H. *The Age of Reconnaissance*. London: Weidenfeld & Nicolson Ltd, 1963.

Patrick. J. Max. "Hawk versus Dove: Francis Bacon's Advocacy of a Holy War by James I against the Turks." *Studies in the Literary Imagination* 4 (1971): 159–173.

Pearce, Roy Harvey. "The Significances of the Captivity Narrative." *American Literature* 19 (1947): 1–20.

———. "The 'Ruines of Mankind': The Indian and the Puritan Mind." *J. H. I.* 13 (1952): 200–217.

Penrose, Boies. *Travel and Discovery in the Renaissance 1420–1620*. New York: Atheneum, 1971. First published in 1952.

Penz, Charles. *Les Captifs Francais du Maroc au XVIIe Siècle (1577–1699)*. Rabat: Imprimerie Officielle, 1944.

Playfair, R. L. *The Scourge of Christendom* (1884).

Porter, A. N., ed. *Atlas of British Overseas Expansion*. New York: Simon & Schuster, 1991.

Powell, William S. *John Pory, 1572–1636*. Chapel Hill: University of North Carolina Press, 1977.

Pringle, Patrick. *Jolly Roger: The Story of the Great Age of Piracy*. New York: W. W. Norton and Company, 1953.

Quinn, David B. *Explorers and Colonies: America, 1500–1625*. London: The Hambledon Press, 1990.

———. *Set Fair for Roanoke: Voyages and Colonies, 1584–1606*. Chapel Hill and London: University of North Carolina Press, 1985.

———. *England and the Discovery of America, 1481–1620*. New York: Alfred A. Knopf,

1974.

―――. ed. *The Hakluyt Handbook*. 2 vols. London: Hakluyt Society, 1974.

Rabb, Theodore K. "The Stirrings of the 1590s and the Return of the Jews to England." *Jewish Historical Society of England—Transactions* 26 (1974–78): 26–33.

"Le Raiss Abdallah Ben Aicha Corsaire de Salé et Amiral de la Flotte Cherifienne." *La Revue Maritime* no. 140. (August 1931): 194–200.

Ralston, David B. *Importing the European Army: The Introduction of European Military Techniques and Institutions into the Extra-European World, 1600–1914*. Chicago: The University of Chicago Press, 1990.

Ransom, David. "Wives for Virginia, 1621." *The William and Mary Quarterly* 3rd series, 48 (1991): 3–18.

Relihan, Constance C. "Suppressing Islam: The Geography of Sidney's Arcadian Landscape." Paper read at the MLA Conference, Chicago, December 1995.

Riley, Stephen T. "Abraham Browne's Captivity by the Barbary Pirates, 1655." In *Seafaring in Colonial Massachusetts*. Boston: Colonial Society of Massachusetts, 1980.

Rosedale, H. G. *Queen Elizabeth and the Levant Company*. London, 1904.

Routh, E. M. G. *Tangier: England's Lost Atlantic Outpost, 1661–1684*. London: John Murray, 1912.

Rowse, A. L. *Homosexuals in History*. London: Dorset Press, 1983. First published in 1977.

Sachse, William L. "The Migration of New Englanders to England, 1640–1660." *American Historical Review* 53 (1948): 251–278.

Said, Edward W. *Orientalism*. New York: Vintage Books, 1979.

Salingar, Leo. "The New World in *The Tempest*." In *Travel and Drama in Shakespeare's Time*. Edited by Jean-Pierre Maquerlot and Michèle Willems. Cambridge: Cambridge University Press, 1996.

Samuel, E. R. "Portuguese Jews in Jacobean London." *Jewish Historical Society of England—Transactions* 18 (1953–55): 171–187.

Schwoebel, Robert. *The Shadow of the Crescent: The Renaissance Image of the Turk (1453–1517)*. New York: St. Martin's Press, 1967.

Seed, Patricia. *Ceremonies of Possesion in Europe's Conquest of the New World, 1492–1640*. Cambridge: Cambridge University Press, 1995.

Senior, C. M. *A Nation of Pirates: English Piracy in its Heyday*. London: David & Charles Newton Abbot, 1976.

Sha'ban, Fuad. *Islam and Arabs in Early American Thought: The Roots of Orientalism in America*. Durham, North Carolina: Acorn Press, 1991.

Shapiro, James. *Shakespeare and the Jews*. New York: Columbia University Press, 1996.

Sheehan, Bernard W. *Savagism and Civility: Indians and Englishmen in Colonial Virginia*. Cambridge: Cambridge University Press, 1980.

Shepherd, Simon. *Marlowe and the Politics of Elizabethan Theatre*. New York: St. Martin's

Press, 1986.

Simmons, William S. "Cultural Bias in New England Puritans' Perception of the Indians." *The William and Mary Quarterly* 38 (1981): 56–72.

Skilliter, Susan. *William Harborne and the Trade with Turkey, 1578–1582*. London: Oxford University Press, 1977.

————. "Three Letters from the Ottoman 'Sultana' Safiye to Queen Elizabeth I." In *Documents from Islamic Chanceries*. Edited by S. M. Stern. Cambridge, Mass.: Harvard University Press, 1965.

Skura, Meredith Anne. "Discourse and the Individual: the Case of Colonialism in *The Tempest*." *Shakespeare Quarterly* 40 (1989): 42–69.

Slotkin, Richard. *Regeneration through Violence: The Mythology of the American Frontier*. Middletown, Connecticut: Wesleyan University Press, 1973.

Smith, Abbot Emerson. *Colonists in Bondage: White Servitude and Convict Labor in America, 1607–1776*. Gloucester, Mass.: Peter Smith, 1965.

Smith, Bruce R. *Homosexual Desire in Shakespeare's England: A Cultural Poetics*. Chicago and London: University of Chicago Press, 1994. First published in 1991.

Smits, David D. " 'Abominable Mixture': Toward the Repudiation of Anglo-Indian Intermarriage in Seventeenth-Century Virginia." *The Virginia Magazine of History and Biography* 95 (1987): 157–193.

Souden, David. " 'Rogues, Whores and Vagabonds'?: Indentured Servant Emigrants to North America and the Case of Mid-Seventeenth Century Bristol." *Social History* 3 (1978): 23–41.

Stannard, David. *American Holocaust*. Oxford: Oxford University Press, 1992.

Symcox, Geoffrey W. "The Battle of the Atlantic, 1500–1700." In *First Images of America*, vol. 1. Edited by F. Chiapelli.

Takaki, Ronald. "*The Tempest* in the Wilderness: The Racialization of Savagery." *Journal of American History* 79 (1992): 892–912.

Taylor, E. G. R. *Late Tudor and Early Stuart Geography 1583–1650*. New York: Octagon Books, 1968. First published in 1934.

Tenenti, Alberto. *Piracy and the Decline of Venice, 1580- 1615*. Translated by Janet and Brian Pullan. Berkeley and Los Angeles: University of California Press, 1967.

Todorov, Tzvetan. *The Conquest of America*. Translated by Richard Howard. New York: Harper Perennial, 1992. First published in 1984.

Tokson, Elliot H. *The Popular Image of the Black Man in English Drama, 1550–1688*. Boston, Mass.: G. K. Hall and Co., 1982.

Toomer, G. J. *Eastern Wisedome and Learning: The Study of Arabic in Seventeenth-Century England*. Oxford: Clarendon Press, 1996.

Trevor-Roper, H. R. *Archbishop Laud, 1573–1645*. London: Macmillan and Co., 1962.

Trexler, Richard C. *Sex and Conquest: Gendered Violence, Political Order, and the European*

Conquest of America. Ithaca, New York: Cornell University Press, 1995.

Turan, Osman. "The Ideal of World Domination among the Medieval Turks." *Studia Islamica* 4 (1955): 77–90.

Tyerman, Christopher. *England and the Crusades 1095–1588*. Chicago and London: University of Chicago Press, 1988.

Vaidon, Lawdom. *Tangier: A Different Way*. Metuchen, New Jersey and London: Scarecrow Press, 1977.

VanDerBeets, Richard. " 'A Thirst for Empire': The Indian Captivity Narrative as Propaganda." *Research Studies* 40 (1972): 207–215.

Vaughan, Alden T. and Edward W. Clark, eds. *Puritans among the Indians: Accounts of Captivity and Redemption 1676–1724*. Cambridge, Mass.: The Belknap Press of Harvard University Press, 1981.

Vaughan, Alden T. and Daniel K. Richter. "Crossing the Cultural Divide: Indians and New Englanders, 1605–1763." *Proceedings of the American Antiquarian Society* 90 (1980), 23–99.

Vaughan, Alden T. *New England Frontier, Puritans and Indians 1620–1675*, 3rd ed. Norman and London: University of Oklahoma Press, 1995.

———. "From White Man to Redskin: Changing Anglo-American Perceptions of the American Indian." *The American Historical Review* 87 (1982): 917–954.

———. " 'Expulsion of the Salvages': English Policy and the Virginia Massacre of 1622." *The William and Mary Quarterly* 3rd. Series, 35 (1978): 57–84.

Vaughan, Virginia Mason. *Othello: A Contextual History*. Cambridge: Cambridge University Press, 1994.

Vella, Andrew P. *An Elizabethan-Ottoman Conspiracy*. Malta: Royal University of Malta, 1972.

Verlinden, Charles. *The Beginnings of Modern Colonization*. Translated by Yvonne Freccero. Ithaca and London: Cornell University Press, 1970.

Viereck, Philip, ed. *The New Land: Discovery, Exploration and Early Settlement of Northeastern United States*. New York: John Day and Co., 1967.

Vitkus, Daniel. "Turning Turk in *Othello*: The Conversion and Damnation of the Moor." *Shakespeare Quarterly* 48 (1997): 145–177.

Wallis, Hellen. "The Cartography of Drake's Voyage." In *Sir Francis Drake and the Famous Voyage, 1577–1580*. Edited by Norman J. W. Thrower. Berkeley, Los Angeles: University of California Press, 1984.

Walzer, Michael. *The Revolution of the Saints: A Study in the Origins of Radical Politics*. New York: Atheneum, 1973. First published in 1965.

Willan, T. S. *Studies in Elizabethan Foreign Trade*. Manchester: Manchester University Press, 1959.

Williams, Neville. *Captains Outrageous: Seven Centuries of Piracy*. New York: Macmillan

Company, 1962.

Wood, Alfred C. *A History of the Levant Company*. London: Oxford University press, 1935.

Wright, Sir Denis. *The English amongst the Persians*. London: Heinemann, 1977.

Wright, J. W. Jr. and Evertt K. Rowson, eds. *Homoeroticism in Classical Arabic Literature*. New York: Columbia University Press, 1997.

Wright, Louis B. *Religion and Empire: The Alliance between Piety and Commerce in English Expansion, 1558–1625*. New York: Octagon Books, 1973. First published in 1943.

Yahya, Dahiru. *Morocco in the Sixteenth Century: Problems and Patterns in African Foreign Policy*. Atlantic Highlands, New Jersey: Humanities Press, 1981.

Yungblut, Laura Hunt. *Strangers Settled Here Amongst Us*. London and New York: Routledge, 1996.

Zinck, Arlette Marie. "Of Arms and the Heroic Reader: The Concept of Psychomachy in Spenser, Milton and Bunyan." Ph.D. dissertation: University of Alberta, 1993.

INDEX

Due to frequent recurrence, entries for Africa,
America, Christians, England, Muslims,
and Turks have not been indexed.

A

a'alaj, 59. *See* renegades.
Abdallah, Mulay, 50, 70
Abraham (Muslim captive), 25
Abraham (Patriarch), 111, 133
Act for the releife of the Captives taken by
    Turkish Moorish and other Pirates, An, 91
Act of Uniformity, 92
Adam, 133–134
Africans; sub-Saharan, 6–7, 113, 170
Age of Discovery, 3, 5, 9, 11, 17–18, 81,
    83–84, 95, 97, 167
al-Ajhouri, Sheikh Ali, 194
al-Ayyashi, Siddy Hamed, 54
Albion, 22, 42, 46, 102, 143
alchemy, 70
Aleppo, 67, 135, 154, 186, 218n96
Alexander VI, Pope, 142
al-Fishtali, Abu Salem, 186
al-Ghalib, Abdallah, 64

Algiers/Algeria, 7, 16, 30, 35, 38, 41, 46,
    74, 80, 87, 89–90, 146–148, 150–152,
    160, 166, 171, 176, 179–180, 201n66,
    207n63, 215n53, 229n31
Allin, Sir Thomas, 164
al-Ma'moon, ash-Sheikh, 116
al-Mansur, Ahmad, 9, 21, 49, 53, 63–64,
    69–70, 87
al-Mawsuli, Hanna, 185–190
Alsop, George, 90
alterity, 15–16, 117, 119. *See also* Other
al-Walid, Mulay, 23, 67
al-Wufrani, Mohammad, 17, 70, 115
Amalekites, 140–141, 158
Andalusia, 24, 57
Andrewes, Lancelot, 152
Anne, Queen (wife of James I), 149
'Annouri, Abd al-Wahid, 33
Appiah, Kwame Anthony, 196n8
Arabia, 99
Arabic, 9, 36, 39, 47, 57–58, 62, 64, 67,
    69, 100, 104, 109, 121, 158, 185–186,
    188, 190
Arabs, 78, 79, 98, 132, 136, 137, 179, 186,
    188, 190
Arundel, Sir Thomas, 98

Augustine, St., 140

Averroes, 209n143

Avicenna, 69, 209n143

Azamur, 112

B

Bacon, Francis, 11, 16, 70, 92, 116, 139, 150–155, 171

Baepler, Paul, 94

Bagg, Sir James, 32

Baghdad, 187

Baines, Sir Thomas, 79

Bainton, Roland, 139

Bajazeth, 6, 13, 51

Baker, Thomas, 118

Ballu, Joffer (Muslim captive), 27

Barbary/ Barbary Coast, 6–7, 10, 15, 20, 22–24, 28–29, 33, 35, 57–60, 62, 64–65, 67, 69–70, 77, 84, 89, 91, 94, 104, 116, 118, 154, 171, 207n68, 217n73

Barbary Company, 10, 23, 33, 67

Barbary Corsairs, 24, 33, 57–58, 60, 91, 94, 104, 171. See also corsairs, pirates

Barbary Merchants, 64

Barbados, 92–93, 197n23

Barret, Robert, 45, 204n8

Barrett, Charles, 29

Barthelemy, Anthony, 14

Bashaw, Ishmael, 173–175

Bassett, Francis, 25, 29

Bayonne, 59

Beacon, Richard, 11

Beaumont, Francis, 74

Beirut, 99

Belkassem, Ahmed, 33

ben Adel, Ahmad, 33

ben Askar, Mohammad, 37

Bendish, Sir Thomas, 218n96

ben Hussein, Ahmad, 35

ben Sa'd, Mohammad, 35

berdache, 109, 219n2

Bergeron, David, 148

Bermuda, 92, 98, 197n23

Bernard, Richard, 224n38

Bernhere, Thomas, 69–70

Bill, John, 153–154

bin Abdallah, Ahmad, 47

bin Aisha, Abdalla, 28

bin Anas, Malek, 194

bin Hadou, Mohammad, 38–39, 41

bin Mohammad, Sidi Ali, 28

bin Qasim, Ahmad, 116, 186, 193

Bishops' Wars, 159

Blake, Robert, 28, 70, 164

Blount, Sir Henry, 52–53

Boston, 111, 132, 166

Bradford, William, 94, 111, 141

Bradshaw, Edmund, 70

Bramforde, Sara, 65

Braudel, Fernand, 55, 83

Brave Memorable and Dangerovs Sea-Fight, A (1636), 73

Bray, Alan, 113, 119–120

Breitwieser, Mitchell Robert, 106

Brereton, John, 196n11

Brightman, Thomas, 130, 159, 223n27, 227n113

Bristol, 145

Brooks, Francis, 53, 183

Browne, Abraham, 182, 214n52

Brussels, 47

Buenos Aires, 188

Bunyan, John, 165

Burg, B. R., 113
Burton, Robert, 21
Butleres, Thomas, 65
Byam, Henry, 62

C

Cabry, Nicholas, 69
Cade, Samuel, 65
Cadiz, 20, 25
Calabria, 76
Calvecho, Mohammed, 23, 35
Calvert, Thomas, 115
Calvin, John, 138
Cambridge, 11, 38, 104
Camden, William, 48
Camoes, Luiz Vaz de, 13, 144, 164
Canaan, Land of, 129, 132–133, 135,
    140–141, 166
Canary Islands, 58
Canup, John, 110
Cape Ann, 97
Cape Cod, 97
Cape of Good Hope, 63, 166
captives, 7, 21, 24–29, 32, 35–36, 40, 43,
    50–51, 57, 60, 63, 71–75, 78–81,
    89–94, 100, 113–114, 119–120, 175
Caracas, 187
Carew, Lord George, 22, 60, 105
Carew, Richard, 143
Caribbean, 59, 83, 88, 96, 100, 109, 116,
    141, 212n9
Carr, R., 9
Cartegena, 100
Carteret, Sir George, 65
Carthage, 137, 179
Cartner, M., 102

Case of many Hundreds of Poor English-
    Captives, in Algier, The (1680), 116
Castiglione, Baldassar, 121
Cathay, 116
Cave, Alfred A., 134
Cecil, William, 48
Cely, Thomas, 65
Cervantes, Miguel de, 13, 73
Chamberlain, John, 34, 38, 52, 61, 89,
    147, 150
Charles I, 10, 22–23, 28, 35–38, 41,
    53–56, 63, 67, 96–97, 154, 157–158,
    163, 165, 226n91
Charles II, 28, 38, 165
Charlestown, 96, 165
China, 135
Cholmeley, Sir Hugh, 203n108
Clark, Edward W. 96
Clarke, Richard, 95
Clarke, William, 218n96
Clements, Joseph, 65
cloth industry, 68; production by Turks, 69
Cocks, R., 60
coffee, 9, 188
Collmer, Robert, 228n127
Columbus, Christopher, 129–130
Connecticut, 10
Constantinople, 25, 67, 136, 155,
    164–165, 174. See also Istanbul
Conversion of a Mahometan to the Christian
    Religion Described in a Letter from Gaifer,
    in England, to Aly-Ben-Hayton, His Friend
    in Turkey, The, 229n20
Cooley, Francis, 116
Coronado, Francisco de, 98, 216n68
corsairs, 26, 33, 56, 59, 62, 65, 74, 94,
    150–151, 160, 175. See also Barbary
    Corsairs, pirates.

Coryat, Thomas, 52, 79, 127
Cotgrave, John, 199n18
Cotton, John, 111, 134
Cotton, Thomas, 65
Coxere, Edward, 52, 182
Craigie, Peter C., 140
Cressy, David, 93
Crete, 163–164
Croatians, 225n52
Cromwell, Oliver, 4, 11, 22, 66, 104, 164
Cromwell, Richard, 22
Crusades/Crusaders, 44, 137, 140, 142–143, 154–155, 157, 160–162, 169
Cushman, Robert, 93, 134
Cyprus, 126, 132

D

D'Acosta, Joseph, 98, 186
D'Avenant, William, 73, 100
D'Avity, Pierre, 222n76
Daborne, Robert, 61
Dale, Sir Thomas, 89
Dandulo, Rigep, 22
Dansker, Simon, 61
Davie, James, 63
Davis, William, 55, 97, 113
Defoe, Daniel, 137, 170–172, 180
Dennis, William, 65
Deptford, 35
Dey, Othman, 62
Dey, Yousef, 62
di Candia, Pedro, 186
Discourse of the Old Company (1625), 85
Donne, John, 118
Drake, Arthur, 62

Drake, Francis, 13, 47, 56, 59, 84, 98, 100, 199n9
du Mont, Sieur, 206n38

E

Eburne, Richard, 11, 89
Eden, Richard, 99, 130
Edinburgh, 162, 174
Egypt, 44, 66, 76, 100, 102, 188, 217n73
El Cid, 13
Eliot, Sir John, 25,
Eliot, John, 138
Elizabeth I, 9–10, 19–21, 33, 44, 46–48, 64, 66, 70, 84, 89, 97, 104, 209n147
Elliot, Adam, 79, 119, 182
Ellis, William, 66
Erdmann, Carl, 139
Esheikh, Mohammad, 23, 157
Ethiopia, 144
Evelyn, John, 22, 39

F

Fairfax, Edward, 143, 153–154, 165
Famous History of the Life and Death of Captain Thomas Stukeley, The, (1605), 49
Fanshawe, Sir Richard, 163
Fenth, John, 61
Fez, 46, 48, 118
Finet, John, 34, 37–38
Fletcher, John, 74
food, bringing Christian and Muslims together, 38
Formes, Elizabeth, 174
Foss, John, 180
Fox, George, 116

Fox, John, 76, 181
France, 10, 13–14, 16, 20, 23, 37, 39, 60,
    73, 84, 131, 137–138, 143, 156, 158,
    171, 180, 206n40
Frederick, Duke, 146
Freigius, Hohannes Thomas, 49
Fry, John, 59
Fuller, Mary C., 84, 107
Fuller, Thomas, 160

G

Gainsford, Thomas, 105, 120, 135
Gascoigne, George, 73
Gates, Sir Thomas, 88–89
Gee, Joshua, 94, 183
Giffard, Captain John, 50, 62
Glanville, Toby, 61
Glassock, Richard, 66
Glover, Sir Thomas, 52
Godfrey of Bulloigns, 157
Godolphin, Sir Francis, 25
Goldberg, Jonathan, 125
Gomorrah, 120
Gondomar, Count, 151
Gorges, Sir Ferdinando, 98
Gorges, Sir William, 98
Gramaye, J. B., 114, 117
Granada, 130
Graves, William, 61
Gray, Robert, 134
Great Migration, 9, 83–84, 89, 92,
    103, 170
Greenblatt, Stephen, 95
Grimeston, Edward, 115, 117, 123,
    222n76
Guinea, 7, 82–83
Gyppes, George, 64

H

Habsburgs, 146
Haget, Paul, 66
Hakluyt, Richard, 11, 17, 20, 48–49, 68–69,
    96, 98–99, 104, 181, 195n6, 216n72
Hall, Joseph, 141–142
Hall, Kim F., 7
Hammer, Meredith, 114–115
Hammet (Muslim captive), 31
Hammett, Vincent (Muslim captive), 25
Hammond, Paul, 119
Harborne, William, 24, 43
Harriot, Thomas, 15
Harrison, John, 10, 29–30, 53, 63, 67, 97,
    138, 154–155
Harrison, William, 84
Harvard College, 106
Hasleton, Richard, 51, 77, 181
Havana, 100, 212n8
Hawkins, John, 97
Henri IV, 56
Henrico College, 106
Henry VIII, 111, 132
Hereford, 69
Herman, John, 64
Herodotus, 102
Heywood, Thomas, 73, 142
Hic Mulier, (1620), 107
Hodgen, Margaret, 14
Hogan, Edmund, 64
Holland, 11, 46, 131, 157, 171
Holy Land, 7, 55, 129, 136–137, 145,
    156–157, 160–166
Holy War, 7, 16, 107, 129, 137, 139, 152,
    157, 160, 162
Homer, 102
homosexuality. See sodomy
Honicombe, Pethericke, 72

Hubert, Etienne, 209n147
Hulme, Peter, 102–103
Hunter, G. K., 7
Hurst Castle, 31

I

Ibn Abi Dinar, 62
Indians, American, 4, 9–10, 15–17, 59,
  95–112, 127, 130–141, 153, 166, 169,
  172–180, 186–190, 195n4 , 215n58,
  216n67, 217n72, 217n84, 219n103,
  229n26
language, 224n30
Interregnum, 4, 38, 73, 144
Iran. See Persia
Ireland, 6, 9, 10–11, 26, 32, 39, 48,
  74–75, 158, 219n103
Iskandaroon, 187
Isle of Wight, 31
Ismail, Mulay, 41, 53, 169, 198n41
Istanbul, 25–26, 34, 37, 42, 44, 52–53, 56,
  65–69, 71, 96, 125, 136, 151
Italy, 13–14, 16, 37, 156
Izmir, 66

J

Jamaica, 215n53
James I, 4, 10, 28, 34–35, 44, 46, 57,
  60–61, 66, 87, 113, 116, 143,
  146–147, 150–152. See also James VI
James II, 28
James VI, 20
Jamestown, 12, 86, 89, 92, 95–96, 131
Janizzaries, 52, 61
Japan, 8, 11, 63, 166

Jaquis, Andrew (Muslim captive), 25
Jason, 159
Jaurar bin Abdallah, Alkaid, 35–37, 157
Jerusalem, 13, 55, 130, 133, 136, 138, 153,
  155, 162, 186
Jews, 3–4, 19, 42, 67, 98, 132–133, 161,
  176, 195n2, 199n18
John, Prester, 76, 144
Johnson, Anthony, 61
Johnson, Edward, 166
Johnson, James Turner, 139–140
Johnson, Richard, 181
Johnson, Robert, 85
Jones, Inigo, 73
Jordan, Winthrop, 112, 125
Josselyn, John, 165

K

Kadir, Djelal, 127
Kellet, Edmund, 155
Khan, Abul Hassan, 203n115
King Philip's War, 100, 112, 225n48
Knight, Francis, 91, 182
Knolles, Richard, 114
Knott, Nathaniel, 140, 157
Knyvett, Sir Henry, 204n8
Kyd, Thomas, 80

L

Lacon, Gertrude, 65
Lane, Ralph, 46, 97
Las Casas, Bartolomé, 110, 189
Laud, Archbishop, 94, 159–160
Lebanon, 98
Leghorn, 30, 66, 151

Leighton, Alexander, 154
Leinster, Marquess of, 48
Leo Africanus, 97, 112, 124
Lepanto, 130, 143, 146, 153–154
lesbianism, 123–124
Lesbos, 124
Letters from the great Turke lately sent vnto the holy Father the Pope (1606), 52
Levant, 4, 7, 8, 10, 14–15, 17, 22, 24, 33, 37, 43–44, 53, 66–67, 88, 96–97, 99–100, 105, 124, 127, 129, 131–132, 134–137, 148, 172, 185, 187–188, 190
Levett, Christopher, 89
Libya, 3
Lithgow, William, 114, 118
Little, David, 139–140
London, 3–7, 12, 19, 21–22, 26, 30, 32–42, 48, 53, 57, 62, 64–69, 75, 79, 82, 86, 88–89, 93, 96–97, 104, 117–118, 140, 142, 145, 158, 162, 164, 173
London Gazette, 38
Lopez, Roderigo Dr., 3
Lords of the Admiralty, 31–32
Lucas, Hamed, 41, 79
Luther, Martin, 155

M

Mahammet (Muslim captive), 31
Mahomet (Muslim captive) 25
Mainwaring, Sir Henry, 60–61
Malek, Abdel, 47, 64, 116, 205–33
Malim, William, 65
Malta/Maltese, 6, 13, 59, 88
Mamora, 58, 61, 154
Manningham, John, 21
Mansfield, Sir Robert, 148

Manwaring, George, 126
Marcum, Robert, 95
Marrakesh, 21, 53
Marranos, 3–4, 19
Marsh, Henry, 79, 139, 155–157
Marvell, Andrew, 98
Maryland, 10, 90, 94
Mason, John, 135, 141
Massachusetts, 10, 87, 97, 111, 134
Massinger, Philip, 73, 104
Mather, Cotton, 94, 138, 141, 166
Mather, Increase, 141
Mayflower, 96, 98
Mead, Joseph, 130, 227n113
Meade, Richard, 102
Mecca, 6, 55
medicine, Islamic, 69
Mellon, William, 88
Memphis (Egypt), 66
Michaelangelo, 121
Middleton, Sir Henry, 56, 182
Milton, John, 14
miscegenation, 40–41
Misque, 188
Mitton, Thomas, 61
Mocadem, Ibrahim, 23
Mogadore, 59
Mohammad III, Sultan, 53, 56
Mohammad IV, Sultan, 186
Monson, Sir William, 58, 62, 207n63, 226n91
Montague, Lady Mary, 114
Moors, 3, 6–7, 10, 20, 30–32, 40–42, 47, 50, 59, 67, 78, 91, 98, 100, 132, 138, 145, 151, 155, 171–172, 176, 178, 199n9, 216n68, 217n76, 219n103
More, Henry, 164
More, Thomas, 8
Morgan, J., 58

Moriscos, 217n75n76
Morocco, 3, 9–11, 21, 23, 28–33, 36- 37,
    41, 44, 46–49, 52–53, 56, 59–60,
    63–66, 69–71, 84, 87, 94, 97, 119,
    138, 143–144, 154, 160, 169, 205n26,
    209n147
Morton, Thomas, 95, 223n14
Moryson, Fynes, 136
Mun, Thomas, 212n15
Munday, Anthony, 181
Munster, Sebastian, 99
Murad, Sultan, 20, 33, 56, 65, 118
Muslim slaves, 57, 200n46
Mutteferrika, Ibraheem, 222n9

N

Naile, Robert, 149
Nazareth, 187
Neoplatonic love, 121
New England, 42, 58, 82, 85, 88, 90, 92,
    94, 96–97, 100, 103, 111, 133, 136,
    153, 165–166, 173, 175, 212n17
New Providence, 197n23
Newes from Sally (1642), 182
Newton, Thomas, 142
Nicholas, Edward, 26
Nicolay, Nicholas, 114, 124
Nova Scotia, 197n23
Nutt, John, 62

O

Oates, Titus, 119
Odyssey, The, 103
Okeley, William, 90, 94, 182
Orientalism, 10, 17

Osborne, Francis, 120
Osman, Cara, 61
Other (Otherness), 3, 10–11, 13–16, 19,
    21, 25, 64–65, 81–82, 95, 106–107,
    109, 112–113, 118, 125, 127, 134,
    142, 169, 172–173, 175, 180
Othman, Caliph, 160
Ottoman Empire, 3, 5, 9, 14, 37, 65–66,
    112, 117, 119–120, 124, 144, 186
Oviedo, Gabriel, 110
Owen, Thomas, 64
Oxford, 38

P

pageant, 13, 17, 139, 144–148, 150–151
Palestine, 39, 85, 129, 132–133, 136–137,
    139, 161
Paris, 116, 186, 193
Parry, William, 126
Patrick, J. Max, 152
Patuxet, 136
Pearce, Roy Harvey, 177
Peckham, Sir George, 133, 136, 153
Peele, George, 47–48
Pellow, Thomas, 53, 71
Penn, Captain Gyles, 65
Penobscot, Mme, 4
Pequot Indians, 135
Percy, George, 89
Persia, 4, 44, 63, 68, 76, 80, 97, 102, 109,
    120–121, 126, 142, 166
Persians, 222n76
Phelps, Thomas, 28, 169, 183
Philip II, 42, 47
Pige, Christopher, 74–75
Pincon, Abel, 126
pirates, 6, 56, 60–61, 188, 206n56. See also

Barbary Corsairs; corsairs

Pitts, Joseph, 53, 71, 79, 169, 183

Plato, 120–122, 162

Platonic love, 121

Plumleigh, Captain, 62

Plymouth, 12, 24–25, 27, 58, 62, 74–75,
 82, 84, 88–89, 92, 94, 98, 132, 136

Pocahontas, 4, 175

Pococke, Edward, 67

Polo, Marco, 132

Poole, 62

Portland, Earl of, 29, 31

Portsmouth, Lord, 31

Pory, John, 97, 112, 124

Potosi, 189

Powhatan, 87, 101

prostitutes; to ransom captives, 41

Purchas, Samuel, 8, 11, 96, 99–101,
 114–117, 123, 136, 182, 211n5

Q

Quakers, 116

Quinn, David Beers, 83, 93

Qur'an, 80, 115, 163, 193

R

R. C., 50

Rabelais, Francois, 73

Rainsborough, William, 32

Raleigh, Sir Walter, 10–11, 13, 56, 98

Rawlins, John, 52, 62, 182

Red Sea, 63, 166

renegades, 25, 52, 59, 63, 71, 93, 205n33,
 215n58

Reys, Jeffera (Muslim captive), 27

Rhazi, 209n143

Rhode Island, 10

Roanoke, 10, 12, 84–85, 95, 211n8

Roberts, Henry, 10, 33, 64, 138,
 143–144

Robinson, Henry, 66

Rochester, Earl of, 119

Roe, Sir Thomas, 22, 26, 43, 52, 57, 97,
 105, 151, 171

Rolfe, Rebecca. See Pocahontas

Rome, 69, 137, 164, 179, 185,

Rome for the Great TURKE, (1664), 164

Ross, Alexander, 163

Rycaut, Paul, 117–118, 121–124

Rymer, Thomas, 41

S

Safi, 47, 65

Sagadahoc, 89

Said, Edward, 17

Saladin, 160

Salamanca, 119

Salee, 10, 23, 29, 30–31, 35, 42, 54, 57,
 59, 61–62, 65–67, 71–73, 82, 91–94,
 103, 105, 140, 157–159, 206n48

Salem, 89, 133

"Samsom," Captain, 62

Sanaa, 89

Sanders, Thomas, 181

Sanderson, John, 118

Sandys, George, 97, 124, 136–137

Santo Domingo, 100

Saracens, 98, 136–137, 142, 153, 161,
 169, 171

Sayer, Ambrose, 62

Scanderberg, 145, 225n62

Scilly Islands, 22

Scotland, 9–10, 20, 39, 75, 120, 143,
    158–159, 162, 173–175
Sebastian, Don, 47
Seed, Patricia, 17
Sepulveda, Juan, 142
Seville, 211n212n8
Sewall, Samuel, 166
Sha'ban (Muslim captive), 25
Shakespeare, William, 4, 6, 7, 13, 87, 102,
    118
Shirley, Sir Anthony, 44, 52, 80, 97, 126
Shirley, Sir Thomas, 52, 67, 124–125
Sidan, Mulay. *See* Zaidan
Sidon, 136
Skydmoore, Ralph, 63
Slotkin, Richard, 93
Smith, John, 58, 65, 88, 97, 181
Smith, N., 101
Smythe, Sir John, 204n8
Smythe, Sir Thomas, 97
Sodom, 119–120
sodomy, 7, 109–110, 113–115, 118–123,
    125–127, 194; associated with royalty,
    116; colonization dependent on, 110;
    denounced in Muslim context, 114;
    Indian stereotype, 111; Islamic refuta-
    tion, 193, 194; justification for Indian
    conquest, 110; relation to a hot climate,
    120; result of repressed instinct, 122
soldiers; Britons in Muslim armies, 45–54
Somer Islands, 84, 97
Spain, 10, 13–16, 19, 23, 31, 35, 37,
    46–47, 53, 57, 73, 76, 89, 94, 100,
    129–131, 138, 143–144, 150–156,
    171, 187–188, 190, 217n75
Spanish Armada, 147
Spenser, Edmund, 14, 225–62
Spice Islands, 11
Spratt, Devereux, 80–81, 182

St. John, Henry, 65
St. Kitts, 197n23
St. Serfe, Thomas, 117
Stannard, David, 139
Stockholm syndrome, 72
Strachey, William, 97, 101, 104
Stukley, Thomas, 47–49, 51, 97
Sudan, 87
Suleyman the Magnificient, Sultan, 129
Sumatra, Sultan of, 40
Suriano, Francesco, 137
Swyer, Robert, 32
Symerons, 101
Symposium, 120–123
Syracuse, 186
Syria, 99
Syriac language, 185–187

T

T. S. [Thomas Smith], 41, 64, 77–79, 81,
    120, 135, 182
taffurs, 169
Tamberlaine Part One, (1590), 51
Tangier, 17, 28, 198n40, 203n108
Tanjawi, Hamet, 28
Tanner, John, 216n60
Tartars, 101
Tasso, Torquato, 13, 143–144, 153, 161,
    164–165
Taylor, John, 146–147
Tempest, The, 4, 102, 196n197n14, 228n9
Tenenti, Alberto, 57, 140
Tetuan, 25, 32, 61
Theseus, 159
Thevet, Andrewe, 99
Thirty Years War, 46, 94
Thousand and One Nights, 188

Thurloe, Secretary John, 218n96

Tift, Joshua, 215n58

Tigris, 188

Timberlake, Henry, 55

Tipton, John, 24

Todorov, Tzvetan, 110

Tokson, Elliot H., 14, 112

Tomson, Jasper, 53

Traherne, Thomas, 164

Traveller's Breviat, The (1601), 46

Trexler, Richard C., 109

Trinity House, 131–132

Tripoli (Lebanon), 99, 132

Tripoli (Libya), 44, 160, 171

Tunisia/Tunis, 3, 23–24, 42–44, 52, 57–58, 60–61, 87, 103, 105, 146, 158, 160, 170–171

Turkey Company, 10, 27, 83, 103

Tuscany, Duke of, 66

Tyerman, Christopher, 140

Tyler, Royall, 228n1

U

umma, 95

Underhill, Captain, 141

Uniate Christian, 186

Urban II, Pope, 157

V

Vandals, 171

Vaughan, Alden, 96

Verney, Sir Francis, 62

Vespucci, Amerigo, 12, 98

Villiers, George, 116

Virgil, 102

Virginia, 10, 15, 57–58, 84–85, 87–88, 91–94, 96–97, 101, 131, 138, 140, 176

W

Wadsworth, James, 182

Wakeman, John, 64

Wales, 39, 93

Waller, Edmund, 140, 158–159, 163

Walsingham, Captain (pirate), 61

Walsingham, Sir Francis, Secretary to Elizabeth I, 46

Walzer, Michael, 159

Wanton, John, 46

Ward, John, 61–62

Wardiyya, Captain. See John Ward

Washington, T., 114

Waterhouse, Edward, 93, 104, 140

Webbe, Edward, 76, 181

West Indies, 9, 11, 85, 99, 131, 188

Weston, Thomas, 95

Weymouth, George, 4, 98

White, Andrew, 94

White, John, 84–85, 89, 93, 98

Wigglesworth, Michael, 141

Wight, John, 65

Willan, T.S., 64

Williams, Captain Roger, 46

Williams, John, 215n60

Williams, Roger, 104

Winchester, 32

Windus, John, 200n29

Wingfield, Captain Edward Maria, 215n58

Winthrop, John, 94, 111

Winwood, Sir Ralph, 147, 150

Wolstenhome Towne, 88

Wood, William, 104

Wright, Edward, 69–70
Wyan, Thomas, 32
Wyndham, Thomas, 33

Y

Yemen, 89

York, Duke of, 28

Z

Zaidan, Mulay, 50, 62
Zante, 60
Zinck, Arlette Marie, 159